D0091465

MODISMOS INGLESES PARA HISPANOS

English Idioms for Spanish Speakers

By
Eugene Savaiano, Ph.D.
Professor Emeritus of Spanish
Wichita State University, Wichita, Kansas
and
Lynn W. Winget, Ph.D.
Professor Emeritus of Spanish
Wichita State University, Wichita, Kansas

All inquiries should be addressed to:
Barron's Educational Series, Inc.
250 Wireless Boulevard
Hauppauge, New York 11788

International Standard Book Number 0-8120-9458-1

Library of Congress Catalog Card Number 95-81412

PRINTED IN THE UNITED STATES OF AMERICA

6789   5500   987654321

Contents

Prólogo

Esta edición de bolsillo está destinada principalmente a españoles y latinoamericanos que tienen interés en el idioma inglés para los propósitos de estudio o de viajes por países de habla inglesa. Esta obra será también útil para anglohablantes que desean aprender modismos españoles mediante la localización de modismos ingleses y subsecuente estudio de su traducción al español. El núcleo de la obra consta de aproximadamente 2.500 modismos ingleses, ordenados alfabéticamente bajo su respectiva palabra clave. Se presentan los modismos, en su mayoría, acompañados de oraciones ilustrativas breves pero completas. Esperamos que este procedimiento ayude a eliminar las frustraciones que a veces experimentan los que consultan diccionarios en que se compilan modismos aislados y sin contexto alguno.

Para los fines de esta edición de bolsillo, se entiende que un modismo puede ser casi cualquier expresión que (1) conste de por lo menos dos palabras en una o ambas de las lenguas en cuestión y (2) se exprese de modo diferente en las dos lenguas ('to be cold' = 'tener frío', o 'to pull one's leg' = 'tomarle el pelo'). Hemos incluido también un número de expresiones que son iguales en las dos lenguas, basándonos en la teoría de que el estudiante querrá tener la seguridad de que efectivamente esto es así. Nos referimos al "buen" estudiante, quien ha aprendido que 'to take place' no es 'tomar lugar' y que 'to have a good time' no es 'tener un buen tiempo' y quien probablemente se resistirá a dar por sentado que 'to take part in' se traduce 'tomar parte en' y bien podrá sentirse agradecido cuando le aseguremos explícitamente que dicha traducción es correcta.

La mayoría de los modismos se hallan en la lengua moderna hablada y el inglés es principalmente el que se habla en los Estados Unidos más bien que el de la Gran Bretaña. Hemos recogido materia tanto de una variedad de fuentes peninsulares e hispanoamericanas con ejemplos del lenguaje coloquial como de diccionarios clásicos, libros de texto y listas de modismos.

Los paréntesis indican la materia que es optativa o bien alternativa. Por ejemplo, 'al (buen) tuntún' implica que la expresión puede ser o 'al tuntún' o 'al buen tuntún', pero 'a (en) nombre de' significa que la expresión puede ser o 'a nombre de' o 'en nombre de', y de ninguna manera podrá interpretarse como 'a en nombre de'.

Para que el diccionario resulte más práctico, hemos incluido un índice inglés-español, listas de abreviaturas, tablas de pesos y medidas y una lista de modismos españoles comunes, con la palabra inglesa entre paréntesis.

En conclusión, queremos expresar nuestros sinceros agradecimientos a todas las personas que de una manera u otra nos han ayudado en la preparación de esta edición de bolsillo, y en especial a nuestros colegas Kenneth Pettersen y John Koppenhaver.

Modismos Ingleses (English Idioms)

a — *uno*

   . . . a . . . — *por (a) . . .*

   He eats five days a week. *Come cinco días por (a la) semana.*

---

about — *acerca de*

   to be about — *tratar de.*

   The novel is about the gaucho. *La novela trata del gaucho.*

   to be about to — *estar a punto de; estar para.*

   He is about to get married. *Está a punto de (para) casarse.*

---

accord — *el acuerdo*

   of one's own accord — *por propia voluntad.*

   He sent it to us of his own accord. *Nos lo mandó por propia voluntad.*

---

according — *conforme*

   according to — *a medida de.*

   They paid me according to the work I did. *Me pagaron a medida de mi trabajo.*

   according to — *de acuerdo con; según, con arreglo a.*

   He built it according to my plans. *Lo construyó de acuerdo con (según; con arreglo a) mis planes.*

---

account — *la cuenta*

   not on any account — *bajo ningún pretexto.*

   I'll not accept on any account. *Bajo ningún pretexto aceptaré.*

   on account of — *a causa de; por motivo de.*

   We went on account of the wedding. *Fuimos a causa de (por motivo de) la boda.*

   to balance the account — *echar la cuenta.*

I balanced the account. *Eché la cuenta.*

to be of no account — *no tener importancia.*
It's of no account. *No tiene importancia.*

to give an account of — *dar cuenta de.*
He gave a good account of himself. *Dio buena cuenta de sí.*

to give an account of — *dar razón de.*
He couldn't give an account of his actions. *No pudo dar razón de sus acciones.*

to keep an account — *llevar una cuenta.*
He keeps an account of all that he spends. *Lleva una cuenta de todo lo que gasta.*

to take into account — *tener en cuenta.*
Take into account that prices have gone up. *Tenga en cuenta que los precios han subido.*

to account — *echar la cuenta*
    to account for — *ser el motivo de.*
That accounts for his attitude. *Es el motivo de su actitud.*

accustomed — *acostumbrado*
    to be accustomed to — *tener la costumbre de.*
We are accustomed to eating at twelve. *Tenemos la costumbre de comer a las doce.*

across — *a través*
    across from — *frente a.*
Across from the church there is a university. *Frente a la iglesia hay una universidad.*

to acknowledge — *reconocer, confesar*
    to acknowledge . . . to be right (to agree with) — *dar la razón a.*
He finally had to acknowledge that I was right (had to agree with me). *Por fin tuvo que darme la razón.*

act — *el acto*

in the act — *en flagrante; con las manos en la masa.*
The policeman caught the thief in the act. *El policía cogió al ladrón en flagrante (con las manos en la masa).*

to be an act of God — *ser un caso de fuerza mayor.*
It was an act of God. *Fue un caso de fuerza mayor.*

to put on an act — *hacer comedia.*
He put on an act when the police stopped him. *Hizo comedia cuando lo detuvo la policía.*

to act — *actuar*

to act as — *hacer las veces de.*
She acts as secretary. *Hace las veces de secretaria.*

to act up — *no funcionar bien.*
My car has been acting up lately. *Últimamente mi coche no está funcionando bien.*

to act up — *comportarse mal.*
They asked him to leave the party because he was acting up. *Le pidieron que se fuera de la fiesta porque se estaba comportando mal.*

action — *la acción*

to suit the action to the word — *unir la acción a la palabra.*
He suits the action to the word. *Une la acción a la palabra.*

to take action against — *proceder en contra de.*
The district attorney took action against the criminals. *El fiscal procedió en contra de los criminales.*

addition — *la adición*

in addition to — *además de.*
In addition to being handsome, he's intelligent. *Además de ser guapo, es inteligente.*

to address — *dirigirse a*

to address as — *tratar de.*
He addressed me as "Miss." *Me trató de señorita.*

ado — *la bulla*

    Much ado about nothing. — *Mucho ruido para nada; Mucho ruido y pocas nueces.*

    without further ado — *sin más ni más.*
    Without further ado, we left. *Sin más ni más, salimos.*

---

advance — *el avance*

    in advance — *de antemano.*
    It's necessary to reserve a room in advance. *Hay que reservar un cuarto de antemano.*

---

advantage — *la ventaja*

    to be to one's advantage — *convenirle.*
    It's to your advantage to arrive on time. *Le conviene llegar a tiempo.*

    to have an advantage over — *llevar una ventaja.*
    She had an advantage over him. *Le llevaba una ventaja.*

    to take advantage of — *abusar de.*
    He took advantage of my generosity. *Abusó de mi generosidad.*

    to take advantage of — *aprovechar; aprovecharse de.*
    They took advantage of the opportunity. *(Se) Aprovecharon (de) la oportunidad.*

---

affair — *el asunto*

    to be one's affair — *corresponderle.*
    It's not his affair. *No le corresponde.*

---

afterwards — *después*

    immediately afterwards — *acto seguido.*
    Immediately afterwards, she left. *Acto seguido, salió.*

---

age — *la edad*

    to act one's age — *comportarse de acuerdo con su edad.*
    He doesn't act his age. *No se comporta de acuerdo con su edad.*

    to be of age — *ser mayor de edad.*
    He's not of age. *No es mayor de edad.*

    to come of age — *llegar a la mayoría de edad.*
    She came of age. *Llegó a la mayoría de edad.*

---

to agree — *convenir*
    not to agree (to disagree) with someone — *hacerle daño.*
    He ate something that didn't agree (that disagreed) with him. *Comió algo que le hizo daño.*

    to agree to — *quedar en (de).*
    We agreed to pay. *Quedamos en (de) pagar.*

agreement — *el acuerdo*
    to be in agreement — *estar conforme; estar de acuerdo.*
    He's in agreement. *Está conforme (de acuerdo).*

    to reach an agreement — *ponerse de acuerdo; llegar a un acuerdo.*
    They reached an agreement. *Se pusieron de acuerdo (Llegaron a un acuerdo).*

---

ahead — *delante*
    to be ahead of — *llevar la delantera (llevar ventaja).*
    As far as rockets are concerned, nobody is ahead of us. *En cuanto a cohetes, nadie nos lleva la delantera (lleva ventaja).*

    to go ahead with — *llevar adelante.*
    We're going ahead with our plans. *Llevamos adelante nuestros planes.*

to aim — *apuntar*
    to aim to — *tener la intención de.*
    He aims to graduate in June. *Tiene la intención de recibirse en junio.*

    to be aiming at (to have designs on) — *tener la mira puesta en.*
    That senator is aiming at (has designs on) the presidency. *Ese senador tiene la mira puesta en la presidencia.*

---

air — *el aire*
    in the air — *en vilo.*
    It is suspended in the air. *Está colgado en vilo.*

    out in the open (air) — *al aire libre.*
    They spent the night out in the open (air). *Pasaron la noche al aire libre.*

to get a breath of fresh air — *tomar el fresco.*
We're getting a breath of fresh air. *Estamos tomando el fresco.*

to give someone the air — *darle calabazas.*
She gave him the air. *Le dio calabazas.*

to put on airs — *darse tono.*
She puts on airs. *Se da tono.*

to vanish into thin air — *desaparecer (repentinamente).*
Once the game was over, the spectators vanished into thin air. *Terminado el partido, los espectadores desaparecieron.*

---

alive — *vivo*

alive and kicking — *vivito y coleando.*
He's still alive and kicking. *Está todavía vivito y coleando.*

---

all — *todo*

above all — *ante todo; sobre todo.*
Above all one must be honest. *Ante todo (Sobre todo) hay que ser honrado.*

after all — *al fin y al cabo.*
It didn't snow after all. *Al fin y al cabo no nevó.*

after all — *en (al) fin de cuentas; después de todo.*
After all, it's my money. *En (Al) fin de cuentas (Después de todo) es mi dinero.*

all at once (all of a sudden) — *de repente; de pronto.*
All at once (All of a sudden) a dog entered. *De repente (De pronto) entró un perro.*

all day long — *todo el día.*

They traveled all day long. *Viajaron todo el día.*

all in all — *en definitiva.*
All in all it was a good game. *En definitiva fue un buen partido.*

all of them — *unos y otros.*
All of them walked away. *Unos y otros se alejaron.*

all over — *por (en) todas partes.*
It's the same all over. *Es igual por (en) todas partes.*

(to be) all right — *(estar) bien (bueno).*
Everything is all right. *Todo está bien (bueno).*

all the better — *tanto mejor; mejor que mejor.*

all the same — *a pesar de todo; no obstante.*
All the same, I think you should stay. *A pesar de todo (No obstante), creo
    que debe quedarse.*

all the same — *de todos modos.*
He came all the same. *Vino de todos modos.*

all the worse — *tanto peor; peor que peor.*

an all-time high — *sin precedentes.*
Our attendance reached an all-time high. *Tuvimos una asistencia sin
    precedentes.*

all told — *en total.*
All told there are ten of us. *En total somos diez.*

for all I know — *que sepa yo.*
For all I know he's not at home yet. *Que sepa yo todavía no está en casa.*

It's all over. — *Ya ha terminado (ya se acabó).*

It's all the same. — *Lo mismo da; Es igual.*

not at all — *en absoluto.*
Do you mind if I smoke? Not at all. *¿Le molesta si fumo? En absoluto.*

not . . . at all — *nada (en absoluto).*
He doesn't speak it at all. *No lo habla nada (en absoluto).*

to be all for — *ser buen partidario de.*
I'm all for liberty. *Soy buen partidario de la libertad.*

to be all in — *estar rendido.*
I'm all in. *Estoy rendido.*

7

to be all man — *ser muy hombre.*
He's all man. *Es muy hombre.*

to be all set — *estar listo; estar dispuesto.*
Everything is all set. *Todo está listo (dispuesto).*

to be all the rage — *estar muy de moda.*
It's all the rage. *Está muy de moda.*

---

alley — *el callejón*
a blind alley — *un callejón sin salida.*
We entered a blind alley. *Nos metimos en un callejón sin salida.*

---

to allow — *dejar*
to allow (to make allowance) for — *tener en cuenta.*
We allowed (made allowance) for his age. *Tuvimos en cuenta su edad.*

---

alone — *solo*
all alone — *a solas.*
She was left all alone. *Se quedó a solas.*

to let (leave) alone — *dejar en paz.*
Let (Leave) me alone. *Déjeme en paz.*

---

along — *a lo largo*
all along — *desde un (el) principio.*
He had it all along. *Lo tenía desde un (el) principio.*

---

to amount — *importar, ascender*
to amount to — *ascender, subir a.*
The bill amounts to ninety dollars. *La cuenta asciende (sube) a noventa dólares.*

to amount to — *reducirse a.*
What it amounts to is that we cannot buy the house. *Se reduce al hecho de que no podemos comprar la casa.*

to amount to — *valer.*
That guy doesn't amount to much. *Ese tipo no vale mucho.*

---

to answer — *contestar*
  to answer one's purpose — *ser adecuado.*
  It didn't answer our purpose. *No nos fue adecuado.*

any — *alguno*
  any minute (time) now — *de un momento a otro; de hoy a mañana.*
  They'll get here any minute (time) now. *Llegarán de un momento a otro*
  (de hoy a mañana).

anything — *algo*
  not to be able to do anything with — *no poder con.*
  He can't do anything with his boss. *No puede con su jefe.*

  not to be able to make anything out of — *no conseguir comprender.*
  I can't make anything out of this letter. *No consigo comprender esta*
  carta.

to appear — *aparecer*
  to appear at (in) — *asomarse a.*
  She appeared at (in) the window. *Se asomó a la ventana.*

appearance — *la apariencia*
  to put in an appearance — *hacer acto de presencia.*
  They put in an appearance. *Hicieron acto de presencia.*

appetite — *el apetito*
  to give one an appetite — *abrirle el apetito.*
  The exercise gave me an appetite. *El ejercicio me abrió el apetito.*

apple — *la manzana*
  the apple of one's eye — *la niña de sus ojos.*
  She's the apple of his eye. *Es la niña de sus ojos.*

  to polish the apple — *hacerle la barba al profesor.*
  He polishes the apple. *Le hace la barba al profesor.*

appointment — *la cita*
  to make an appointment with — *citarse con.*
  He made an appointment with the manager. *Se citó con el gerente.*

argument — *la discusión, la disputa*
  to get into arguments — *entrar en disputas.*
  He never gets into arguments. *Nunca entra en disputas.*

to arise — *levantarse*
  to arise from — *obedecer a.*
  It arises from a lack of respect. *Obedece a una falta de respeto.*

arm — *el brazo*
  arm in arm — *cogidos del brazo.*
  They were walking arm in arm. *Andaban cogidos del brazo.*

  at arm's length — *a distancia.*
  He kept her at arm's length. *La mantuvo a distancia.*

  to rise up in arms — *alzarse en armas.*
  They rose up in arms. *Se alzaron en armas.*

army — *el ejército*
  to join the army — *incorporarse a filas.*
  He'll join the army. *Se incorporará a filas.*

around — *alrededor*
  to be around . . . — *rondar ya . . .*
  He's around thirty. *Ronda ya los treinta años.*

arrangement — *el arreglo*
  to make arrangements — *tomar las medidas necesarias.*
  I made arrangements to see her. *Tomé las medidas necesarias para verla.*

as — *como*
  as a child — *de niño.*
  As a child he cried a lot. *De niño lloraba mucho.*

  as for — *lo que es; en cuanto a.*
  As for my father, he agrees. *Lo que es (En cuanto a) mi padre, está de acuerdo.*

  as yet — *hasta ahora.*
  As yet they haven't arrived. *Hasta ahora no han llegado.*

ashamed — *avergonzado*
   to be ashamed — *tener vergüenza; darle vergüenza.*
   I'm ashamed. *Tengo vergüenza (Me da vergüenza).*

aside — *aparte, al lado*
   aside from — *aparte de.*
   Aside from boxing he doesn't like sports. *Aparte del boxeo no le gustan los deportes.*

asleep — *dormido*
   to fall asleep — *conciliar el sueño.*
   I couldn't fall asleep. *No pude conciliar el sueño.*

astonished — *asombrado*
   to be astonished at — *asombrarse de (con).*
   They were astonished at his ideas. *Se asombraron de (con) sus ideas.*

astray — *extraviado*
   to lead astray — *llevar por mal camino.*
   His friends led him astray. *Sus amigos le llevaron por mal camino.*

at — *en, a*
   at about . . . — *a eso de la(s) . . .*
   They are coming at about four. *Vienen a eso de las cuatro.*

   at (for) less than — *en menos de.*
   You get them at (for) less than three pesos. *Se consiguen en menos de tres pesos.*

   to live at — *vivir en.*
   He lives at the Smiths'. *Vive en casa de los Smith.*

to attend — *atender, asistir*
   to attend to — *ocuparse de.*
   Isn't there anyone to attend to that matter? *¿No hay quien se ocupe de ese asunto?*

attention — *la atención*

    to attract one's attention — *llamarle la atención.*
    It attracted my attention. *Me llamó la atención.*

    to call one's attention to — *llamarle la atención sobre.*
    He called our attention to the mistake. *Nos llamó la atención sobre el error.*

    to pay attention — *prestar (poner) atención; hacer caso.*
    He never pays attention. *Nunca presta (pone) atención (Nunca hace caso).*

avail — *el provecho*

    to avail oneself of — *valerse de.*
    You must avail yourself of all the resources you can. *Debes valerte de todos los recursos que puedes.*

    to be of no avail — *ser inútil.*
    It was of no avail. *Fue inútil.*

available — *disponible*

    to make available to someone — *facilitarle.*
    He made his car available to me. *Me facilitó su coche.*

average — *el promedio*

    on the average — *por término medio.*
    It rains once a month, on the average. *Llueve una vez al mes, por término medio.*

awake — *despierto*

    to be wide awake — *estar completamente despierto.*
    I'm wide awake. *Estoy completamente despierto.*

    wide-awake — *muy listo.*
    He's a wide-awake boy. *Es un muchacho muy listo.*

aware — *enterado*

    to be aware of — *estar al tanto de.*
    I'm aware of the problems. *Estoy al tanto de los problemas.*

axe — *el hacha (f)*
   to have an axe to grind — *tener algún fin interesado.*
   He always has an axe to grind. *Siempre tiene algún fin interesado.*

B

baby — *el nene*
   to cry like a baby — *llorar a lágrima viva.*
   When he heard the news, he cried like a baby. *Al oír la noticia, lloró a lágrima viva.*

back — *la espalda*
   by . . . back — *a lomo de . . . .*
   He went by mule back. *Fue a lomo de mula.*

   on one's back — *a cuestas.*
   I was carrying it on my back. *Lo llevaba a cuestas.*

   to be back — *estar de vuelta.*
   She's back. *Está de vuelta.*

   to break one's back — *partirse el espinazo.*
   They break their backs digging. *Se parten el espinazo cavando.*

   to have one's back to the wall — *encontrarse entre la espada y la pared.*
   We had our backs to the wall. *Nos encontramos entre la espada y la pared.*

   to have one's back turned — *estar dando la espalda.*
   She had her back (turned) to me. *Me estaba dando la espalda.*

   to turn one's back — *volver (dar) la espalda.*
   I turned my back on her. *Le volví (di) la espalda.*

to back — *moverse hacia atrás, respaldar*
   to back down — *volverse atrás.*
   He backed down. *Se volvió atrás.*

   to back out — *retirarse; romper su compromiso, echarse atrás.*
   He was going with us but backed out. *Iba con nosotros pero se retiró (rompió su compromiso; se echó atrás).*

13

to back someone up — *apoyar.*
His family backed him up. *Su familia lo apoyó.*

to back up — *marchar atrás.*
He didn't know how to back up. *No sabía hacer marchar atrás el coche.*

back(ward) — *atrás*
  back(ward) — *hacia atrás.*
  She looked back(ward). *Miró hacia atrás.*

bacon — *el tocino*
  to bring home the bacon — *tener éxito.*
  They brought home the bacon. *Tuvieron éxito.*

bad — *malo*
  from bad to worse — *de mal en peor.*
  His luck is going from bad to worse. *Su suerte va de mal en peor.*

bag — *la bolsa*
  to be in the bag — *ser cosa hecha.*
  It's in the bag. *Es cosa hecha.*

  to leave holding the bag — *dejar con la carga en las costillas.*
  She left me holding the bag. *Me dejó con la carga en las costillas.*

  to let the cat out of the bag — *escapársele el secreto.*
  He let the cat out of the bag. *Se le escapó el secreto.*

baker — *el panadero*
  a baker's dozen — *una docena de fraile.*
  He gave her a baker's dozen. *Le dio una docena de fraile.*

ball — *la pelota*
  That's the way the ball bounces. *Así es la vida.*

  to have a lot on the ball — *tener capacidad.*
  He's got a lot on the ball. *Tiene gran capacidad.*

  to get all balled up — *hacerse bolas; estar hecho un lío.*
  He got all balled up. *Se hizo bolas (Está hecho un lío).*

to get the ball rolling — *empezar.*
They'll get the ball rolling tomorrow. *Empezarán mañana.*

to have a ball — *divertirse mucho; pasarlo en grande.*
We had a ball. *Nos divertimos mucho (Lo pasamos en grande).*

to keep the ball rolling — *mantener el interés.*
He did it to keep the ball rolling. *Lo hizo para mantener el interés.*

to play ball with — *obrar en armonía con.*
He had to play ball with his boss in order to succeed. *Tuvo que obrar en armonía con su jefe para tener éxito.*

---

bandwagon — *el carro de banda de música*
  to get on the bandwagon — *unirse a la mayoría.*
  It's best to get on the bandwagon. *Es mejor unirse a la mayoría.*

bang — *el estrépito*
  to go over with a bang — *ser un éxito tremendo.*
  It went over with a bang. *Fue un éxito tremendo.*

---

to bank — *depositar (dinero)*
  to bank on — *contar con.*
  You can't bank on his help. *No puedes contar con su ayuda.*

bargain — *la ganga*
  to strike a bargain — *cerrar un trato (llegar a un acuerdo).*
  After arguing for an hour, they struck a bargain. *Después de una hora de discusión, cerraron un trato (llegaron a un acuerdo).*

---

bark — *el ladrido*
  His bark is worse than his bite. — *Perro ladrador, poco mordedor.*

---

barrel — *el barril*
  to have over a barrel — *tener agarrado de las greñas.*
  I couldn't help it. He had me over a barrel. *No pude más. Me tenía agarrado de las greñas.*

---

to base — *basar, fundar*
  to base oneself (one's opinion) on — *fundarse en.*
  I'm basing myself (my opinion) on what he said last week. *Me fundo en lo que dijo la semana pasada.*

basis — *la base*
  to be on a first-name basis — *tutearse.*
  They're on a first-name basis. *Se tutean.*

bat — *el murciélago*
  like a bat out of hell — *como alma que lleva el diablo.*
  He took off like a bat out of hell. *Salió como alma que lleva el diablo.*

He took off like a
bat out of hell.
*Salió como alma
que lleva el diablo.*

to bat — *golpear*
  to go to bat for — *defender.*
  He went to bat for his employees. *Defendió a sus empleados.*

to bawl — *vocear*
  to bawl out — *regañar.*
  The teacher bawled out the kid who broke the window. *El maestro regañó al chico que rompió la ventana.*

bay — *la bahía*
  to hold at bay — *tener a raya.*
  They held us at bay. *Nos tuvieron a raya.*

to be — *ser, estar*

as it were — *por decirlo así.*

He's the father, as it were, of the modern novel. *Es el padre, por decirlo así, de la novela moderna.*

How are you? — *¿Qué tal?*

. . . -to-be — *futuro . . . .*

She's his wife-to-be. *Es su futura esposa.*

to be becoming — *quedarle (irle) muy bien.*

Her skirt is becoming to her. *La falda le queda (va) muy bien.*

to be onto someone — *conocerle el juego.*

Since we're already onto him, he can't fool us. *Como ya le conocemos el juego, no nos puede engañar.*

---

beam — *la viga; el rayo*

to be off the beam — *estar despistado.*

He's slightly off the beam. *Está un poco despistado.*

---

bean — *el frijol, la judía*

to spill the beans — *descubrirlo todo.*

He spilled the beans. *Lo descubrió todo.*

---

to bear — *cargar*

to bear with someone — *ser paciente.*

Please bear with us a little longer. *Haga el favor de ser paciente un poco más.*

---

to beat — *batir*

it beats me — *no tengo ni idea.*

It beats me why he does that. *No tengo ni idea por qué hace eso.*

to beat one to it — *cogerle (tomarle) la delantera.*

I tried to get there first but Mario beat me to it. *Quise llegar primero pero Mario me cogió (tomó) la delantera.*

---

because — *porque*

because of — *a (por) causa de.*

We're staying because of our parents. *Nos quedamos a (por) causa de nuestros padres.*

---

to become — *hacerse, llegar a ser*
  what has become of — *qué ha sido de, qué se ha hecho.*
  What has become of the maid? *¿Qué ha sido de la criada? (¿Qué se ha hecho la criada?)*

---

becoming — *conveniente*
  to be becoming to — *sentarle bien.*
  That dress is very becoming to her. *Ese vestido le sienta muy bien.*

---

bed — *la cama*
  a bed of roses — *un lecho de rosas.*
  His life was not a bed of roses. *Su vida no era un lecho de rosas.*

  to be sick in bed — *estar en cama.*
  He's sick in bed. *Está en cama.*

  to go to bed with the chickens — *acostarse con las gallinas.*
  They go to bed with the chickens. *Se acuestan con las gallinas.*

  to make the bed — *hacer (arreglar) la cama.*
  She made the bed. *Hizo (Arregló) la cama.*

  to put to bed — *reducir a cama.*
  The cold put me to bed. *El resfriado me redujo a cama.*

  to stay in bed — *guardar cama.*
  He stayed in bed two days. *Guardó cama dos días.*

---

bee — *la abeja*
  a bee in one's bonnet — *una idea fija en la mente.*
  She's got a bee in her bonnet. *Tiene una idea fija en la mente.*

---

beeline — *la línea recta*
  to make a beeline for — *salir disparado hacia.*
  We made a beeline for the dining room. *Salimos disparados hacia el comedor.*

---

behalf — *el favor*
  on behalf of — *en nombre de.*
  He welcomed them on behalf of the president. *Les dio la bienvenida en nombre del presidente.*

  on one's behalf — *a su favor.*
  He wrote on my behalf. *Escribió a mi favor.*

behind — *detrás*
  from behind — *de espaldas.*
  She was attacked from behind. *Fue atacada de espaldas.*

to believe — *creer*
  believe it or not — *aunque parezca mentira.*
  Believe it or not, it's true. *Aunque parezca mentira, es la verdad.*

  to make believe — *hacer como.*
  He made believe he didn't know. *Hizo como si no lo supiera.*

bell — *la campana*
  to ring a bell — *sonarle (a algo conocido).*
  That name rings a bell. *Ese nombre me suena (a algo conocido).*

to belong — *pertenecer*
  where one belongs — *donde le llaman.*
  I don't go where I don't belong. *No voy a donde no me llaman.*

belt — *el cinturón*
  to tighten one's belt — *apretar el cinturón.*
  We had to tighten our belts. *Tulvimos que apretar el cinturón.*

beneath — *abajo*
  to feel it beneath one — *tener a menos.*
  She doesn't feel it beneath her to cook. *No tiene a menos cocinar.*

benefit — *el beneficio*
  the benefit of the doubt — *un margen de confianza.*
  They gave us the benefit of the doubt. *Nos concedieron un margen de confianza.*

to be of benefit — *ser útil.*
It will be of benefit to us. *Nos será útil.*

---

bent — *encorvado, inclinado*
    to be bent on — *empeñarse en.*
    He's bent on proving me wrong. *Se empeña en probar que yo estoy equivocado.*

---

beside — *cerca de, junto a*
    to be beside oneself — *estar fuera de sí.*
    She's beside herself. *Está fuera de sí.*

---

besides — *además*
    besides — *además de; a más de.*
    Besides being too small, she can't sing. *Además de (A más de) ser muy pequeña, no sabe cantar.*

---

best — *mejor*
    at best — *en el mejor de los casos.*
    We'll win five games at best. *Ganaremos cinco partidos en el mejor de los casos.*

    at one's best — *en uno de sus mejores momentos.*
    He wasn't at his best. *No estaba en uno de sus mejores momentos.*

    to do one's best — *hacer lo posible.*
    He does his best. *Hace lo posible.*

    to make the best of — *sacar el mejor partido posible de.*
    He made the best of the situation. *Sacó el mejor partido posible de la situación.*

    with the best of them — *como el más pintado.*
    He can dance the tango with the best of them. *Sabe bailar el tango como el más pintado.*

---

to bet — *apostar*
    I'll bet — *a que.*
    I'll bet that it will rain. *A que llueve.*

    You bet! — *¡Ya lo creo!*

---

better — *mejor*

Better late than never. — *Más vale tarde que nunca.*

for better or for worse — *para bien o para mal.*
She got married, for better or for worse. *Se casó para bien o para mal.*

one's better half — *su cara mitad; su media naranja.*
My better half will accompany me. *Mi cara mitad (media naranja) me acompañará.*

to be better — *valer más.*
It is better to wait. *Más vale esperar.*

to be better off — *estar mejor.*
He's better off here. *Está mejor aquí.*

to get better — *mejorarse.*
She's getting better. *Se está mejorando.*

to get the better of — *poder más que.*
He got the better of me. *Pudo más que yo.*

to think better of it — *cambiar de opinión.*
I was about to go but I thought better of it. *Estaba para ir pero cambié de opinión.*

---

big — *grande*
The bigger they come, the harder they fall. *De gran subida, gran caída.*

---

bill — *la cuenta*
to foot the bill — *pagar la cuenta.*
My father didn't want to foot the bill. *Mi padre no quiso pagar la cuenta.*

---

bind — *el apuro*
to get in a bind — *meterse en un apuro.*
By trying to help them, I got in a bind. *Tratando de ayudarlos, me metí en un apuro.*

---

binge — *la juerga*
to go on a binge — *ir de juerga.*
They are going on a binge. *Van de juerga.*

---

bird — *pájaro*

A bird in the hand is worth two in the bush. — *Vale más pájaro en mano que ciento volando.*

birds of a feather — *de la misma calaña.*
They're birds of a feather. *Son de la misma calaña.*

Birds of a feather flock together — *Dios los cría y ellos se juntan.*

naked as a jay bird (as the day he was born) — *en cueros.*
He went out on the street naked as a jay bird (as the day he was born). *Salió a la calle en cueros.*

The early bird gets the worm. — *Al que madruga, Dios le ayuda.*

to kill two birds with one stone — *matar dos pájaros de (en) un tiro.*

---

birth — *el nacimiento*

to give birth to — *dar a luz a.*
She gave birth to a son. *Dio a luz a un hijo.*

---

bit — *pedacito; el freno, el bocado; moneda antigua*

a good bit — *una buena cantidad.*
He left a good bit in the basket. *Dejó una buena cantidad en la canasta.*

every bit — *todo.*
I understood every bit of it. *Lo entendí todo.*

not a bit — *ni pizca.*
He doesn't eat a bit of meat. *No come ni pizca de carne.*

quite a bit — *bastante.*
He dances quite a bit. *Baila bastante.*

to do one's bit — *apartar su granito de arena.*
He always does his bit. *Siempre aparta su granito de arena.*

to take the bit in one's teeth — *rebelarse.*
He took the bit in his teeth and said no. *Se rebeló y dijo que no.*

two-bit — *de poco valor.*
He's a two-bit artist. *Es un artista de poco valor.*

---

to bite — *morder*

    to bite off more than one can chew — *medir mal sus propias fuerzas.*

    He bit off more than he can chew. *Midió mal sus propias fuerzas.*

black — *negro*

    in black and white — *por escrito.*

    I want to see it in black and white. *Lo quiero ver por escrito.*

    in the black — *con superávit.*

    The company is operating in the black. *La compañía funciona con superávit.*

blame — *la culpa*

    to be to blame — *tener la culpa.*

    We're not to blame for her death. *No tenemos la culpa de su muerte.*

    to put (lay) the blame on — *echarle la culpa a.*

    First he put (laid) the blame on Philip and then shifted the blame on to us.
        Primero le echó la culpa a Felipe y luego nos la echó a nosotros.

blank — *blanco*

    to be blank — *estar en blanco.*

    This page is blank. *Esta página está en blanco.*

    to draw a blank — *no conseguirlo.*

    I tried to find him but I drew a blank. *Quise encontrarlo pero no lo
        conseguí.*

blanket — *la manta*

    a wet blanket — *un aguafiestas.*

    He's a wet blanket. *Es un aguafiestas.*

to bleed — *sangrar*

    to bleed white (dry) — *sangrar de las venas.*

    His relatives are bleeding him white (dry). *Sus parientes lo están
        sangrando de las venas.*

blind — *ciego*

    In the land of the blind the one-eyed is king. — *En tierra de ciegos, el
        tuerto es rey.*

to blindfold — *vendar los ojos*
    to be able to do it blindfolded — *saber hacerlo a ojos cerrados.*
    He can do that blindfolded. *Sabe hacer eso a ojos cerrados.*

block — *el bloque*
    to knock someone's block off — *romperle la cabeza.*
    He threatened to knock his block off. *Amenazó (con) romperle la cabeza.*

blood — *la sangre*
    in cold blood — *a sangre fría.*
    They killed him in cold blood. *Lo mataron a sangre fría.*

    to sweat blood — *sudar la gota gorda.*
    She was sweating blood preparing for her exam. *Sudaba la gota gorda preparándose para el examen.*

    You can't get blood out of a turnip. *Nadie puede dar lo que no tiene.*

blow — *el golpe*
    to come to blows — *llegar a las manos; liarse a mamporros.*
    They came to blows. *Llegaron a las manos (Se liaron a mamporros).*

to blow — *soplar*
    to blow down — *echar al suelo.*
    The wind blew down the sign. *El viento echó al suelo el letrero.*

    to blow hot and cold — *pasar de un extremo a otro.*
    The team blows hot and cold. *El equipo pasa de un extremo a otro.*

    to blow out — *reventarse.*
    His tire blew out (on him). *Se le reventó la llanta.*

    to blow over — *pasar (olvidarse).*
    They are angry now, but don't worry, it will blow over soon. *Están enojados ahora, pero no te preocupes, pronto pasará (se olvidará).*

    to blow up — *explotar; volar.*
    The engineer blew up the bridge. *El ingeniero explotó (voló) el puente.*

blue — *azul*
    out of the blue — *como caído de las nubes.*

He appeared out of the blue. *Apareció como caído de las nubes.*

to have the blues — *sentir tristeza.*
He's got the blues. *Siente tristeza.*

---

board — *la tabla*
across-the-board — *general.*
They gave everyone an across-the-board raise. *Dieron a todos un aumento general de sueldo.*

---

to boast — *jactarse*
to boast of — *echárselas de.*
He boasts of being smart. *Se las echa de listo.*

---

body — *el cuerpo*
in a body — *en comitiva.*
They came in a body to complain. *Vinieron en comitiva para quejarse.*

over one's dead body — *pasando por encima de su cadáver.*
You'll take it over my dead body. *Se lo llevará pasando por encima de mi cadáver.*

---

bone — *el hueso*
a bone of contention — *la manzana de la discordia.*
It's a bone of contention with him. *Es la manzana de la discordia con él.*

to have a bone to pick — *tener que habérselas.*
I've got a bone to pick with you. *Tengo que habérmelas con usted.*

to make no bones about it — *no andar con rodeos en decirlo.*
He didn't like it and made no bones about it. *No le gustó y no anduvo con rodeos en decirlo.*

---

boner — *el error*
to pull a boner — *meter la pata.*
He pulled a boner. *Metió la pata.*

---

book — *el libro*
in my book — *en mi concepto.*

In my book, Madrid is a beautiful city. *En mi concepto, Madrid es una ciudad hermosa.*

the good book — *la Biblia.*
It is found in the good book. *Se encuentra en la Biblia.*

to crack a book — *abrir un libro (para estudiarlo).*
Even though he never cracks a book, he always gets good grades. *Aunque nunca abre un libro, siempre saca buenas notas.*

to keep books — *llevar libros.*
He keeps books for a publishing house. *Lleva libros para una casa editorial.*

to know like a book — *conocer a fondo.*
I know him like a book. *Lo conozco a fondo.*

to throw the book at — *castigar con todo rigor.*
The army threw the book at him. *El ejército lo castigó con todo rigor.*

---

boot — *la bota*
to die with one's boots on — *morir al pie del cañón; morir vestido.*
They died with their boots on. *Murieron al pie del cañón (Murieron vestidos).*

---

to bore — *aburrir, fastidiar*
to bore to death (bore stiff) — *matar de aburrimiento.*
My brother is bored to death (bored stiff) by that professor's lectures. *A mi hermano le matan de aburrimiento las conferencias de ese profesor.*

---

boredom — *el aburrimiento, el fastidio*
to die of boredom — *aburrirse como una ostra.*
I die of boredom at my aunt's parties. *Me aburro como una ostra en las fiestas de mi tía.*

---

born — *nacido*
to be born lucky — *nacer de pie(s).*
Everybody in that family is born lucky. *Todos los de esa familia nacen de pie(s).*

to be born yesterday — *ser niño.*
I wasn't born yesterday. *No soy niño.*

---

both — *ambos*
  both . . . and . . . — *tanto . . . como . . .; lo mismo . . . que . . .*
  Both the heat and the cold bother her. *Tanto el calor como el frío (Lo mismo el calor que el frío) la molestan.*

---

to bother — *molestar*
  don't bother — *no se moleste.*
  Don't bother to get up. *No se moleste en levantarse.*

  to bother about — *molestarse con.*
  They don't want to bother about my problems. *No quieren molestarse con mis problemas.*

---

bottom — *el fondo*
  at the bottom of the ladder — *sin nada.*
  He began at the bottom of the ladder. *Empezó sin nada.*

  at the bottom of the page — *al pie (al final) de la página.*
  It's at the bottom of the page. *Está al pie (final) de la página.*

  Bottoms up! — *¡Salud! (dicho al brindar).*

  to get to the bottom — *aclarar.*
  We got to the bottom of the mystery. *Aclaramos el misterio.*

  to knock the bottom out of — *echar abajo.*
  It knocked the bottom out of his project. *Echó abajo su proyecto.*

---

bound — *obligado*
  to be bound for — *ir rumbo a; ir con destino a.*
  I'm bound for home. *Voy rumbo a (con destino a) mi casa.*

  to be bound to — *tener que; estar destinado a.*
  It's bound to rain. *Tiene que (Está destinado a) llover.*

---

to bow — *inclinarse*
  to bow out — *dejar de participar.*
  He bowed out. *Dejó de participar.*

---

boy — *el muchacho*
  to be someone's fair-haired boy — *ser pu preferido (predilecto).*

He was the professor's fair-haired boy. *Era el preferido (predilecto) del profesor.*

---

brain — *el cerebro*
  to rack one's brains (to beat one's brains out) — *calentarse (romper; devanarse) la cabeza.*
  He racked his brains (beat his brains out). *Se calentó (Rompió) (Se devanó) la cabeza.*

---

brand — *la marca*
  brand new — *flamante.*
  He was sporting a brand new wristwatch. *Lucía un flamante reloj de pulsera.*

---

bread — *el pan*
  to know which side one's bread is buttered on — *arrimarse al sol que más calienta (saber lo que le conviene).*
  I know which side my bread is buttered on. *Me arrimo al sol que más calienta (Sé lo que me conviene).*

  to put on bread and water — *poner a pan y agua.*
  They put him on bread and water. *Lo pusieron a pan y agua.*

---

break — *la oportunidad; la interrupción*
  to give someone a break — *echarle una mano; darle una oportunidad.*
  She gave me a break. *Me echó una mano (Me dio una oportunidad).*

  to have a good break — *tener buena suerte.*
  He had a good break. *Tuvo buena suerte.*

  to take a break — *tomarse un descanso.*
  They took a break every day at ten. *Se tomaban un descanso todos los días a las diez.*

---

to break — *romper*
  to be broke — *estar sin blanca.*
  I'm broke. *Estoy sin blanca.*

  to break down — *romperse.*
  The washing machine broke down. *La lavadora se rompió.*

  to break even — *cubrir gastos.*

We can't break even. *No podemos cubrir gastos.*

to break in — *estrenar.*
We broke in our typewriter. *Estrenamos nuestra máquina de escribir.*

to break in — *formar.*
It takes a month to break in a new secretary. *Hace falta un mes para formar a una secretaria.*

to break into — *entrar (por fuerza) en.*
A thief broke into my office. *Un ladrón entró (por fuerza) en mi oficina.*

to break loose — *escaparse.*
He broke loose from his cell. *Se escapó de su celda.*

to break off — *romper; terminar.*
They broke off their friendship. *Rompieron (Terminaron) su amistad.*

to break one's spirit — *doblegarle el ánimo.*
They broke his spirit. *Le doblegaron el ánimo.*

to break out — *estallar.*
War broke out. *Estalló la guerra.*

to break out in tears — *deshacerse en lágrimas.*
She breaks out in tears easily. *Se deshace en lágrimas fácilmente.*

---

breakdown — *la avería*
  a nervous breakdown — *un colapso nervioso; una crisis nerviosa.*
  She suffered a nervous breakdown. *Sufrió un colapso nervioso (una crisis nerviosa).*

---

breast — *el pecho*
  to make a clean breast of it — *confesarlo todo.*
  He made a clean breast of it. *Lo confesó todo.*

---

breath — *el aliento*
  all in one breath — *todo de un aliento.*
  He said it all in one breath. *Lo dijo todo de un aliento.*

  in the same breath — *casi al mismo tiempo.*
  She consented to come and in the same breath said that she couldn't.
    Consintió en venir y casi al mismo tiempo dijo que no podía.

to be out of breath — *estar sin aliento.*
I'm out of breath. *Estoy sin aliento.*

to catch one's breath — *recobrar el aliento.*
We don't have time to catch our breath. *No tenemos tiempo para recobrar el aliento.*

to catch one's breath (i.e., to gasp) — *tomar aliento.*
We caught our breath. *Tomamos aliento.*

to take one's breath away — *dejarle boquiabierto; asombrarle.*
Her intelligence took my breath away. *Su inteligencia me dejó boquiabierto (me asombró).*

to waste one's breath — *perder el tiempo.*
I wasted my breath teaching him to speak Spanish. *Perdí el tiempo enseñándole a hablar español.*

under one's breath — *en voz baja.*
He said it under his breath. *Lo dijo en voz baja.*

---

bridge — *el puente*

    to burn one's bridges behind one — *quemar sus naves.*
    He burned his bridges behind him. *Quemó sus naves.*

---

to bring — *traer*

    to bring about — *causar.*
    The flood was brought about by the rains. *La inundación fue causada por las lluvias.*

    to bring back — *devolver.*
    He brought back my book. *Me devolvió el libro.*

    to bring down the house — *hacer venirse abajo el teatro.*
    Her song brought down the house. *Su canción hizo venirse abajo el teatro.*

    to bring out — *dar (sacar) a luz.*
    He brought out his last novel in 1910. *Dio (Sacó) a luz su última novela en 1910.*

    to bring out — *presentar.*
    The factory brought out a new model of the airplane. *La fábrica presentó un nuevo modelo de avión.*

to bring out — *sacar.*
She brought out her best dishes. *Sacó su mejor vajilla.*

to bring someone to (around) — *reanimar.*
We brought him to (around) with artificial respiration. *Lo reanimamos con respiración artificial.*

to bring (pull) up — *arrimar.*
Bring (Pull) up a chair. *Arrime una silla.*

to bring up — *criar; educar.*
Since she was an orphan, her grandparents brought her up. *Como era huérfana, la criaron (educaron) sus abuelos.*

to bring up — *sacar a relucir.*
He brought up all my shortcomings. *Sacó a relucir todos mis defectos.*

---

broad — *ancho*
It's as broad as it is long. — *Lo mismo de un modo que del otro.*

---

brow — *la frente*
   to knit one's brow — *fruncir el ceño.*
   She knitted her brow when she saw me. *Frunció el ceño cuando me vio.*

---

brunt — *la fuerza*
   to bear the brunt — *llevar el peso.*
   I bore the brunt of the responsibility. *Llevé el peso de la responsabilidad.*

---

to brush — *cepillar*
   to brush up on — *repasar.*
   They're brushing up on their English. *Están repasando su inglés.*

---

buck — *la ficha*
   to pass the buck — *echar la carga.*
   He passed the buck to me. *Me echó la carga a mí.*

   to buck — *encorvarse*
   Buck up! — *¡Anímese!*

---

bud — *el pimpollo*
  to nip in the bud — *cortar de raíz.*
  Our plan was nipped in the bud. *Nuestro plan fue cortado de raíz.*

to bug — *molestar*
  What's bugging her? — *¿Qué mosca la ha picado?*

What's bugging her?
¿Qué mosca la ha picado?

to build — *construir*
  to build up — *amasar.*
  We have built up a large fortune. *Hemos amasado una gran fortuna.*

  to build up — *aumentar.*
  We built up our stock. *Aumentamos nuestras existencias.*

bull — *el toro*
  to take the bull by the horns — *agarrar al toro por los cuernos.*
  They took the bull by the horns and made the decision. *Agarraron al toro
    por los cuernos y tomaron la decisión.*

bullet — *la bala*
  to put a bullet through someone — *pegarle un tiro.*
  They put a bullet through him. *Le pegaron un tiro.*

to bump — *topar*
  to bump into — *darse de cara con.*

We bumped into him at the university. *Nos dimos de cara con él en la universidad.*

to bump off — *matar, despachar.*
The gangster bumped off his rival. *El gangster mató (despachó) a su rival.*

to burst — *estallar*
    to burst out laughing (crying) — *romper (echarse) a reír (llorar)* .
    He burst out laughing (crying). *Rompió (Se echó) a reír (llorar).*

bush — *el arbusto*
    to beat around the bush — *andar por las ramas; andar con rodeos.*
    She always beats around the bush. *Siempre anda por las ramas (con rodeos).*

business — *el negocio*
    It's his (her, etc.) business. — *Allá él (ella, etc.).*

    It's my business. — *Es cosa mía.*

    it's none of . . . 's business — *no es cuenta de. . . .*
    It's none of John's business. *No es cuenta de Juan.*

    that business about — *lo (eso) de.*
    That business about the murder grieves me. *Lo (Eso) del asesinato me da pena.*

    to get down to business — *ponerse a la obra.*
    We're wasting time. Let's get down to business. *Estamos perdiendo tiempo. Pongámonos a la obra.*

    to mean business — *hablar en serio.*
    I mean business. *Hablo en serio.*

    to mind one's own business — *no meterse en lo que no le toca.*
    He told her to mind her own business. *Le dijo que no se metiera en lo que no le tocaba.*

    to work up a good business — *poner a flote un buen negocio.*
    They worked up a good business. *Pusieron a flote un buen negocio.*

but — *pero*
    No buts about it! — *¡No hay pero que valga!*

to butter — *untar con mantequilla*
  to butter up — *chuparle las medias.*
  That student likes to butter up the professor. *A ese alumno le gusta chuparle las medias al profesor.*

to buy — *comprar*
  to buy out — *comprar.*
  I bought out his business. *Compré su negocio.*

  to buy up — *adquirir; acaparar.*
  I bought up all the land I could. *Adquirí (Acaparé) todo el terreno que pude.*

Cain — *Caín*
  to raise Cain — *armar un alboroto.*
  When he sees it, he'll raise Cain. *Cuando lo vea, armará un alboroto.*

cake — *el pastel*
  That takes the cake! — *¡Eso sí que es el colmo!*

  to take the cake (i.e., to take the prize) — *llevarse la palma.*
  Her dance took the cake. *Su baile se llevó la palma.*

Her dance took the cake.
Su baile se llevó la palma.

call — *la llamada*

    to have a close call — *salvarse por los pelos.*
    We had a close call. *Nos salvamos por los pelos.*

    within call — *al alcance de la voz.*
    Stay within call. *Quédese al alcance de mi voz.*

to call — *llamar*

    to call down (i.e., to chide) — *regañar.*
    Her teacher called her down. *Su maestra la regañó.*

    to call for — *merecer.*
    This calls for a celebration. *Esto merece una fiesta.*

    to call for — *requerir.*
    That calls for a lot of patience. *Requiere mucha paciencia.*

    to call for — *venir a buscar.*
    He called for me at ten. *Vino a buscarme a las diez.*

    to call on — *visitar a.*
    We called on Mrs. López. *Visitamos a la señora de López.*

    to call up — *llamar por teléfono.*
    He called me up. *Me llamó por teléfono.*

candle — *la vela*

    not to hold a candle to — *no poder compararse con.*
    He can't hold a candle to his sister. *No puede compararse con su hermana.*

    to burn the candle at both ends — *gastar locamente las fuerzas.*
    He burns the candle at both ends. *Está gastando locamente sus fuerzas.*

canoe — *la canoa*

    to paddle one's own canoe — *bastarse a sí mismo.*
    From the time he was a child, he was used to paddling his own canoe.
       Desde niño estaba acostumbrado a bastarse a sí mismo.

capacity — *la capacidad*

    in the capacity of — *en calidad de.*
    He's here in the capacity of program director. *Está aquí en calidad de
       director del programa.*

carbon — *el carbón*
   to make a carbon — *sacar una copia (en papel carbón).*
   He made a carbon of it. *Sacó una copia (en papel carbón).*

---

card — *la carta*
   to put one's cards on the table — *poner las cartas boca arriba; poner
      las cartas sobre la mesa.*
   When we put our cards on the table we understood each other. *Al poner
      las cartas boca arriba (sobre la mesa) nos entendimos.*

---

care — *el cuidado*
   in care of — *al cuidado de.*
   I left it in care of the manager. *Lo dejé al cuidado del gerente.*

   That takes care of that (So much for that). — *Asunto terminado.*

   to take care of — *cuidar a.*
   She takes care of her children. *Cuida a sus hijos.*

   to take care of — *ocuparse (encargarse) de.*
   He took care of the matter. *Se ocupó (Se encargó) del asunto.*

---

to care — *cuidar*
   not to be able to care less — *no importarle lo más mínimo.*
   He couldn't care less. *No le importaba lo más mínimo.*

---

careful — *cuidadoso*
   Be careful! — *¡Tenga cuidado!*

   be careful not to . . . — *cuidado con. . . .*
   Be careful not to fall! *¡Cuidado con caerse!*

---

carpet — *la alfombra*
   to have someone on the carpet — *echarle una reprimenda.*
   They had me on the carpet. *Me echaron una reprimenda.*

---

to carry — *llevar*
   to carry out — *llevar a cabo; efectuar*
   He carried out the plan. *Llevó a cabo (Efectuó) el proyecto.*

to carry the ball — *encargarse de todo; tener toda la responsabilidad.*
He carries the ball. *Se encarga de todo (Tiene toda la responsabilidad).*

---

cart — *la carreta*
   to put the cart before the horse — *tomar el rábano por las hojas; empezar la casa por el tejado.*
   That's putting the cart before the horse. *Eso es tomar el rábano por las hojas (empezar la casa por el tejado).*

   to upset the apple cart — *echar todo a perder.*
   He upset the apple cart with his comments. *Echó todo a perder con sus comentarios.*

---

case — *el caso*
   as the case may be — *según el caso.*
   They come in the morning or in the afternoon, as the case may be. *Vienen por la mañana o por la tarde según el caso.*

   in any case — *de todas formas.*
   In any case, I'll accept. *De todas formas, aceptaré.*

   in case — *en caso de.*
   In case you know, call us. *En caso de saber, llámenos.*

   just in case — *por si acaso; por si las moscas.*
   Take two more, just in case. *Llévese dos más, por si acaso (por si las moscas).*

   to have a case — *tener un argumento convincente.*
   They don't have a case. *No tienen un argumento convincente.*

---

cash — *el dinero contante*
   cash on the barrel head — *en dinero contante y sonante.*
   He wanted me to pay him cash on the barrel head. *Quería que yo le pagara en dinero contante y sonante.*

   to pay (spot) cash — *pagar al contado; pagar con dinero contante.*
   He pays (spot) cash. *Paga al contado (con dinero contante).*

   to send C. O. D. — *mandar contra reembolso.*
   He sent it C. O. D. *Lo mandó contra reembolso.*

---

to cast — *echar*

    to cast responsibilities on one — *echarle encima responsabilidades.*
    They cast many responsibilities on him. *Le echaron encima muchas responsabilidades.*

cat — *el gato*

    All cats are alike in the dark. — *De noche todos los gatos son pardos.*

    copycat — *un imitador.*
    He's a copycat. *Es un imitador.*

    There are more ways than one to skin a cat. — *Hay muchos modos de matar pulgas.*

    to let the cat out of the bag — *descubrirlo todo; revelar el secreto.*
    He let the cat out of the bag. *Lo descubrió todo (Reveló el secreto).*

    to rain cats and dogs (pitchforks) — *llover a cántaros (llover chuzos).*
    It's raining cats and dogs (pitchforks). *Está lloviendo a cántaros (Llueve chuzos).*

catch — *la presa, el botín*

    to be a good catch — *ser un buen partido.*
    That girl is a good catch. *Esa chica es un buen partido.*

to catch — *coger, asir*

    to catch hold of — *agarrar.*
    I caught hold of it. *Lo agarré.*

    to catch on — *tener eco.*
    It's a good idea, but I doubt that it will catch on. *Es una buena idea, pero dudo que tenga eco.*

    to catch on to — *entender.*
    He didn't catch on to the plan. *No entendió el plan.*

    to catch up with — *alcanzar; dar alcance.*
    He caught up with us. *Nos alcanzó (dio alcance).*

ceiling — *el cielo raso, el techo (interior)*

    to hit the ceiling — *ponerse como una fiera; poner el grito en cielo.*

She hit the ceiling when she found out what her sister had done. *Se puso como una fiera (Puso el grito en el cielo) al saber lo que había hecho su hermana.*

certain — *cierto*
  a certain — *un tal.*
  A certain Mr. Pérez told me. *Me lo dijo un tal señor Pérez.*

  for certain — *a ciencia cierta.*
  I know it for certain. *Lo sé a ciencia cierta.*

  on a certain — *uno de tantos.*
  On a certain Monday, they went away. *Uno de tantos lunes se marcharon.*

chance — *la ocasión, la oportunidad; el azar*
  by chance — *por casualidad.*
  Do you by chance have my book? *¿Tiene por casualidad mi libro?*

  to let the chance slip by — *perder la ocasión.*
  We let the chance slip by. *Perdimos la ocasión.*

  to stand a chance — *tener la posibilidad (probabilidad).*
  He doesn't stand a chance of winning. *No tiene ninguna posibilidad (probabilidad) de ganar.*

  to take a chance — *aventurarse.*
  I don't want to take a chance. *No quiero aventurarme.*

character — *el carácter*
  to be quite a character — *ser un tipo original.*
  He's quite a character. *Es un tipo original.*

charge — *el cargo*
  to be in charge — *estar a cargo; estar al frente.*
  He's in charge of the group. *Está a cargo (al frente) del grupo.*

  to take charge — *hacerse cargo; encargarse de.*
  He took charge of the clerks. *Se hizo cargo (Se encargó) de los dependientes.*

charity — *la caridad*
  Charity begins at home. — *La caridad bien entendida empieza por uno mismo.*

chase — *la caza*
   a wild-goose chase — *una empresa hecha sin provecho.*
   It turned out to be a wild-goose chase. *Resultó ser una empresa hecha sin provecho.*

to cheat — *defraudar; hacer trampas*
   to cheat on one's spouse — *engañar al cónyuge.*
   They accused her of cheating on her husband. *La acusaron de haber engañado a su marido.*

to check — *verificar; detener, refrenar*
   to check in (out) — *registrarse (marcharse).*
   He checked in on Monday and checked out on Wednesday. *Se registró en el hotel el lunes y se marchó el miércoles.*

   to check oneself — *refrenarse.*
   He was about to say it but he checked himself. *Estaba a punto de decirlo pero se refrenó.*

   to check up on — *hacer indagaciones sobre.*
   He checked up on his students. *Hizo indagaciones sobre sus alumnos.*

   to check with — *consultar.*
   Check with me before you leave. *Consúlteme antes de salir.*

check-up — *el reconocimiento*
   to give a check-up — *hacer un reconocimiento general.*
   The doctor gave me a check-up. *El médico me hizo un reconocimiento general.*

to cheer — *animar*
   to cheer up — *animarse.*
   I cheered up when I saw her. *Me animé cuando la vi.*

chest — *el pecho*
   to throw out one's chest — *sacar el pecho.*
   He threw out his chest. *Sacó el pecho.*

chestnut — *la castaña*
   to pull someone's chestnuts out of the fire — *sacarle las castañas del fuego.*
   We were always pulling his chestnuts out of the fire. *Siempre le sacábamos las castañas del fuego.*

chicken — *la gallina, el pollo*
   Don't count your chickens before they are hatched. — *No venda la piel del oso antes de haberlo cazado.*

chin — *la barba, el mentón*
   to keep one's chin up — *no desanimarse.*
   Keep your chin up. *No se desanime.*

chip — *la astilla*
   to be a chip off the old block. — *De tal palo, tal astilla.*

   to have a chip on one's shoulder — *ser muy provocador; ser un resentido.*
   He always has a chip on his shoulder. *Es muy provocador (un resentido).*

circle — *el círculo*
   a vicious circle — *un círculo vicioso.*
   Life is a vicious circle. *La vida es un círculo vicioso.*

   to go around in circles — *dar vueltas.*
   Why don't we drop this? We're just going around in circles and not getting anywhere. *¿Por qué no dejamos esto? Estamos dando vueltas sin llegar a ninguna parte.*

circumstance — *la circunstancia*
   under no circumstances (not under any circumstances) — *de ningún modo; en ningún caso.*
   Under no circumstances am I going to do that (I'm not going to do that under any circumstances). *De ningún modo (En ningún caso) voy a hacer eso.*

   under the circumstances — *dadas las circunstancias; en estas circunstancias.*

Under the circumstances it's the only thing we can do. *Dadas las circunstancias (En estas circunstancias) es lo único que podemos hacer.*

---

clean — *limpio*
    to come clean — *confesarlo todo.*
    He came clean. *Lo confesó todo.*

---

to clean — *limpiar*
    to clean out — *dejar sin nada.*
    They cleaned us out. *Nos dejaron sin nada.*

---

cleaners — *la tintorería*
    to take to the cleaners — *dejar en la calle.*
    Don't play poker with them. They'll take you to the cleaners. *No juegues al póker con ellos. Te dejarán en la calle.*

---

clear — *claro*
    clear-cut — *bien delimitado.*
    It's a clear-cut plan. *Es un plan bien delimitado.*

    to be in the clear — *estar libre de culpa.*
    He's in the clear. *Está libre de culpa.*

    to make clear — *dar a entender; sacar en claro.*
    She made it clear that she wasn't interested. *Dio a entender (Sacó en claro) que no tenía interés.*

---

to clear — *aclarar*
    to clear up — *clarificar; poner en claro.*
    He cleared up the matter with his explanation. *Clarificó (Puso en claro) el asunto con su explicación.*

    to clear up — *despejarse; aclararse.*
    By eleven it had cleared up. *Para las once se había despejado (aclarado).*

---

clock — *el reloj*
    around the clock — *día y noche.*
    We worked around the clock. *Trabajamos día y noche.*

    to wind the clock — *dar cuerda al reloj.*
    I wound the clock. *Di cuerda al reloj.*

---

close — *el fin*
  to draw to a close — *tocar a su fin; estar para terminar.*
  The year is drawing to a close. *El año está tocando a su fin (está para terminar).*

---

close — *cerca*
  to get close to . . . — *frisar en los . . . años.*
  He's getting close to 75. *Frisa en los setenta y cinco años.*

---

cloud — *la nube*
  cloud nine — *el séptimo cielo.*
  He's on cloud nine. *Está en el séptimo cielo.*

  Every cloud has a silver lining. — *No hay mal que por bien no venga.*

  to be (up) in the clouds — *estar en las nubes.*
  It is useless to ask him for advice; he's always up in the clouds. *Es inútil pedirle consejos; siempre está en las nubes.*

---

coast — *la costa*
  The coast is clear. — *Ya no hay moros en la costa.*

---

cock — *el gallo*
  the cock of the walk — *el gallito del lugar.*
  He always wanted to be the cock of the walk. *Siempre quería ser el gallito del lugar.*

---

cocktail — *el cóctel*
  to mix (up) a cocktail — *preparar un cóctel.*
  He mixed us (up) a cocktail. *Nos preparó un cóctel.*

---

coincidence — *la coincidencia*
  by coincidence — *por casualidad.*
  He found out by mere coincidence. *Lo supo por pura casualidad.*

---

cold — *el frío; el resfriado, el catarro*
  to catch cold — *coger catarro.*
  He caught cold in the rain. *Cogió catarro en la lluvia.*

to leave out in the cold — *dejar colgado.*
We were left out in the cold. *Nos dejaron colgados.*

---

cold — *frío*
to be cold (the weather) — *hacer frío.*
It's cold today. *Hace frío hoy.*

to be cold (a person) — *tener frío.*
I'm cold. *Tengo frío.*

---

collar — *el cuello*
to get hot under the collar — *enojarse, enfadarse.*
He got hot under the collar when he heard the news. *Se enojó (se enfadó)
al oír la noticia.*

white collar — *de oficina.*
He was looking for a white-collar job. *Buscaba un empleo de oficina.*

---

color — *el color*
to call to the colors — *llamar a filas.*
He was called to the colors. *Lo llamaron a filas.*

to lend color — *dar color.*
The presence of the gypsies lent color to the scene. *La presencia de los
gitanos le daba color a la escena.*

---

to come — *venir*
Come and get it! — *¡A comer!*

Come on! — *¡Vamos!*

come to think of it — *ahora caigo en que.*
Come to think of it, he sent me one. *Ahora caigo en que me mandó uno.*

Come what may (Come hell or high water) — *contra viento y marea.*
She's going to marry him come what may (come hell or high water). *Va a
casarse con él contra viento y marea.*

How come? — *¿Cómo se explica?*

I'm coming! — *¡Allá voy!*

to come about — *suceder.*

How did it come about? *¿Cómo sucedió?*

to come across — *encontrarse con.*
I came across an old photo. *Me encontré con una vieja foto.*

to come along — *acompañar.*
She asked me to come along. *Me pidió que la acompañara.*

to come along — *andar.*
How's your aunt coming along? *¿Cómo anda su tía?*

to come back — *regresar.*
Come straight back. *Regrese en seguida (sin detenerse).*

to come down — *venir hacia abajo.*
He was coming down. *Venía hacia abajo.*

to come down to — *reducirse a.*
What it comes down to is that they didn't want to go. *A lo que se reduce es que no querían ir.*

to come from — *ser de.*
He comes from Malta. *Es de Malta.*

to come in handy — *servir bien.*
The tool came in handy. *La herrarmienta me sirvió bien.*

to come off — *caérsele.*
A button came off. *Se me cayó un botón.*

to come out ahead — *salir ganando.*
If they listen to my advice they'll come out ahead. *Si escuchan mis consejos saldrán ganando.*

to come out well (badly) — *salir bien (mal).*
He came out well (badly) in his exam. *Salió bien (mal) en su examen.*

to come to — *volver en sí.*
He seemed dazed when he came to. *Parecía ofuscado cuando volvió en sí.*

to come to pass — *cumplirse.*
If it comes to pass, we'll be without funds. *Si se cumple, estaremos sin fondos.*

to come true — *realizarse.*
His dream came true. *Su sueño se realizó.*

comfort — *el consuelo*
   to be cold comfort — *ser un pobre consuelo.*
   What he said was cold comfort. *Lo que dijo fue un pobre consuelo.*

comfortable — *cómodo*
   to be very comfortable — *estar muy a gusto; muy bien; a sus anchas.*
   We are very comfortable here. *Estamos muy a gusto (muy bien; a nuestras anchas) aquí.*

command — *el dominio*
   to have a good command — *dominar bien.*
   He has a good command of Spanish. *Domina bien el español.*

commotion — *la conmoción*
   to cause a commotion — *armar un alboroto.*
   He caused a commotion. *Armó un alboroto.*

company — *la compañía*
   to keep company with — *cortejar a.*
   He keeps company with his secretary. *Corteja a su secretaria.*

   to keep someone company — *hacerle compañía.*
   She's keeping him company. *Le hace compañía.*

   to part company — *tomar rumbos distintos.*
   They were good friends for several years but they finally parted company. *Fueron buenos amigos por varios años pero al fin tomaron rumbos distintos.*

to compel — *compeler*
   to be compelled to — *verse forzado (obligado) a.*
   He's compelled to leave the city. *Se ve forzado (obligado) a marcharse de la ciudad.*

to concern — *concernir, interesar*
   as far as I'm concerned — *por lo que a mí se refiere; por lo que a mí me toca.*
   As far as I'm concerned, take it. *Por lo que a mí se refiere (me toca) lléveselo.*

To whom it may concern. — *A quien le corresponda; a quien pueda interesar.*

---

conclusion — *la conclusión*
  to jump to conclusions — *juzgar a la ligera.*
  She likes to jump to conclusions. *Le gusta juzgar a la ligera.*

---

to confide — *confiar*
  to confide in — *hacer una confidencia.*
  He confided in us. *Nos hizo una confidencia.*

---

conformity — *la conformidad*
  to be in conformity with — *estar de conformidad con.*
  It's in conformity with our laws. *Está de conformidad con nuestras leyes.*

---

conscience — *la conciencia*
  a clear conscience — *una conciencia limpia.*
  My conscience is clear. *Mi conciencia está limpia.*

---

consideration — *la consideración*
  out of consideration for — *por consideración a.*
  She rests out of consideration for her health. *Descansa por consideración a su salud.*

---

to consist — *consistir*
  to consist of — *constar de.*
  It consists of five parts. *Consta de cinco partes.*

---

conspicuous — *conspicuo*
  to be conspicuous by one's absence — *brillar por su ausencia.*
  She's conspicuous by her absence. *Brilla por su ausencia.*

  to make oneself conspicuous — *llamar la atención.*
  He always makes himself conspicuous. *Siempre llama la atención.*

---

construction — *la construcción*
  under construction — *en obras.*
  There is a dam under construction. *Hay una presa en obras.*

---

contrary — *contrario*
  on the contrary — *al contrario.*
  She's not ugly. On the contrary, she's very pretty. *No es fea. Al contrario, es muy bonita.*

control — *el control*
  to be under control — *andar perfectamente.*
  Everything is under control. *Todo anda perfectamente.*

convenience — *la comodidad*
  at one's earliest convenience — *a la primera oportunidad.*
  Answer at your earliest convenience. *Conteste a la primera oportunidad.*

convenient — *cómodo*
  to be more convenient — *resultar más cómodo.*
  It's more convenient to fly. *Resulta más cómodo tomar el avión.*

conversation — *la conversación*
  to strike up a conversation — *entablar una conversación.*
  He likes to strike up a conversation with strangers. *Le gusta entablar una conversación con desconocidos.*

to convince — *convencer*
  to be convinced — *estar persuadido de.*
  I'm convinced that it's correct. *Estoy persuadido de que es correcto.*

cook — *el cocinero*
  Too many cooks spoil the broth. — *Tres al saco, y el saco en tierra.*

to cook — *cocinar*
  to cook one's goose — *firmar su sentencia de muerte; perderlo todo.*
  Now he's cooked his goose! *Ya ha firmado su sentencia de muerte (lo ha perdido todo).*

cookie — *la galleta (dulce)*
  That's the way the cookie crumbles. — *Así es la vida.*

cool — *fresco; sereno*
> **to keep cool** — *conservar la serenidad.*
> He kept cool. *Conservó la serenidad.*

> **to lose one's cool** — *perder la cabeza.*
> When he heard the accusation, he lost his cool. *Al oír la acusación perdió la cabeza.*

---

to cool — *serenarse; refrescarse*
> Cool off! — *¡Serénese!*

> **to cool off** — *enfriarse.*
> My tea cooled off. *Mi té se enfrió.*

---

core — *el corazón, el centro*
> **to the core** — *hasta la médula; de pies a cabeza.*
> He's stingy to the core. *Es tacaño hasta la médula (de pies a cabeza).*

---

corner — *el rincón*
> **to look out of the corner of one's eye** — *mirar de reojo.*
> She's looking at us out of the corner of her eye. *Nos está mirando de reojo.*

---

cost — *la costa*
> **at all cost** — *a todo trance; a toda costa; cueste lo que cueste.*
> She'll do it at all cost. *Lo hará a todo trance (a toda costa; cueste lo que cueste).*

---

to count — *contar*
> **to count** — *entrar en la cuenta.*
> It doesn't count. *No entra en la cuenta.*

> **to count on** — *contar con.*
> He's counting on us. *Cuenta con nosotros.*

> **to count out** — *no contar con.*
> I'm counting you out. *No cuento con usted.*

---

counter — *el mostrador*
> **over the counter** — *libremente.*

Liquor is not sold over the counter here. *No se venden licores libremente aquí.*

under the counter (table) — *en secreto.*
He buys his gold under the counter (table). *Compra el oro en secreto.*

---

courage — *el ánimo*
to pluck up one's courage — *recobrar ánimo.*
I plucked up my courage and entered. *Recobré ánimo y entré.*

---

course — *el curso*
in due course — *a su debido tiempo.*
You'll know in due course. *Sabrá a su debido tiempo.*

in the course of time — *con el transcurso del tiempo.*
In the course of time the Moors left Spain. *Con el transcurso del tiempo, los moros salieron de España.*

of course — *claro; desde luego; por supuesto.*
Of course, it's not true. *Claro (Desde luego; Por supuesto) que no es verdad.*

of course — *cómo no.*
You have it? Of course! *¿Lo tiene? ¡Cómo no!*

---

courtesy — *la cortesía*
out of courtesy — *por cortesía.*
I invited her out of courtesy. *La invité por cortesía.*

---

crack — *la grieta; el instante; la prueba*
at the crack of dawn — *al romper el alba.*
We left at the crack of dawn. *Salimos al romper el alba.*

to make cracks about — *burlarse de.*
He makes cracks about her. *Se burla de ella.*

to take a crack at — *probar.*
I took a crack at tennis when I was 15. *Probé el tenis cuando tenía 15 años.*

---

to crack — *agrietarse*
to crack up — *estrellarse.*
The plane cracked up. *El avión se estrelló.*

---

to crawl — *arrastrarse*
  to crawl in — *entrar a gatas.*
  He crawled in. *Entró a gatas.*

---

crazy — *loco*
  to drive one crazy (mad) — *volverle loco; sacarle de las casillas.*
  She's driving me crazy (mad). *Me vuelve loco (Me saca de mis casillas).*

  to go crazy — *volverse loco.*
  He went crazy. *Se volvió loco.*

---

credit — *el crédito*
  on credit — *a crédito; al fiado.*
  We buy on credit. *Compramos a crédito (al fiado).*

  to give credit — *dar mérito.*
  You've got to give him a lot of credit. *Hay que darle mucho mérito.*

---

creeps — *el hormigueo*
  to give one the creeps — *darle escalofríos.*
  It gives me the creeps. *Me da escalofríos.*

---

crime — *el crimen*
  Crime doesn't pay. — *No hay crimen sin castigo.*

---

to cross — *cruzar*
  to cross out — *tachar.*
  He crossed out the last line. *Tachó la última línea.*

---

cross-country — *a campo traviesa*
  to go cross-country — *ir (a) campo traviesa.*
  They're going cross-country. *Van (a) campo traviesa.*

---

crow — *el cuervo*
  as the crow flies — *a vuelo de pájaro.*
  It's ten miles as the crow flies. *Está a diez millas a vuelo de pájaro.*

to make someone eat crow — *hacerle tragar saliva; hacerle sufrir la humillación.*

They made him eat crow. *Le hicieron tragar saliva (sufrir la humillación).*

---

crush — *el aplastamiento*
  to have a crush on — *estar encaprichado con; estar perdido por.*
  She has a crush on her boss. *Está encaprichada con (Está perdida por) su jefe.*

---

to crush — *aplastar*
  to be crushed by — *quedarse abrumado con.*
  We were crushed by his death. *Nos quedamos abrumados con su muerte.*

---

crust — *la corteza*
  the upper crust — *la alta sociedad.*
  He likes to mix with the upper crust. *Le gusta mezclarse con la alta sociedad.*

---

cry — *el grito*
  to be a far cry from — *distar mucho de ser.*
  This is a far cry from what I expected. *Esto dista mucho de ser lo que esperaba.*

---

to cry — *gritar; llorar*
  to cry out — *lanzar un grito.*
  I cried out. *Lancé un grito.*

---

cucumber — *el pepino*
  cool as a cucumber — *como si nada.*
  He listened to the bad news cool as a cucumber. *Escuchó la mala noticia como si nada.*

---

cudgel — *el garrote*
  to take up the cudgels for — *defender con vehemencia a; salir en defensa de.*
  He took up the cudgels for his brother. *Defendió con vehemencia a (Salió en defensa de) su hermano.*

---

cuff — *el puño*
   to speak off the cuff — *hablar improvisado.*
   She spoke off the cuff. *Habló improvisado.*

cup — *la taza*
   not to be one's cup of tea — *no ser de su gusto.*
   Baseball is not my cup of tea. *El béisbol no es de mi gusto.*

to cure — *curar*
   What can't be cured must be endured. — *A lo hecho, pecho.*

to cut — *cortar*
   cut and dried — *decidido de antemano.*
   It was all cut and dried. *Todo fue decidido de antemano.*

   to be cut out for — *tener talento para.*
   He's not cut out to be an artist. *No tiene talento para ser artista.*

   to cut class — *faltar a clase.*
   He cut class. *Faltó a clase.*

   to cut in — *interrumpir.*
   She cut in on our conversation. *Interrumpió nuestra conversación.*

   to cut off — *cortar.*
   They cut off the end. *Cortaron el extremo.*

   to cut off — *no dejar continuar.*
   He was trying to tell a joke, but his wife cut him off. *Trataba de contar un chiste, pero su mujer no lo dejó continuar.*

   to cut out — *dejar de.*
   He cut out smoking. *Dejó de fumar.*

   to cut (clip) out — *recortar.*
   She cut out my picture from the newspaper. *Recortó mi retrato del periódico.*

   to cut short — *interrumpir.*
   He cut short his visit. *Interrumpió su visita.*

   to cut up — *cortar en pedazos.*
   He cut up the melon. *Cortó en pedazos el melón.*

D

to dare — *atreverse*
  I dare you to! — *¡A ver si se atreve!*

dark — *oscuro*
  to get dark — *hacerse de noche.*
  I want to get there before it gets dark. *Quiero llegar antes que se haga de noche.*

  to keep in the dark — *tener a obscuras.*
  He kept her in the dark. *La tenía a obscuras.*

darling — *el predilecto*
  to be . . . 's darling — *ser el ojo derecho de. . . .*
  She's her father's darling. *Es el ojo derecho de su padre.*

date — *la fecha*
  at an early date — *en fecha próxima.*
  We'll decide at an early date. *Decidiremos en fecha próxima.*

  out of date — *anticuado; pasado de moda.*
  The book is out of date. *El libro es anticuado (pasado de moda)*

  to be up to date — *estar al corriente; estar al tanto.*
  He's up to date on everything. *Está al corriente (al tanto) de todo.*

  to be up to date — *estar al día.*
  The book's not up to date. *El libro no está al día.*

  to bring up to date (on) — *poner al corriente (al día) de.*
  He brought us up to date on the issue. *Nos puso al corriente (al día) del problema.*

  to date — *hasta la fecha.*
  To date it hasn't been seen. *Hasta la fecha no se ha visto.*

to date — *datar*
  to date — *salir con.*

He dates my sister. *Sale con mi hermana.*

to date back to — *remontar a; datar de.*
It dates back to the Middle Ages. *Remonta a (Data de) la Edad Media.*

---

dawn — *el alba*
  at (the break of) dawn — *al rayar (romper) el alba (al amanecer).*
  He got up at (the break of) dawn. *Se levantó al rayar (romper) el alba (al amanecer).*

  to dawn on — *occurrírsele.*
  Suddenly it dawned on me that she was lying. *De repente me di cuenta de que estaba mintiendo.*

day — *el día*
  as plain as day — *tan claro como el agua.*
  It's as plain as day. *Está tan claro como el agua.*

It's as plain as day.
Está tan claro como el agua.

  by the day — *día por día.*
  He gets fatter by the day. *Se va engordando día por día.*

  day in and day out — *día tras día.*
  He swims day in and day out. *Nada día tras día.*

  day-to-day — *cotidiano.*
  His day-to-day activities are interesting. *Sus actividades cotidianas son interesantes.*

  for one's days to be numbered — *tener los días contados.*
  His days are numbered. *Tiene los días contados.*

from day to day — *de día en día.*
We live from day to day. *Vivimos de día en día.*

one of these days — *un día de éstos.*
One of these days, we'll visit you. *Un día de éstos lo visitaremos.*

the next day — *al (el) día siguiente.*
I got it the next day. *Lo tuve al (el) día siguiente.*

this very day — *hoy mismo.*
I need it this very day. *Lo necesito hoy mismo.*

to call it a day — *dar el día por terminado.*
At 8:30 p.m. they called it a day. *A las ocho y media de la noche dieron el día por terminado.*

to have a day off — *tener un día libre.*
I've got a day off. *Tengo un día libre.*

to save for a rainy day — *guardar para un caso de emergencia.*
They are saving it for a rainy day. *Lo guardan para un caso de emergencia.*

---

daylight — *la luz del día*
in broad daylight — *en pleno día.*
It happened in broad daylight. *Pasó en pleno día.*

to begin to see daylight — *empezar a ver el fin.*
We're beginning to see daylight. *Empezamos a ver el fin.*

---

dead — *muerto*
dead tired — *muerto de cansancio.*
He came home dead tired. *Llegó a casa muerto de cansancio.*

in the dead of winter — *en lo más frío del invierno.*
Even in the dead of winter he took a walk every day. *Hasta en lo más frío del invierno daba un paseo todos los días.*

to be dead set against — *oponerse decididamente.*
I'm dead set against it. *Me opongo decididamente.*

to be dead to the world — *estar profundamente dormido.*
He's dead to the world. *Está profundamente dormido.*

to play dead (to play possum) — *hacer(se) el muerto.*
He played dead (played possum). *(Se) hizo el muerto.*

---

deaf — *sordo*

to be stone deaf — *estar sordo como una tapia.*
He's stone deaf. *Está sordo como una tapia.*

deal — *el negocio*

a square deal — *trato equitativo.*
The Indian hasn't always had a square deal. *El indio no siempre ha tenido trato equitativo.*

by a good deal — *ni con mucho.*
He didn't achieve his goal by a good deal. *No realizó su fin, ni con mucho.*

It's a deal. — *Trato hecho.*

to get a raw deal — *jugarle una mala pasada.*
He got a raw deal. *Le jugaron una mala pasada.*

death — *la muerte*

a struggle to the death — *una lucha a muerte.*
It's a struggle to the death. *Es una lucha a muerte.*

to be at death's door — *estar en las últimas.*
They say that his father is at death's door. *Se dice que su padre está en las últimas.*

to be frightened to death — *estar muerto de susto.*
I was frightened to death. *Estaba muerto de susto.*

to beat to death — *matar a palos.*
They beat him to death. *Lo mataron a palos.*

to die a natural death — *morirse de muerte natural.*
He died a natural death. *Se murió de muerte natural.*

to freeze to death — *partírsele de frío los huesos.*
He's freezing to death. *Se le parten de frío los huesos.*

to starve to death — *morir de hambre.*
He starved to death. *Murió de hambre.*

decision — *la decisión*

to make a decision — *tomar una determinación (decisión).*
We must make a decision. *Tenemos que tomar una determinación (decisión).*

deck — *la cubierta*
   to hit the deck — *levantarse (y ponerse a trabajar).*
   When I worked for my uncle, I had to hit the deck at six every morning.
      Cuando trabajaba para mi tío, tenía que levantarme a las seis todas las mañanas.

delivery — *la entrega*
   home delivery — *servicio a domicilio.*
   No home delivery. *No hacemos servicio a domicilio.*

demonstration — *la demostración*
   to give a demonstration — *hacer una demostración.*
   Give us a demonstration. *Háganos una demostración.*

to depend — *depender*
   That depends. — *Según y conforme.*

   to depend on — *depender de.*
   It depends on you. *Depende de usted.*

description — *la descripción*
   a blow-by-blow description — *una descripción con pelos y señales.*
   He gave us a blow-by-blow description. *Nos dio una descripción con pelos y señales.*

desert — *el merecido*
   to give someone his just deserts — *darle lo suyo.*
   He gives each one his just deserts. *Da a cada cual lo suyo.*

despair — *la desesperación*
   to sink into despair — *echarse a la desesperación.*
   He sank into despair. *Se echó a la desesperación.*

detour — *el desvío*
   to make a detour — *dar un rodeo.*
   I made a detour. *Di un rodeo.*

devil — *el diablo*

  between the devil and the deep blue sea — *entre la espada y la pared.*

  I found myself between the devil and the deep blue sea. *Me encontré entre la espada y la pared.*

  Speak of the devil. — *Hablando del ruin de Roma, luego asoma.*

  there will be the devil to pay — *ahí será el diablo.*

  If you do that there will be the devil to pay. *Si hace eso ahí será el diablo.*

  to give the devil his due — *ser justo, hasta con el diablo.*

  You've got to give the devil his due. *Hay que ser justo, hasta con el diablo.*

  to raise the devil — *armar un alboroto.*

  They went out and raised the devil. *Salieron y armaron un alboroto.*

to die — *morir*

  to be dying to — *reventar de ganas de.*

  He was dying to see that film. *Reventaba de ganas de ver esa película.*

  to die away (down) — *desaparecer; cesar.*

  The noise died away (down). *El ruido desapareció (cesó).*

  to die laughing — *morirse (ahogarse) de risa.*

  They died laughing. *Se murieron (ahogaron) de risa.*

  to die of sorrow — *reventar de dolor.*

  He died of sorrow. *Reventó de dolor.*

  to die out — *acabarse; apagarse.*

  The fire died out. *El fuego se acabó (se apagó).*

  to die out — *desaparecer completamente.*

  That legend died out. *Esa leyenda desapareció completamente.*

die-hard — *intransigente*

  die-hard — *empedernido.*

  He's a die-hard Republican. *Es un republicano empedernido.*

diet — *la dieta, el régimen*

  to be on a diet — *estar a dieta (régimen).*

  He's on a diet. *Está a dieta (régimen).*

to go on a diet — *ponerse a régimen (dieta).*
I went on a diet. *Me puse a régimen (dieta).*

---

difference — *la diferencia*
It makes no difference. — *Es igual; Lo mismo da.*
What difference does it make? — *¿Qué más da?*

---

difficulty — *la dificultad*
with utmost difficulty — *a duras penas.*
He reached it with utmost difficulty. *Lo alcanzó a duras penas.*

---

dig — *el codazo*
to take a dig at — *lanzar una sátira contra.*
He took a dig at the editor. *Lanzó una sátira contra el redactor.*

---

to dig — *cavar*
to dig in — *poner manos a la obra.*
We all had to dig in in order to finish it. *Todos tuvimos que poner manos a la obra para terminarlo.*

to dig up — *desenterrar.*
They dug up an old scandal. *Desenterraron un viejo escándalo.*

---

dime — *moneda de diez centavos*
to be a dime a dozen — *abundar como la mala hierba.*
These days English teachers are a dime a dozen. *Hoy en día los profesores de inglés abundan como la mala hierba.*

---

dint — *la fuerza*
by dint of — *a (en) fuerza de; a costa de.*
He learned it all by dint of studying. *Lo aprendió todo a (en) fuerza (a costa) de estudiar.*

---

discouraged — *desalentado*
to get discouraged — *caérsele las alas (del corazón).*
He got discouraged. *Se le cayeron las alas (del corazón).*

---

dish — *el plato*
  to do the dishes — *lavar los platos.*
  She does the dishes. *Lava los platos.*

disposal — *la disposición*
  to put at one's disposal — *poner a su disposición.*
  I put myself at his disposal. *Me puse a su disposición.*

distance — *la distancia*
  in the distance — *a lo lejos.*
  They could be seen in the distance. *Se veían a lo lejos.*

ditch — *la zanja*
  to the last ditch — *hasta quemar el último cartucho.*
  He'll fight to the last ditch. *Luchará hasta quemar el último cartucho.*

to do — *hacer*
  and be done with it — *de una vez.*
  Buy it and be done with it. *Cómprelo de una vez.*

  How are you doing? — *¿Cómo le va?*

  How do you do? — *Mucho gusto en conocerle.*

  That does it! — *¡No faltaba más!*
  That does it! I'll never speak to her again. *¡No faltaba más! ¡Nunca volveré a hablarle!*

  to do away with — *deshacerse de.*
  They did away with the evidence. *Se deshicieron de la prueba.*

  to do over — *volver a hacer.*
  He did his work over. *Volvió a hacer su trabajo.*

  to do with — *hacer de.*
  What have you done with my sword? *¿Qué ha hecho de mi espada?*

  to do without — *pasar(se) sin; prescindir de.*
  He can't do without his coffee. *No puede pasar(se) sin (prescindir de) su café.*

  What is done is done. — *Lo hecho, hecho está (A lo hecho, pecho).*

dog — *perro*

Every dog has his day. — *A cada santo le llega su fiesta.*

Let sleeping dogs lie. — *Deje las cosas como son.*

to be the dog in the manger — *ser como el perro del hortelano.*
Give it to me if you don't want it. Don't be the dog in the manger.
  Dámelo a mí si tú no lo quieres. No seas como el perro del hortelano.

to go to the dogs — *echarse a perder.*
He's going to the dogs. *Se está echando a perder.*

to put on the dog — *darse tono (aires).*
He likes to put on the dog. *Le gusta darse tono (aires).*

top dog — *el gallito del lugar.*
Mr. Jiménez is (the) top dog around here. *El señor Jiménez es el gallito
  del lugar por aquí.*

You can't teach an old dog new tricks. — *No se puede conseguir que un
  viejo cambie de ideas.*

doll — *la muñeca*

to play dolls — *jugar a las muñecas.*
They're playing dolls. *Están jugando a las muñecas.*

to doll — *engalanar*

to doll up — *engalanarse.*
She got all dolled up to go to the party. — *Se engalanó para ir a la fiesta.*

door — *la puerta*

next door — *al lado.*
Next door there's a doctor. *Al lado hay un médico.*

to darken one's door — *poner los pies en la casa.*
He never darkened my door again. *No volvió a poner los pies en mi casa.*

To lock the barn door after the horse has been stolen. — *Asno muerto,
  la cebada al rabo.*

to show to the door (i.e., show out) — *despedir en la puerta.*
With his usual politeness, he showed me to the door. *Con la cortesía de
  siempre, me despidió en la puerta.*

to show to the door (i.e., throw out) — *pedir que salga.*

Offended by my actions, he showed me to the door. *Ofendido por mis acciones, me pidió que saliera.*

to slam the door — *dar un portazo.*
She slammed the door. *Dio un portazo.*

to slam the door in someone's face — *cerrarle (darle con) la puerta en las narices.*
She slammed the door in my face. *Me cerró (Me dio con) la puerta en las narices.*

dot — *el punto*
    on the dot — *en punto.*
    They left at six on the dot. *Salieron a las seis en punto.*

doubt — *la duda*
    beyond the shadow of a doubt — *sin sombra de duda.*
    He is the guilty one beyond the shadow of a doubt. *El es el culpable sin sombra de duda.*

    no doubt — *sin duda.*
    He's no doubt right. *Sin duda tiene razón.*

    to be in doubt — *estar en duda.*
    The outcome is in doubt. *El resultado está en duda.*

    to cast doubt on — *poner en duda.*
    They cast doubt on her conduct. *Pusieron en duda su conducta.*

down — *abajo*
    to be down and out — *no tener donde caerse muerto.*
    She's down and out. *No tiene donde caerse muerta.*

    to get down to work — *ponerse a trabajar; aplicarse al trabajo.*
    He got down to work. *Se puso a trabajar (Se aplicó al trabajo).*

    when it comes right down to it — *a la hora de la verdad.*
    When it came right down to it, he refused to accept. *A la hora de la verdad no quiso aceptar.*

downhill — *cuesta abajo*
    to be downhill all the way — *ser cosa de coser y cantar (ser cuesta abajo).*

Our work will be downhill all the way. *Nuestro trabajo será cosa de coser y cantar (será cuesta abajo).*

to go downhill — *ir de capa caída.*
She's been going downhill lately. *Va de capa caída últimamente.*

---

to drag — *arrastrar*
    to drag off — *llevarse a rastras.*
    They dragged her off. *Se la llevaron a rastras.*

---

drain — *el desaguadero*
    to go down the drain — *no servir de nada.*
    All our efforts have gone down the drain. *Todos nuestros esfuerzos no han servido de nada.*

---

to draw — *extraer; tirar; dibujar*
    to draw someone out — *sonsacarle.*
    They couldn't draw him out. *No pudieron sonsacarle.*

    to draw up — *preparar.*
    I drew up a plan. *Preparé un plan.*

---

to dream — *soñar*
    to dream about — *soñar con.*
    I dream about my work. *Sueño con mi trabajo.*

---

to dress — *vestirse*
    to dress down — *echar un rapapolvo.*
    He dressed me down for arriving late. *Me echó un rapapolvo por haber llegado tarde.*

    to dress in — *vestirse de.*
    She dresses in velvet. *Se viste de terciopelo.*

---

driver — *el conductor*
    a hit-and-run driver — *un automovilista que se da a la fuga.*
    He was run over by a hit-and-run driver. *Fue atropellado por un automovilista que se dio a la fuga.*

to drive — *conducir, manejar*

  to drive at — *querer decir.*

  We didn't know what he was driving at. *No sabíamos lo que quería decir.*

  to drive (one) crazy — *sacar(le) de sus casillas.*

  Her way of talking drives me crazy. *Su manera de hablar me saca de mis casillas.*

to drop — *dejar caer*

  to drop a line — *poner unas líneas.*

  We dropped him a line. *Le pusimos unas líneas.*

  to drop in on — *visitar inesperadamente.*

  The neighbors dropped in on us last night. *Los vecinos nos visitaron inesperadamente anoche.*

  to drop in (by) to say hello — *pasar para saludar.*

  They dropped in (by) to say hello. *Pasaron para saludar.*

  to drop out — *dejar de asistir.*

  He dropped out of my class. *Dejó de asistir a mi clase.*

drunk — *borracho*

  to get dead drunk — *emborracharse a muerte.*

  We got dead drunk. *Nos emborrachamos a muerte.*

during — *durante*

  during the day (night) — *de día (noche).*

  He sleeps during the day (night). *Duerme de día (noche).*

to dry — *secar*

  to dry out — *secarse.*

  This shirt will never dry out. *Esta camisa no se secará nunca.*

  to dry up — *secarse.*

  The field dried up. *El campo se secó.*

duck — *el pato*

  to be a dead duck — *estar listo (quedar frito).*

  I'm a dead duck if my brother finds out about it. *Estoy listo (Quedo frito) si lo llega a saber mi hermano.*

dumbfounded — *atónito, pasmado*
  to be dumbfounded — *perder el habla.*
  When we saw him dressed as a clown, we were dumbfounded. *Al verle vestido de payaso perdimos el habla.*

dusk — *el crepúsculo*
  at dusk — *al atardecer; al oscurecer.*
  It began at dusk. *Empezó al atardecer (al oscurecer).*

dust — *el polvo*
  to bite the dust — *morder el polvo.*
  He bit the dust. *Mordió el polvo.*

Dutch — *holandés*
  to be in Dutch — *estar en un apuro.*
  He's in Dutch with his family. *Está en un apuro con su familia.*

  to go Dutch — *pagar cada uno lo suyo.*
  We went Dutch. *Cada uno pagó lo suyo.*

duty — *el deber*
  to be on duty — *estar de servicio (de turno).*
  She's on duty. *Está de servicio (de turno).*

  to report for duty — *acudir al trabajo.*
  He reports for duty at eight. *Acude a su trabajo a las ocho.*

  to shirk one's work — *faltar a las obligaciones.*
  He shirked his work. *Faltó a sus obligaciones.*

eager — *ansioso*
  to be eager to — *tener empeño (interés) en; estar ansioso de.*
  He's eager to learn. *Tiene empeño (interés) en (Está ansioso de) aprender.*

ear — *el oído, la oreja*
  by ear — *al (de) oído.*
  She plays by ear. *Toca al (de) oído.*

  to be all ears — *ser todo oídos; abrir los oídos.*
  It's a good idea to be all ears when they're explaining things like that. *Es conveniente ser todo oídos (abrir los oídos) cuando están explicando cosas así.*

  to go in one ear and out the other — *entrar por un oído y salir por el otro.*
  Everything he said to her went in one ear and out the other. *Todo lo que le decía le entraba por un oído y le salía por el otro.*

  to have someone's ear — *tener influencia con. . . .*
  I don't have the president's ear. *No tengo influencia con el presidente.*

  to play by ear — *tocar de oído.*
  He plays the piano by ear. *Toca el piano de oído.*

  to prick up one's ears — *aguzar el oído (los oídos).*
  When he heard her voice, he pricked up his ears. *Al oír su voz, aguzó el oído (los oídos).*

  to talk one's ear off — *hablar hasta por los codos.*
  He talks your ear off. *Habla hasta por los codos.*

  to turn a deaf ear — *hacerse (el) sordo.*
  He turned a deaf ear. *Se hizo (el) sordo.*

  up to one's ears — *hasta los ojos.*
  I'm up to my ears in work. *Estoy hasta los ojos en trabajo.*

early — *temprano*
  early in — *a primera hora de; muy de.*

It rained early in the morning. *Llovió a primera hora de la mañana (muy de mañana).*

---

earth — *la tierra*
   how on earth — *cómo diablos.*
   How on earth did you do it? *¿Cómo diablos lo hizo?*

   to come down to earth — *bajar de las nubes.*
   He wouldn't come down to earth. *No quería bajar de las nubes.*

---

ease — *la tranquilidad, la comodidad*
   to be (ill) at ease — *estar a (dis)gusto.*
   I'm never (ill) at ease in this atmosphere. *Nunca estoy a (dis)gusto en este ambiente.*

---

easy — *fácil*
   Easy come, easy go. — *Lo que el agua trae el agua lleva.*

   to make things easy — *dar toda clase de facilidades.*
   He made things easy for them. *Les dio toda clase de facilidades.*

   to take it easy — *descansar.*
   Take it easy for a few days. *Descanse por unos días.*

---

to eat — *comer*
   to eat out — *comer en un restaurante.*
   We ate out last night. *Comimos en un restaurante anoche.*

   What's eating you? — *¿Qué mosca le ha picado?*

---

edge — *el borde*
   to be on edge — *estar nervioso.*
   Everyone is on edge. *Todo el mundo está nervioso.*

   to have the edge on someone — *llevarle la ventaja.*
   She has the edge on me. *Me lleva la ventaja.*

   to set one's teeth on edge — *darle dentera.*
   It sets my teeth on edge. *Me da dentera.*

---

to edge — *avanzar de lado*
    to edge in — *abrir paso poco a poco.*
    We were able to edge in. *Pudimos abrir paso poco a poco.*

effect — *el efecto*
    in effect — *en pie; en vigor.*
    It is still in effect. *Sigue en pie (en vigor).*

    to go into effect — *entrar en vigor.*
    It went into effect yesterday. *Entró en vigor ayer.*

    to have a bad effect — *hacer mal efecto.*
    It has a bad effect on them. *Les hace mal efecto.*

egg — *el huevo*
    a nest egg — *los ahorros.*
    He has quite a nest egg in the bank. *Tiene muchos ahorros en el banco.*

    to lay an egg — *poner un huevo.*
    She lays an egg a day. *Pone un huevo al día.*

    to put all one's eggs in one basket — *jugarlo todo a una carta.*
    He put all his eggs in one basket. *Lo jugó todo a una carta.*

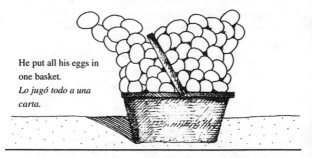

He put all his eggs in
one basket.
*Lo jugó todo a una
carta.*

elbow — *el codo*
    to rub elbows with — *rozarse mucho (tratar) con.*
    He rubs elbows with lawyers. *Se roza mucho (trata) con abogados.*

to elbow — *codear*
    to elbow one's way through — *abrirse paso a codazos.*
    They had to elbow their way through. *Tuvieron que abrirse paso a codazos.*

element — *el elemento*
    to be in one's element — *estar en su elemento.*
    When it's a question of dancing the tango, they're in their element.
        Cuando es cuestión de bailar el tango, están en su elemento.

eleventh — *undécimo*
    eleventh-hour — *de la última hora.*
    It was an eleventh-hour decision. *Fue una decisión de la última hora.*

end — *el fin*
    at the end of — *a fines de.*
    They arrived at the end of March. *Llegaron a fines de marzo.*

    at the end of — *al cabo (fin) de.*
    At the end of one hour, it was over. *Al cabo (fin) de una hora, se terminó.*

    at the end of — *al final de.*
    They live at the end of the street. *Viven al final de la calle.*

    at the end of nowhere — *en el quinto infierno.*
    They live at the end of nowhere. *Viven en el quinto infierno.*

    no end of — *un sin fin (la mar) de.*
    He has no end of problems. *Tiene un sin fin (la mar) de problemas.*

    to bring to an end — *dar fin a.*
    The storm brought the outing to an end. *La tormenta dio fin al paseo.*

    to come to a bad end — *acabar mal.*
    He came to a bad end. *Acabó mal.*

    to come to an end — *acabarse.*
    The dispute came to an end. *La disputa se acabó.*

    to come to an untimely end — *tener un final inesperado.*
    His life came to an untimely end. *Su vida tuvo un final inesperado.*

    to make (both) ends meet — *pasar con lo que se tiene.*
    It's hard to make (both) ends meet. *Es difícil pasar con lo que se tiene.*

to put an end to — *acabar con.*
They put an end to their quarrels. *Acabaron con sus peleas.*

to the bitter end — *hasta la muerte.*
He struggled to the bitter end. *Luchó hasta la muerte.*

to end — *terminar*
to end up by — *acabar (terminar) por.*
They ended up by getting married. *Acabaron (terminaron) por casarse.*

Where will it all end? — *¿Dónde va a parar?*

English — *el inglés*
in plain English — *sin rodeos.*
He told it to her in plain English. *Se lo dijo sin rodeos.*

to enjoy — *gozar*
to enjoy oneself — *pasarlo bien.*
Enjoy yourself. *Que lo pase bien.*

enough — *bastante, suficiente*
Enough is enough! — *¡Basta ya!*

It's enough to make you cry (laugh). — *Es para llorar (reír).*

not to be enough — *no alcanzar.*
There isn't enough money. *No alcanza el dinero.*

to be enough — *bastar.*
Seeing it once is enough for me. *Me basta con verlo una vez.*

to be more than enough — *sobrar.*
There's more than enough water. *Sobra agua.*

equal — *igual*
to be equal to — *estar a la altura de.*
I'm not equal to this task. *No estoy a la altura de esta tarea.*

equally — *igualmente*
to treat equally — *tratar por igual.*
They treat us equally. *Nos tratan por igual.*

errand — *recado, mandado*
   to run an errand — *hacer un mandado.*
   He's running an errand for his father. *Está haciendo un mandado por su padre.*

   to send on an errand — *enviar a un recado.*
   She sent me on an errand. *Me envió a un recado.*

eve — *la víspera*
   to be on the eve of — *estor en vísperas de.*
   He was on the eve of his promotion to colonel. *Estaba en vísperas de su ascenso a coronel.*

even — *aun, hasta; igualmente, con uniformidad*
   even so — *con todo (así y todo).*
   Even so, we have the best there is. *Con todo (Así y todo) tenemos lo mejor que hay.*

   not even — *ni siquiera.*
   Not even the water was good. *Ni siquiera el agua era buena.*

   to be even — *estar en paz.*
   We're even. *Estamos en paz.*

   to break even — *ni ganar ni perder.*
   They broke even. *Ni ganaron ni perdieron.*

   to get even with — *pagársela.*
   I'll get even with them. *Me la pagarán.*

event — *el suceso*
   in any event — *en todo caso; de todas maneras.*
   In any event we'll do everything possible. *En todo caso (De todas maneras) haremos todo lo posible.*

ever — *jamás*
   ever since — *desde entonces.*
   He's been cold ever since. *Desde entonces ha tenido frío.*
   ever since — *desde que.*

Ever since she found out the truth, she refuses to visit us. *Desde que supo la verdad, se niega a visitarnos.*

forever and ever — *para siempre jamás.*
They've left forever and ever. *Se han marchado para siempre jamás.*

if ever — *si alguna vez.*
If ever you come to México, visit us. *Si alguna vez viene a México, visítenos.*

every — *cada*
every other . . . — *un . . . sí y otro no.*
We go every other day. *Vamos un día sí y otro no.*

evil — *malo*
evil-minded — *mal pensado.*
He's evil-minded. *Es mal pensado.*

example — *el ejemplo*
to set an example — *servir de (dar) ejemplo.*
She sets an example for her daughters. *Sirve de (Da) ejemplo a sus hijas.*

excess — *el exceso*
to excess — *en demasía.*
He drank to excess. *Tomaba en demasía.*

exchange — *el cambio*
in exchange for — *a cambio de.*
I gave him my watch in exchange for his lighter. *Le di mi reloj a cambio de su encendedor.*

excuse — *la excusa*
to use as an excuse — *tomar de pretexto.*
She used it as an excuse to miss class. *Lo tomó de pretexto para faltar a la clase.*

to excuse — *excusar*
excuse me — *con permiso.*
Excuse me. I have to leave. *Con permiso. Tengo que marcharme.*

excuse me — *perdone.*
Excuse me! I didn't see you. *¡Perdone! No lo vi.*

expected — *esperado*
   when least expected — *el día menos pensado; cuando menos se piense.*
   It will arrive when least expected. *Llegará el día menos pensado (cuando menos se piense).*

expense — *el gasto*
   at the expense of — *a expensas (costa) de.*
   He won at the expense of his friends. *Ganó a expensas (costa) de sus compañeros.*

   to go to the expense — *meterse en gastos.*
   He didn't want to go to the expense. *No quiso meterse en gastos.*

explanation — *la explicación*
   to ask for explanations — *pedir cuentas.*
   She always asked him for explanations. *Siempre le pedía cuentas.*

extent — *el grado*
   to a great extent — *en gran parte.*
   To a great extent it is due to his good health. *Se debe en gran parte a su buena salud.*

   to some extent — *hasta cierto punto.*
   To some extent, that is true. *Hasta cierto punto es verdad.*

   to such an extent — *a tal punto.*
   It irritated him to such an extent that he refused to go. *Lo molestó a tal punto que se negó a ir.*

eye — *el ojo*
   An eye for an eye and a tooth for a tooth — *Ojo por ojo, diente por diente.*

   in the public eye — *en la escena (a la luz) pública.*
   He is no longer in the public eye. *Ya no está en la escena (a la luz) pública.*
   There is more to it than meets the eye. — *La cosa tiene más miga de lo que parece.*

to catch one's eye — *captarle la atención.*
She caught my eye. *Me captó la atención.*

to cry one's eyes out — *llorar a mares.*
She cried her eyes out. *Lloró a mares.*

to have an eye for — *tener mucha vista para.*
She has an eye for beauty. *Tiene mucha vista para la belleza.*

to keep an eye on — *no perder de vista.*
She kept an eye on him. *No lo perdió de vista.*

to keep an eye on — *vigilar a.*
Keep an eye on that kid. *Vigile a ese chico.*

to keep one's eyes peeled — *tener los ojos abiertos.*
Keep your eyes peeled. *Tenga los ojos abiertos.*

to lay eyes on — *echar la vista encima.*
He never laid eyes on them again. *Nunca volvió a echarles la vista encima.*

to raise one's eyes — *levantar la vista.*
She didn't raise her eyes. *No levantó la vista.*

to see eye to eye — *estar de acuerdo.*
We don't see eye to eye on anything. *No estamos de acuerdo en nada.*

to turn a blind eye — *hacer la vista gorda.*
I saw it but turned a blind eye. *Lo vi pero hice la vista gorda.*

without batting an eye — *sin pestañear.*
He lied without batting an eye. *Mintió sin pestañear.*

---

eyesight — *la vista*
  to have bad eyesight — *andar mal de la vista.*
  I have bad eyesight. *Ando mal de la vista.*

F

face — *la cara*
  face down — *boca abajo.*
  He fell face down. *Se cayó boca abajo.*

face to face — *frente a frente; cara a cara.*
They discussed it face to face. *Lo discutieron frente a frente (cara a cara).*

face up — *boca arriba.*
They found him face up. *Lo encontraron boca arriba.*

in the face — *a la cara.*
They look each other in the face. *Se miran a la cara.*

in the face of . . . — *frente a.*
He was brave in the face of death. *Fue valiente frente a la muerte.*

on the face of it — *a juzgar por las apariencias.*
On the face of it, I can't accept it. *A juzgar por las apariencias, no lo puedo aceptar.*

right to one's face — *en la cara.*
I told him right to his face. *Se lo dije en la cara.*

to fall flat on one's face — *caer de bruces.*
I fell flat on my face. *Caí de bruces.*

to get red in the face — *subírsele el pavo; ruborizarse.*
She got red in the face. *Se le subió el pavo (Se ruborizó).*

to keep a straight face — *contener la risa.*
She couldn't keep a straight face. *No pudo contener la risa.*

to lose face — *sufrir una pérdida de prestigio.*
They lost face in that deal. *Sufrieron una pérdida de prestigio en ese negocio.*

to make a face — *hacer una mueca.*
She tasted it and made a face. *Lo probó e hizo una mueca.*

to make an about-face — *cambiar de opinión (decisión).*
He made an about-face. *Cambió de opinión (decisión).*

to save face — *salvar las apariencias.*
He saved face by paying the fine. *Salvó las apariencias pagando la multa.*

to show one's face — *asomar la cara.*
She wouldn't show her face. *No quería asomar la cara.*

---

to face — *encararse con*
  to face — *dar (frente) a.*

It faces the river. *Da (frente) al río.*

to face (up to) it — *hacer frente a la situación (a las consecuencias).*
There's so much to do I can't face (up to) it. *Hay tanto que hacer que no puedo hacer frente a la situación (a las consecuencias).*

fact — *el hecho*
in fact — *en efecto.*
He'll be here soon. In fact, he's coming tomorrow. *Estará aquí muy pronto. En efecto viene mañana.*

the fact is — *el caso (ello) es.*
The fact is that no one knows. *El caso (Ello) es que nadie lo sabe.*

to get down to the facts — *ir al asunto.*
Let's get down to the facts. *Vamos al asunto.*

fail — *la falta*
without fail — *sin falta.*
Come tomorrow without fail. *Venga mañana sin falta.*

to fail — *faltar a; dejar de*
to fail to — *dejar de.*
Don't fail to see it. *No deje de verlo.*

to fail to show up for — *faltar a.*
He failed to show up for the appointment. *Faltó a la cita.*

fair — *justo*
fair and square — *con absoluta honradez.*
He treated us fair and square. *Nos trató con absoluta honradez.*

faith — *la fe*
in good (bad) faith — *de buena (mala) fe.*
He did it in good (bad) faith. *Lo hizo de buena (mala) fe.*

to pin one's faith on — *tener puesta la esperanza en.*
She had pinned her faith on graduating. *Tenía puesta su esperanza en graduarse.*

to fall — *caer*

    to fall apart — *deshacerse.*
    The club has fallen apart. *El club se ha deshecho.*

    to fall behind — *retrasarse.*
    I have fallen behind in my studies. *Me he retrasado en mis estudios.*

    to fall flat — *fracasar.*
    His report fell flat. *Su informe fracasó.*

    to fall for — *prendarse de.*
    He fell for her. *Se prendó de ella.*

    to fall for — *tragar(se).*
    Nobody's going to fall for a lie like that. *Nadie va a tragar(se) una mentira así.*

    to fall in love with — *enamorarse de.*
    He fell in love with his teacher. *Se enamoró de su maestra.*

    to fall off — *caerse de.*
    He fell off the ladder. *Se cayó de la escalera.*

    to fall off — *disminuir.*
    The quality of his work is falling off. *La calidad de su trabajo está disminuyendo.*

    to fall short — *no llegar a ser.*
    It fell short of being a masterpiece. *No llegó a ser una obra maestra.*

    to fall through — *fracasar.*
    Our plans fell through. *Nuestros planes fracasaron.*

falling-out — *la riña*

    to have a falling-out — *reñirse con.*
    I've had a falling-out with her. *Me he reñido con ella.*

family — *la familia*

    to be like one of the family — *ser muy de adentro.*
    He's like one of the family. *Es muy de adentro.*

fan — *el aficionado*

    to be a fan of — *ser aficionado a.*
    He's a movie fan. *Es aficionado al cine.*

fancy — *la fantasía*

    to strike one's fancy — *encapricharse de.*
    The new styles have struck her fancy. *Se ha encaprichado de las nuevas modas.*

    to take a fancy to — *prendarse de.*
    He took a fancy to his secretary. *Se prendó de su secretaria.*

far — *lejos*

    as far as one knows — *que sepa uno.*
    As far as we know, it's not true. *Que sepamos nosotros, no es verdad.*

    by far — *con mucho.*
    It's by far the cheapest. *Es con mucho el más barato.*

    far and near — *en (por) todas partes.*
    He has traveled far and near. *Ha viajado en (por) todas partes.*

    Far be it from me! — *¡Dios me libre!*

    Far from it! — *¡Ni mucho menos! (¡Ni con mucho!).*

    far into the night — *hasta las altas horas de la noche.*
    We studied far into the night. *Estudiamos hasta las altas horas de la noche.*

    so far — *en lo que va de.*
    So far this winter it hasn't snowed. *En lo que va de invierno no ha nevado.*

    That's going too far. — *Eso es demasiado fuerte.*

    to come from far and wide — *venir de todas partes.*
    They came from far and wide. *Vinieron de todas partes.*

    to come from far away — *venir de lejos.*
    They come from far away. *Vienen de lejos.*

    to go far — *ir lejos.*
    With all that talent, he'll go far. *Con tanto talento irá lejos.*

farther — *más lejos*

    farther on — *más allá.*
    It's farther on. *Está más allá.*

fashion — *la moda*
   after a fashion — *a su modo.*
   He described it after a fashion. *Lo describió a su modo.*

   to go out of fashion — *pasar de moda.*
   They went out of fashion. *Pasaron de moda.*

fashionable — *elegante*
   to become fashionable — *ponerse de moda.*
   They became fashionable last year. *Se pusieron de moda el año pasado.*

fast — *rápido; firme*
   to hold fast — *mantenerse firme.*
   He held fast in his decision. *Se mantuvo firme en su decisión.*

   to pull a fast one — *engañar.*
   He pulled a fast one on us. *Nos engañó.*

fat — *la grasa*
   The fat is in the fire. — *El mal ya está hecho; La cosa ya no tiene remedio.*

   to live off the fat of the land — *nadar en la abundancia.*
   They are living off the fat of the land. *Nadan en la abundancia.*

fate — *el hado, la suerte*
   to leave to one's fate — *dejar a su suerte.*
   I left him to his fate. *Lo dejé a su suerte.*

fault — *la culpa*
   it's . . . 's fault — *la culpa es de. . . .*
   It's your fault, not Mary's. *La culpa es suya, no de María.*

   to be at fault — *ser el culpable; tener la culpa.*
   He's at fault. *Es el culpable (Tiene la culpa).*

   to find fault with — *criticar; encontrar defectos en.*
   He finds fault with all I do. *Critica (Encuentra defectos en) todo lo que hago.*

favor — *el favor*
   in one's favor — *a su favor.*

It was decided in my favor. *Se decidió a mi favor.*

to be in favor of — *estar por.*
I'm in favor of attending. *Estoy por asistir.*

to decide in favor of — *optar por.*
We decided in favor of riding horseback. *Optamos por montar a caballo.*

---

feather — *la pluma*
Fine feathers don't make fine birds. — *Aunque la mona se vista de seda, mona se queda.*
It's a feather in his cap. — *Se ha apuntado un tanto; Es un triunfo personal.*

---

fed — *alimentado*
to be fed up with — *estar harto de; estar hasta la coronilla de.*
I'm fed up with this. *Estoy harto (hasta la coronilla) de esto.*

---

feed — *el alimento*
chicken feed — *una insignificancia; dinero menudo.*
All I have left is chicken feed. *Todo lo que me queda es una insignificancia (dinero menudo).*

---

to feel — *sentir*
to feel bad — *sentirse apenado.*
He feels bad because he failed. *Se siente apenado por haber salido mal.*

to feel free — *no vacilar.*
Feel free to let me know if I can help you. *No vacile en avisarme si puedo ayudarlo.*

to feel like — *tener ganas de.*
I feel like sleeping. *Tengo ganas de dormir.*

to feel like a new person — *sentirse como nuevo.*
I feel like a new man. *Me siento como nuevo.*

---

feelings — *la sensibilidad*
hard feelings — *rencor.*
He left with hard feelings. — *Salió con rencor.*

for one's feelings to be hurt — *estar muy sentido.*

My feelings are hurt. *Estoy muy sentido.*

mixed feelings — *reacciones diversas.*
His talk was received with mixed feelings. *Su charla fue acogida con reacciones diversas.*

to hurt one's feelings — *ofenderle.*
She hurt our feelings. *Nos ofendió.*

---

fence — *la cerca, la valla*
    to be on the fence — *estar indeciso; no querer comprometerse.*
    I don't know whether they're going to be on our side; they're still on the fence. *No se si van a ponerse de nuestra parte; todavía están indecisos (no quieren comprometerse).*

---

fiddle — *el violín*
    to be as fit as a fiddle — *estar de buena salud.*
    He's as fit as a fiddle. *Está de buena salud.*

    to play second fiddle — *hacer el papel de segundón.*
    He has to play second fiddle. *Tiene que hacer el papel de segundón.*

---

to fiddle — *tocar el violín*
    to fiddle with — *jugar nerviosamente con.*
    She was fiddling with her ring. *Jugaba nerviosamente son su anillo.*

---

fifty — *cincuenta*
    to go fifty-fifty — *ir a medias.*
    Let's go fifty-fifty. *Vamos a medias.*

---

figure — *la figura*
    to cut a fine figure — *causar una buena impresión.*
    He always cuts a fine figure. *Siempre causa una buena impresión.*

---

to figure — *figurar*
    to figure on — *contar con.*
    Let's figure on going. *Contemos con que vamos.*

    to figure out — *entender.*
    I can't figure out what he said. *No entiendo lo que dijo.*

to **figure up (out)** — *calcular.*
Figure up (out) what I owe you. *Calcule cuánto le debo.*

file — *la fila*
in single file — *en fila india*
They advanced in single file. *Avanzaron en fila india.*

on file — *archivado.*
I have it on file. *Lo tengo archivado.*

fill — *el hartazgo*
to have one's fill of — *hartarse de.*
I've had my fill of this. *Me he hartado de esto.*

to fill — *llenar*
to fill in (out) — *llenar.*
Fill in (out) this form. *Llene este formulario.*

to fill in for — *suplir.*
They filled in for us during the meeting. *Nos suplieron durante la reunión.*

to fill the gap — *llenar un vacío.*
It fills the gap. *Llena un vacío.*

to find — *encontrar*
to find out — *saber; enterarse de.*
He found out that she was married. *Supo (Se enteró de) que ella estaba casada.*

finder — *el hallador*
Finders keepers, losers weepers. — *Quien fue a Sevilla perdió su silla.*

finger — *el dedo*
to get one's fingers burnt — *pillarse los dedos.*
He got his fingers burnt. *Se pilló los dedos.*

to lay a finger on — *poner la mano encima.*
Don't lay a finger on my child. *No le ponga la mano encima a mi hijo.*

not to lift a finger — *no querer hacer nada.*
He didn't lift a finger. *No quiso hacer nada.*

to slip through one's fingers — *escapársele de las manos.*
I let it slip through my fingers. *Lo dejé escapárseme de las manos.*

to wrap (twist) . . . around one's little finger — *manejar a . . . a su antojo.*
He wraps (twists) his mother around his little finger. *Maneja a su madre a su antojo.*

fire — *el fuego*
to hang fire — *estar en suspenso.*
Too many decisions are still hanging fire. *Demasiadas decisiones todavía están en suspenso.*

to catch fire — *incendiarse.*
The house caught fire. *La casa se incendió.*

to open fire — *abrir fuego.*
They opened fire. *Abrieron fuego.*

to set fire to — *prender (pegar) fuego a.*
They set fire to the building. *Prendieron (Pegaron) fuego al edificio.*

to fire — *disparar, hacer fuego; despedir*
Fire away! — *¡Dispare!*

first — *primero*
at first — *al (en un) principio.*
At first, I accepted it. *Al (En un) principio lo acepté.*

first and foremost — *ante todo.*
First and foremost, we must try harder. *Ante todo tenemos que esforzarnos más.*

First come, first served. — *Servirán primero a los que lleguen primero.*

to come first — *ser lo primero.*
His work comes first. *Su trabajo es lo primero.*

fish — *el pez*
to drink like a fish — *beber como una esponja.*
They fired him because he drank like a fish. — *Lo despidieron porque bebía como una esponja.*

fishing — *la pesca*
  to go fishing — *ir de pesca.*
  We went fishing. *Fuimos de pesca.*

fit — *el ajuste; el ataque*
  by fits and starts — *a rachas, a empujones; sin regularidad.*
  He always works by fits and starts. *Siempre trabaja a rachas (a empujones; sin regularidad).*

  to feel fit — *sentirse bien.*
  She feels fit again. *Se siente bien otra vez.*

  to see fit — *juzgar conveniente; tener a bien.*
  They saw fit to sell it. *Juzgaron conveniente (Tuvieron a bien) venderlo.*

  to throw (to have) a fit — *poner el grito en el cielo; darle un patatús.*
  When she saw it, she threw (had) a fit. *Cuando lo vio, puso el grito en el cielo (le dio un patatús).*

to fit — *ajustar*
  to fit in — *estar de acuerdo.*
  It doesn't fit in with my ideas. *No está de acuerdo con mis ideas.*

  to fit in — *llevarse bien.*
  He doesn't fit in with our group. *No se lleva bien con nuestro grupo.*

flame — *la llama*
  an old flame — *un viejo amor.*
  She met an old flame. *Se encontró con un viejo amor.*

  to burst into flames — *inflamarse.*
  It burst into flames. *Se inflamó.*

flash — *el relámpago*
  a flash in the pan — *humo de pajas.*
  The idea was only a flash in the pan. *La idea fue sólo humo de pajas.*

  in a flash — *de un salto.*
  He was here in a flash. *Estuvo aquí de un salto.*

flat — *plano*
   to fall flat — *caer de plano; caer de redondo.*
   He fell flat on the floor. *Cayó de plano (redondo) al suelo.*

   to leave someone flat — *dejarlo plantado.*
   His wife left him flat. *Su esposa lo dejó plantado.*

flat-footed — *de pies achatados*
   to catch flat-footed — *coger de sorpresa.*
   The decision caught us flat-footed. *La decisión nos cogió de sorpresa.*

flesh — *la carne*
   in the flesh — *en persona.*
   We were surprised to see the president himself there in the flesh. *Nos sorprendió ver allí al propio presidente en persona.*

flight — *el vuelo*
   charter flight — *vuelo especial.*
   They went by charter flight. *Fueron por vuelo especial.*

   to take flight — *alzar el vuelo.*
   After the robbery, the thieves took flight. *Después del robo los ladrones alzaron el vuelo.*

to flock — *congregarse*
   to flock together — *andar juntos.*
   The foreigners always flock together. *Los extranjeros siempre andan juntos.*

floor — *el piso*
   to ask for (to take) the floor — *pedir (tomar) la palabra.*
   He asked for (took) the floor. *Pidió (Tomó) la palabra.*

floor — *el suelo*
   to pace the floor (pace up and down) — *pasearse de un lado para (a) otro.*
   Waiting for the doctor's decision, he paced the floor (paced up and down). *Esperando la decisión del médico, se paseaba de un lado para (a) otro.*

to fly — *volar*
    to fly by — *pasar volando.*
    This month has flown by. *Este mes ha pasado volando.*

fond — *cariñoso*
    to be fond of — *tener afición a.*
    We are fond of music. *Tenemos afición a la música.*

food — *la comida*
    to give food for thought — *dar que pensar.*
    His speech gave us food for thought. *Su discurso nos dio que pensar.*

fool — *el tonto*
    to be nobody's fool — *no tener pelo de tonto.*
    He's nobody's fool. *No tiene pelo de tonto.*

    to make a fool of someone — *ponerle en ridículo.*
    He made a fool of her. *La puso en ridículo.*

    to make a fool of oneself — *hacer el ridículo.*
    He's making a fool of himself. *Está haciendo el ridículo.*

    to play (act) the fool — *hacer el tonto.*
    He played (acted) the fool. *Hizo el tonto.*

to fool — *tontear, engañar*
    to fool around — *perder tiempo; malgastar el tiempo.*
    They fired him because he fools around too much. *Lo despidieron porque pierde demasiado tiempo (malgasta el tiempo).*

foolproof — *a prueba de mal trato*
    a foolproof method — *un método infalible.*
    It's a foolproof method. *Es un método infalible.*

foot — *el pie*
    on foot — *a pie.*
    They're going on foot. *Van a pie.*

    to drag one's feet — *tardar en obrar.*

Salaries were not raised because the president dragged his feet. *No se realizó el aumento de los sueldos porque el rector tardó en obrar.*

to have one's feet on the ground — *estar bien plantado.*

I think you can have confidence in him. He seems to have his feet on the ground. *Creo que puedes confiar en él. Parece estar bien plantado.*

to put one's best foot forward — *esmerarse en hacer lo mejor posible.*

She put her best foot forward in order to impress him. *Se esmeró en hacer lo mejor posible para impresionarlo.*

to put one's foot down —*oponerse enérgicamente.*

Raúl wanted to learn karate, but his father put his foot down. *Raúl quería aprender karate, pero su padre se opuso enérgicamente.*

to put one's foot in one's mouth — *meter la pata.*

He put his foot in his mouth. *Metió la pata.*

He put his foot in his mouth.
Metió la pata.

to set foot in — *poner los pies en; pisar.*

He refuses to set foot in that house. *Se niega a poner los pies en (pisar) esa casa.*

---

for — *por, para*

for — *(desde) hace.*

I've been here for an hour. *Estoy aquí (desde) hace una hora.*

to be for — *preferir.*

I'm for going to the beach. *Prefiero ir a la playa.*

---

force — *la fuerza*
  by sheer force — *a viva fuerza.*
  She succeeded by sheer force. *Lo logró a viva fuerza.*

  in force — *en masa.*
  His friends visited him in force. *Sus amigos lo visitaron en masa.*

  to be in force — *estar en vigor.*
  The law is no longer in force. *La ley ya no está en vigor.*

forest — *el bosque*
  You cannot see the forest for the trees. — *Los árboles no dejan ver el bosque.*

form — *la forma*
  for form's sake (as a matter of form) — *por (pura) fórmula.*
  For form's sake (As a matter of form), he asked us if we wanted to go along. *Por (pura) fórmula nos preguntó si queríamos acompañarlo.*

frame — *el marco*
  to be in a good frame of mind — *estar de buen humor.*
  Today he is not in a very good frame of mind. *Hoy no está de muy buen humor.*

free — *libre*
  free — *de balde; gratis.*
  They sent it to me free. *Me lo mandaron de balde (gratis).*

  to go scot free — *salir impune.*
  He went scot free. *Salió impune.*

  to set free — *poner en libertad.*
  They set him free. *Lo pusieron en libertad.*

friend — *el amigo*
  a fair-weather friend — *un amigo del buen viento (de circunstancias).*
  He's a fair-weather friend. *Es un amigo del buen viento (de circunstancias).*

  A friend in need is a friend indeed. — *En el peligro se conoce al amigo.*

89

to make friends with — *hacerse amigos.*
They made friends with us immediately. *Se hicieron amigos nuestros en seguida.*

---

friendship — *la amistad*
  to strike up a friendship — *trabar amistad.*
  He struck up a friendship with us. *Trabó amistad con nosotros.*

---

from — *de*
  from . . . to . . . — *de . . . en . . . .*
  We went from town to town. *Fuimos de pueblo en pueblo.*

---

fruit — *la fruta, el fruto*
  to bear fruit — *dar frutos.*
  It doesn't bear fruit. *No da frutos.*

---

fuel — *el combustible*
  to add fuel to the flames — *echar aceite al fuego.*
  She always adds fuel to the flames. *Siempre echa aceite al fuego.*

---

fun — *la diversión*
  for fun — *por gusto; por divertirse.*
  We did it for fun. *Lo hicimos por gusto (por divertirnos).*

  to have fun — *divertirse.*
  They had fun. *Se divirtieron.*

  to make fun of — *burlarse de.*
  She made fun of me. *Se burló de mí.*

---

funny — *gracioso*
  to be funny — *tener gracia; ser gracioso.*
  It's funny. *Tiene gracia (Es gracioso).*

  to strike one funny — *parecerle raro.*
  He strikes me funny. *Me parece raro.*

---

fuss — *la alharaca*
  It's not worth making such a fuss over. — *No es para tanto.*

to make a fuss over — *hacer muchas alharacas.*
She made a fuss over having to prepare the supper. *Hizo muchas alharacas porque tenía que preparar la cena.*

to raise a terrible fuss — *poner el grito en el cielo; armar un escándalo tremendo.*
When she found out, she raised a terrible fuss. *Cuando lo supo, puso el grito en el cielo (armó un escándalo tremendo).*

---

future — *el futuro*
in the future — *en lo sucesivo.*
There will be some in the future. *Habrá unos en lo sucesivo.*

in the near future — *en un futuro próximo.*
I'll write in the near future. *Escribiré en un futuro próximo.*

G

to gain — *ganar*
to gain on — *ir alcanzando.*
Let's run faster. They're gaining on us. *Corramos más de prisa. Nos van alcanzando.*

---

game — *el juego, la partida*
to play a game — *echar una partida.*
They played a game of cards. *Echaron una partida de naipes.*

---

gap — *la sima*
the generation gap — *el conflicto generacional.*
The generation gap is evident. *El conflicto generacional es evidente.*

---

gas — *el gas, la gasolina*
Step on it (the gas)! — *¡Apresúrese!*

---

general — *general*
in general — *por lo general; por regla general.*
In general he dresses well. *Por lo general (Por regla general) se viste bien.*

---

to get — *conseguir*

Get it out of your head! — *¡Quíteselo de la cabeza!*

not to get over — *no acostumbrarse a.*
We can't get over it. *No podemos acostumbrarnos a la idea.*

There's no getting around it — *no hay que darle vueltas.*
There's no getting around it, she made a mistake. *No hay que darle vueltas, ha cometido un error.*

There's no getting away from it. — *La cosa es clara.*

to get ahead — *prosperar.*
It's hard to get ahead in the world. *Es difícil prosperar en el mundo.*

to get along — *irlo pasando.*
Although her husband is dead, she is getting along. *Aunque está muerto su esposo, ella lo va pasando.*

to get along well — *defenderse bien.*
She gets along well in Spanish. *Se defiende bien en español.*

to get along with — *llevarse bien con.*
She gets along with everyone. *Se lleva bien con todos.*

to get along without — *pasarse sin.*
I can't get along without coffee. *No puedo pasarme sin café.*

to get away — *escaparse.*
The thief got away. *El ladrón se escapó.*

to get away with it — *no ser castigado.*
He lied and got away with it. *Mintió y no fue castigado.*

to get back — *volver.*
We got back at ten. *Volvimos a las diez.*

to get back at — *pagar en la misma moneda.*
He played a dirty trick on me, but I'm going to get back at him. *Me jugó una mala pasada, pero le voy a pagar en la misma moneda.*

to get by — *ir tirando.*
We're getting by. *Vamos tirando.*

to get by one — *escapársele a uno.*
The meaning of his speech got by us. *El significado de su discurso se nos escapó.*

to get cheaply — *salirle barato.*

We got it cheaply. *Nos salió barato.*

to get going — *ponerse en marcha.*
We got going at six. *Nos pusimos en marcha a las seis.*

to get involved in — *entregarse a.*
I got involved in Red Cross work. *Me entregué al trabajo de la Cruz Roja.*

to get it — *caer en la cuenta.*
I get it. *Caigo en la cuenta.*

to get off — *bajar (salir; apearse de).*
He got off the train. *Bajó (Salió, Se apeó) del tren.*

to get on — *subir a.*
He got on the bus. *Subió al autobús.*

to get over — *restablecerse (curarse) de.*
She got over the flu. *Se restableció (se curó) de la gripe.*

to get ready — *prepararse.*
They all got ready to leave. *Todos se prepararon para salir.*

to get there — *llegar.*
We got there at one. *Llegamos a la una.*

to get through — *pasar.*
We finally got through. *Por fin pasamos.*

to get through — *terminar.*
We got through working at ten. *Terminamos el trabajo a las diez.*

to get to — *poder.*
I never got to see it. *Nunca pude verlo.*

to get together — *ponerse de acuerdo.*
They finally got together. *Por fin, se pusieron de acuerdo.*

to get together — *reunirse.*
They got together to decide. *Se reunieron para decidir.*

to get up — *levantarse.*
She gets up at six. *Se levanta a las seis.*

to get what is coming to one — *recibir lo merecido.*
It looks as if they have finally gotten what was coming to them. *Parece que por fin han recibido lo merecido.*

What's gotten into him? — *¿Qué mosca le ha picado?*

ghost — *el fantasma*
   to give up the ghost — *entregar el alma.*
   He gave up the ghost. *Entregó el alma.*

gift — *el regalo*
   to have the gift of gab — *ser de mucha labia.*
   He has the gift of gab. *Es un hombre de mucha labia.*

   to present with a gift — *hacer un regalo.*
   He presented me with a gift. *Me hizo un regalo.*

to give — *dar*
   to give away — *regalar.*
   He gives away his old shoes. *Regala sus zapatos viejos.*

   to give in — *darse por vencido; doblar la cabeza.*
   He gave in. *Se dio por vencido (Dobló la cabeza).*

   to give off — *producir.*
   It gives off a bad odor. *Produce un mal olor.*

   to give out — *acabarse.*
   The beer gave out. *Se acabó la cerveza.*

   to give out — *repartir.*
   He gave out one bottle to each employee. *Repartió una botella a cada
      empleado.*

   to give to understand — *dar a entender.*
   He gave me to understand that he was boss. *Me dio a entender que
      mandaba él.*

   to give up — *dejar de.*
   He gave up smoking. *Dejó de fumar.*

   to give up — *rendirse.*
   When they surrounded him he gave up. *Cuando lo rodearon, se rindió.*

glad — *alegre*
   How glad we are! — *¡Cuánto nos alegramos!*

   to be glad to see someone — *tener mucho gusto en verlo.*
   I'm glad to see you. *(Tengo) mucho gusto en verlo.*

glance — *la ojeada*
   at first glance — *a primera vista.*
   At first glance he doesn't impress me. *A primera vista no me impresiona.*

to glance — *lanzar una mirada*
   to glance at — *lanzar una mirada.*
   She glanced at me. *Me lanzó una mirada.*

   to glance over — *examinar de paso.*
   I glanced over his examination. *Examiné de paso su examen.*

glove — *el guante*
   to fit like a glove — *sentarle muy bien.*
   His coat fits like a glove. *Su abrigo le sienta muy bien.*

   to handle with kid gloves — *tener entre algodones; tratar con sumo cuidado.*
   She handles him with kid gloves. *Lo tiene entre algodones (Lo trata con sumo cuidado).*

go — *marcha, movimiento; tentativa*
   to be on the go — *estar en actividad; no pararse.*
   He's always on the go. *Siempre está en actividad (Nunca se para).*

   to have a go at it — *probarlo.*
   He had a go at it but failed. *Lo probó pero fracasó.*

   to have lots of go — *tener mucha energía.*
   He has lots of go. *Tiene mucha energía.*

to go — *ir*
   Go on! — *¡Qué va! (¡Qué tontería!)*

   How goes it? (How's it going?) —*¿Qué tal?*

   not to be able to go on — *no poder más.*
   He can't go on. *No puede más.*

   to be enough to go around — *alcanzar.*
   There aren't enough chairs to go around. *No alcanzan las sillas.*

   to go — *para llevar.*
   I want a pizza to go. *Quiero una pizza para llevar.*

to go ahead — *seguir adelante.*
They are going ahead with the work. *Siguen adelante con el trabajo.*

to go all out — *echar la casa por la ventana.*
She went all out to celebrate my birthday. *Echó la casa por la ventana para celebrar mi cumpleaños.*

She went all out to
celebrate my birthday.
*Echó la casa por la
ventana para celebrar mi
cumpleaños.*

to go all out — *hacer un esfuerzo supremo.*
They went all out. *Hicieron un esfuerzo supremo.*

to go along with — *aceptar; apoyar.*
He won't go along with our plans. *No quiere aceptar (apoyar) nuestros planes.*

to go around — *ir por.*
He goes around the university as if he were lost. *Va por la universidad como si estuviera perdido.*

to go as far as to say — *atreverse a decir.*
I won't go as far as to say that she's smart. *No me atrevo a decir que sea lista.*

to go astray — *extraviarse.*
The book I sent went astray. *El libro que mandé se extravió.*

to go back on one's word — *no cumplir su palabra.*
He went back on his word. *No cumplió su palabra.*

to go bad — *descomponerse.*
His carburetor went bad. *Su carburador se descompuso.*

to go bad — *echarse a perder.*
The fruit went bad. *La fruta se echó a perder.*

to go for — *ser atraído por.*

He goes for tall girls. *Es atraído por las muchachas altas.*

to go get — *ir a buscar.*
Go get me a book. *Vaya a buscarme un libro.*

to go in for — *ser aficionado a.*
We go in for jai alai. *Somos aficionados al jai alai.*

to go off — *explotar.*
The bomb went off. *La bomba explotó.*

to go on — *seguir.*
He goes on day after day. *Sigue día tras día.*
He goes on smoking. *Sigue fumando.*

to go out — *salir.*
He went out alone. *Salió solo.*

to go smoothly — *ir sobre ruedas.*
Things went smoothly at first. *Al principio todo fue sobre ruedas.*

to go straight — *seguir la vía recta.*
When he got out of jail he went straight. *Al salir de la cárcel siguió la vía recta.*

to go through — *aprobarse.*
My request went through. *Mi petición se aprobó.*

to go through — *pasar.*
It went through the test. *Pasó la prueba.*

to go through — *sufrir.*
She has to go through an operation. *Tiene que sufrir una operación.*

to go with — *hacer juego con.*
It doesn't go with this tie. *No hace juego con esta corbata.*

to go wrong — *ir por mal camino.*
Her son went wrong. *Su hijo fue por mal camino.*

to go wrong — *salir mal.*
Everything went wrong today. *Todo me salió mal hoy.*

to have . . . to go — *quedarle. . . .*
You have five minutes to go. *Le quedan cinco minutos.*

to make a go of — *tener (lograr) éxito en.*
He didn't make a go of his business. *No tuvo (logró) éxito en sus negocios.*

God — *Dios*

  God willing — *Si Dios quiere (Dios mediante)*

  God willing, we'll spend Christmas together. *Pasaremos las pascuas juntos, si Dios quiere (Dios mediante).*

gold — *el oro*

  All that glitters is not gold. — *No es oro todo lo que reluce.*

  to be as good as gold — *ser más bueno que el pan.*

  He's as good as gold. *Es más bueno que el pan.*

good — *bueno*

  for good — *para siempre.*

  She left home for good. *Salió de se casa para siempre.*

  good and . . . — *bien . . .*

  We got home good and tired. *Llegamos a casa bien cansados.*

  to be as good as done — *poder darse por hecho.*

  It's as good as done. *Puede darse por hecho.*

  to be good enough to — *tener la bondad de.*

  He was good enough to help me. *Tuvo la bondad de ayudarme.*

  to be good for — *servir (ser de provecho) para.*

  It's no good for anything. *No sirve (No es de provecho) para nada.*

  to be up to no good — *estar tramando algo.*

  Don't trust him. He's up to no good. *No te fíes de él. Está tramando algo.*

  to do one good (harm) — *venirle bien (mal).*

  It has done me good (harm). *Me ha venido bien (mal).*

  to make good — *prosperar.*

  He's making good in his new job. *Está prosperando en su nuevo puesto.*

  what good is it (what's the good of) — *para qué (sirve).*

  What good is it to work (What's the good of working) all day? *¿Para qué (sirve) trabajar todo el día?*

  when one is good and ready — *cuando le parezca.*

  I'll do it when I'm good and ready. *Lo haré cuando me parezca.*

goodbye — *adiós*
  to wave goodbye — *decir adiós con la mano.*
  He waved goodbye to her. *Le dijo adiós con la mano.*

goose — *el ganso*
  They killed the goose that laid the golden eggs. — *Mataron la gallina de los huevos de oro.*
  What's sauce for the goose is sauce for the gander. — *La ley es ley para todos.*

grain — *el grano*
  not a grain of truth — *ni pizca de verdad.*
  There's not a grain of truth in what he says. *No hay ni pizca de verdad en lo que dice.*

  to go against the grain — *repugnarle.*
  It went against the grain. *Me repugnó.*

to grant — *conceder*
  to take for granted — *dar por sentado (supuesto; hecho).*
  I took it for granted. *Lo di por sentado (supuesto; hecho).*

grass — *la hierba*
  a grass widow — *una viuda de paja.*
  She's a grass widow. *Es viuda de paja.*

  The grass is always greener on the other side of the fence. — *La gallina de la vecina pone más huevos que la mía.*

  to let grass grow under one's feet — *dormirse en las pajas.*
  He doesn't let grass grow under his feet. *No se duerme en las pajas.*

to grin — *sonreírse bonachonamente*
  to grin and bear it — *poner a mal tiempo buena cara.*
  He'll have to grin and bear it. *Tendrá que poner a mal tiempo buena cara.*

grip — *el asimiento, el agarro*
  to come to grips with — *afrontar; enfrentarse con*

He won't come to grips with his situation. *No quiere afrontar (enfrentarse con) su situación.*

---

to groom — *asear*
    to be well groomed — *estar muy compuesto (acicalado).*
    He's always well groomed. *Siempre está muy compuesto (acicalado).*

---

ground — *la tierra*
    to be on firm ground — *estar en lo firme.*
    When they say it's impossible, they're on firm ground. *Al decir que es imposible están en lo firme.*

    to stand one's ground — *mantenerse firme.*
    Despite the criticism, he stood his ground. *A pesar de la crítica, se mantuvo firme.*

---

to grow — *crecer, cultivar*
    grown-ups — *personas mayores.*
    It's for grown-ups. *Es para personas mayores.*

    to grow on one — *gustarle más.*
    The more I look at it the more it grows on me. *Cuanto más lo miro, (tanto) más me gusta.*

    to grow out of it — *quitársele.*
    He stutters but he'll grow out of it. *Tartamudea pero se le quitará.*

---

grudge — *el rencor*
    to bear (to hold) a grudge — *guardar rencor.*
    He never bears (holds) a grudge. *Nunca guarda rencor.*

---

guard — *la guardia*
    to be on one's guard — *estar sobre aviso.*
    He's always on his guard. *Siempre está sobre aviso.*

    to catch one off one's guard — *cogerle desprevenido.*
    They caught us off our guard. *Nos cogieron desprevenidos.*

    to guard against — *guardarse de.*
    You ought to guard against eating too much. *Debe guardarse de comer demasiado.*

---

guess — *la suposición*
  Your guess is as good as mine. — *Usted sabe tanto como yo.*

to guess — *suponer, adivinar*
  I guess so. — *Creo que sí*

gun — *el arma de fuego*
  to jump the gun — *precipitarse.*
  He jumped the gun in making the announcement. *Se precipitó al hacer el anuncio.*

  to stick to one's guns — *no dar el brazo a torcer.*
  In spite of all the arguments, he stuck to his guns. *A pesar de todos los argumentos, no dio el brazo a torcer.*

H

hair — *el pelo*
  to let one's hair down — *sincerarse.*
  Finally he let his hair down with me. *Por fin se sinceró conmigo.*

  to make one's hair stand on end — *ponerle los pelos de punta.*
  Her story made our hair stand on end. *Su historia nos puso los pelos de punta.*

Her story made our hair stand on end.
Su historia nos puso los pelos de punta.

to part one's hair — *peinarse con raya.*
He parts his hair. *Se peina con raya.*

to split hairs — *andar en quisquillas; pararse en pelillos.*
That's splitting hairs. *Eso es andar en quisquillas (pararse en pelillos).*

to turn a hair — *inmutarse.*
He didn't turn a hair when he found it out. *No se inmutó cuando lo supo.*

---

half — *medio*
to cut in half — *partir por la mitad.*
They cut the apple in half. *Partieron la manzana por la mitad.*

half . . . and half . . . — *entre . . . y. . . .*
He said it half joking and half serious. *Lo dijo entre chistoso y serio.*

half closed — *a medio cerrar.*
We found the door half closed. *Encontramos la puerta a medio cerrar.*

half done — *a medias.*
He leaves things half done. *Deja las cosas a medias.*

---

hammer — *el martillo*
to fight hammer and tongs — *luchar con todas sus fuerzas.*
We fought hammer and tongs to save him. *Luchamos con todas nuestras fuerzas para salvarlo.*

---

hand — *la mano*
by hand — *a mano.*
They used to write all their letters by hand. *Escribían todas sus cartas a mano.*

Don't bite the hand that feeds you. — *No muerdas la mano que te da de comer.*

hand in hand — *cogidos de la mano.*
They approached hand in hand. *Se acercaron cogidos de la mano.*

on the one hand, . . . ; on the other, . . . — *de (por) un lado, . . . ; de (por) otro, ...*
On the one hand she likes her work; on the other, she gets tired of sitting. *De (por) un lado, le gusta su trabajo; de (por) otro, se cansa de estar sentada.*

on the other hand — *en cambio; al contrario.*

This one, on the other hand, is ours. *Este, en cambio (al contrario), es el nuestro.*

on the other hand — *por otra parte (otro lado).*

On the other hand, we may need more. *Por otra parte (otro lado) puede ser que nos haga falta más.*

to be an old hand — *ser experto.*

He's an old hand at golf. *Es un experto jugador de golf.*

to be hand in glove — *ser uña y carne.*

They're hand in glove. *Son uña y carne.*

to be on hand — *estar disponible.*

He's never on hand when I need him. *Nunca está disponible cuando lo necesito.*

to change hands — *cambiar de dueño.*

The hotel changed hands. *El hotel cambió de dueño.*

to clap one's hands (to applaud) — *aplaudir.*

He clapped his hands (applauded). *Aplaudió.*

to clap one's hands — *dar palmadas.*

He clapped his hands to attract the waiter's attention. *Dio unas palmadas para llamarle la atención al camarero.*

to get out of hand — *desmandarse.*

The situation got out of hand. *La situación se desmandó.*

to give someone a big hand — *darle fuertes aplausos.*

They gave her a big hand. *Le dieron fuertes aplausos.*

to go from hand to hand — *ir de mano en mano.*

It went from hand to hand. *Fue de mano en mano.*

to have a free hand — *tener carta blanca (plena libertad).*

He has a free hand in his job. *Tiene carta blanca (plena libertad) en su trabajo.*

to have at hand — *tener a mano.*

He had it at hand. *Lo tenía a mano.*

to have in hand — *tener entre manos.*

She has her work well in hand. *Tiene su trabajo entre manos.*

to have in one's hands — *tener en su poder.*
I have in my hands your letter. *Tengo en mi poder su grata.*

to have the upper hand — *dominar la situación.*
He had the upper hand. *Dominaba la situación.*

to keep one's hand in — *seguir teniendo práctica.*
He's studying Spanish just to keep his hand in. *Estudia español sólo para
    seguir teniendo práctica.*

to lay one's hands on — *encontrar.*
I can't lay my hands on that report. *No puedo encontrar ese informe.*

to lend (to give) a hand — *dar (echar) una mano.*
He lent (gave) me a hand. *Me dio (echó) una mano.*

to live from hand to mouth — *vivir al día.*
The poor man lives from hand to mouth. *El pobre vive al día.*

to play right into one's hands — *redundar en su beneficio.*
What he did played right into our hands. *Lo que hizo redundó en nuestro
    beneficio.*

to put one's hands on one's hips — *ponerse en (de) jarras.*
She put her hands on her hips. *Se puso en (de) jarras.*

to shake hands with — *dar (estrechar) la mano (a).*
He shook hands with me. *Me dio (estrechó) la mano.*

to wait on hand and foot — *cuidar a cuerpo de rey.*
She waits on her children hand and foot. *Cuida a sus hijos a cuerpo
    de rey.*

to wash one's hands of — *lavarse las manos de.*
He washed his hands of that enterprise. *Se lavó las manos de esa empresa.*

to win hands down — *ganar sin ninguna dificultad.*
We won hands down. *Ganamos sin ninguna dificultad.*

to work hand in hand — *trabajar en buena armonía.*
They work hand in hand. *Trabajan en buena armonía.*

with a steady hand — *con pulso firme.*
He aims with a steady hand. *Apunta con pulso firme.*

handful — *el puñado*
   by the handful — *a manos llenas.*
   He wasted money by the handful. *Malgastó dinero a manos llenas.*

handwriting — *la escritura, la letra*
   to be in one's own handwriting — *ser de su puño y letra.*
   It's in his own handwriting. *Es de su puño y letra.*

   to see the handwriting on the wall — *comprender el presagio de peligro.*
   He saw the handwriting on the wall. *Comprendió el presagio de peligro.*

to hang — *colgar*
   to hang on someone's words — *estar pendiente de sus palabras.*
   She hangs on his words. *Está pendiente de sus palabras.*

hard — *duro*
   to be hard — *costar trabajo.*
   It's hard for us to imagine. *Nos cuesta trabajo imaginarlo.*

   to take something hard — *tomarlo a pecho.*
   He took it hard. *Lo tomó a pecho.*

hard-hearted — *duro de corazón*
   to be hard-hearted — *tener corazón de piedra.*
   He's hard-hearted. *Tiene corazón de piedra.*

haste — *la prisa*
   in great haste — *a escape; a toda prisa.*
   He took off in great haste. *Se despidió a escape (a toda prisa).*

   Haste makes waste. — *Vísteme despacio que tengo prisa.*

hat — *el sombrero*
   to be old hat — *ser muy anticuado.*
   His ideas are old hat. *Sus ideas son muy anticuadas.*

   to remove one's hat — *descubrirse.*
   They removed their hats reverently. *Se descubrieron con reverencia.*

   to take off one's hat to — *descubrirse ante.*

I take off my hat to his courage. *Me descubro ante su valor.*

to talk through one's hat — *decir tonterías (disparates).*
As usual, he's talking through his hat. *Como de costumbre dice tonterías (disparates).*

to wear many hats — *desempeñar muchos cargos al mismo tiempo.*
As president of the university, he wears many hats. *Como rector de la universidad desempeña muchos cargos al mismo tiempo.*

---

hatchet — *el hacha*
    to bury the hatchet — *hacer las paces.*
    They buried the hatchet. *Hicieron las paces.*

---

haul — *el tirón*
    Over the long haul — *a la larga.*
    Over the long haul it will be to our advantage. *A la larga será para nuestro provecho.*

---

to have — *tener*
    had better — *mejor.*
    You had better stay. *Mejor sería que se quedara.*

    to be had — *ser engañado.*
    You've been had. *Fue engañado.*

    to have had it — *no poder más.*
    I've had it! *¡No puedo más!*

    to have it in for — *tenérsela jurada.*
    He's got it in for us. *Nos la tiene jurada.*

    to have it out — *poner las cosas en claro; habérselas.*
    He had it out with his wife. *Puso las cosas en claro (Se las ha habido) con su esposa.*

    to have on — *tener puesto.*
    He has on his new suit. *Tiene puesto su traje nuevo.*

    to have to — *tener que.*
    He has (He's got) to find a job. *Tiene que encontrar empleo.*

    to have to do with — *tener que ver con.*

They have nothing to do with this company. *No tienen nada que ver con esta compañía.*

---

haves — *los ricos*
the haves and the have-nots — *los ricos y los pobres.*
It's a matter of the haves and the have-nots. *Es cuestión de los ricos y los pobres.*

---

havoc — *el estrago*
to play havoc with — *destruir.*
The wind played havoc with our kite. *El viento destruyó nuestra cometa.*

---

hay — *el heno*
to hit the hay — *irse a la cama.*
Let's hit the hay. *Vámonos a la cama.*

to make hay while the sun shines — *batir el hierro cuando está al rojo.*
It's better to make hay while the sun shines. *Es mejor batir el hierro cuando está al rojo.*

---

head — *la cabeza*
at the head — *por delante; a la cabeza.*
There's a horseman at the head. *Viene un jinete por delante (a la cabeza).*

head first (on one's head) — *de cabeza.*
They all fell head first (on their heads). *Todos se cayeron de cabeza.*

head on — *de cabeza.*
They met head on. *Se encontraron de cabeza.*

Heads or tails? — *¿Cara o cruz?*

not to be able to make head or tail (out) of something — *no verle ni pies ni cabeza.*
I cannot make head or tail (out) of it. *No le veo ni pies ni cabeza.*

to be head and shoulders above one — *aventajarle en mucho.*
As for singing, he's head and shoulders above me. *En cuanto a cantar, me aventaja en mucho.*

to be head over heels in love — *estar perdidamente enamorado.*
He's head over heels in love. *Está perdidamente enamorado.*

to beat one's head against a wall — *topar con una pared.*
I think you're beating your head against a wall. *Creo que está topando con una pared.*

to bury one's head in the sand — *cerrar los ojos a la realidad.*
She buried her head in the sand. *Cerró los ojos a la realidad.*

to come to a head — *estar que arde.*
Things are coming to a head. *La cosa está que arde.*

to go to one's head — *subírsele a la cabeza.*
His success went to his head. *Su éxito se le subió a la cabeza.*

to keep one's head — *quedarse con calma.*
He kept his head despite the tragedy. *Se quedó con calma a pesar de la tragedia.*

to lose one's head — *perder los estribos (la cabeza).*
She lost her head. *Perdió los estribos (la cabeza).*

to make one's head swim — *aturdirse.*
It made my head swim. *Me aturdió.*

to put heads together — *consultarse mutuamente.*
We put our heads together. *Nos consultamos mutuamente.*

to take into one's head — *metérsele en la cabeza.*
She took it into her head to get married. *Se le metió en la cabeza casarse.*

---

headache — *dolor de cabeza*
  to have a headache — *dolerle la cabeza.*
  I have a headache. *Me duele la cabeza.*

---

healthy — *sano*
  to look healthy — *tener buen ver; lucir bien.*
  She looks very healthy. *Tiene muy buen ver (Luce bien).*

---

to hear — *oír*
  to hear — *oír decir.*
  I heard it's true. *Oí decir que es verdad.*

  to hear about — *oír hablar de.*
  Have you heard about the game? *¿Ha oído hablar del partido?*

to hear from — *recibir noticias de.*
I heard from my daughter. *Recibí noticias de mi hija.*

---

heart — *el corazón*

after one's own heart — *como le gustan a uno.*
He's a boy after my own heart. *Es un chico como a mí me gustan.*

at heart — *en el fondo.*
At heart, he's generous. *En el fondo es generoso.*

Take heart! — *¡Anímese!; ¡Cobre aliento!*

to bare one's heart — *abrir el pecho.*
Last night my daughter bared her heart to me. *Anoche mi hija me abrió su pecho.*

to carry one's heart on one's sleeve — *tener el corazón en la mano.*
He carries his heart on his sleeve. *Tiene el corazón en la mano.*

to do one's heart good — *alegrarle el corazón.*
It did my heart good. *Me alegró el corazón.*

to eat one's heart out — *consumirse de pena.*
She's eating her heart out over her husband's death. *Se está consumiendo de pena por la muerte de su esposo.*

to get to the heart of the problem — *llegar al fondo del problema.*
We wanted to get to the heart of the problem. *Queríamos llegar al fondo del problema.*

to have one's heart in one's mouth — *tener el corazón en un puño.*
I had my heart in my mouth. *Tenía el corazón en un puño.*

to have one's heart set on — *tener la esperanza puesta en.*
He had his heart set on going to college. *Tenía la esperanza puesta en asistir a una universidad.*

to know by heart — *saber de memoria (al dedillo).*
I know it by heart. *Lo sé de memoria (al dedillo).*

to learn by heart — *aprender de memoria.*
I learned it by heart. *Lo aprendí de memoria.*

to take to heart — *tomar a pecho(s).*
He took what I said to heart. *Tomó a pecho(s) lo que dije.*

heaven — *el cielo*

   Good heavens! — *¡Dios mío!; ¡Válgame Dios!*

   Heaven forbid! — *¡Dios nos (me) libre!*

heed — *la atención*

   to take heed — *hacer caso.*

   I'm sorry you didn't take heed to what I said. *Siento que no haya hecho caso de lo que dije.*

heel — *el tacón, el talón*

   to be hard on one's heels — *pisarle los talones.*

   They were hard on his heels. *Le pisaban los talones.*

   to be well heeled — *ser muy rico.*

   He's well heeled. *Es muy rico.*

   to cool one's heels — *hacer antesala.*

   They left him cooling his heels. *Lo dejaron haciendo antesala.*

   to take to one's heels — *echar a correr; poner pies en polvorosa.*

   He took to his heels. *Echó a correr (Puso pies en polvorosa).*

hell — *el infierno*

   come hell or high water — *contra viento y marea.*

   We'll get to San Francisco come hell or high water. *Llegaremos a San Francisco contra viento y marea.*

   until hell freezes over — *hasta el día del juicio.*

   He can stay in jail until hell freezes over. *Puede quedarse en la cárcel hasta el día del juicio.*

to help — *ayudar*

   It can't be helped (It's beyond help). — *No hay (No tiene más) remedio.*

   not to be able to help — *no poder menos de.*

   He can't help loving her. *No puede menos de amarla.*

   to help out — *ayudar.*

   He always helps out. *Siempre ayuda.*

   to help someone out — *sacarle del apuro.*

   He helped us out. *Nos sacó del apuro.*

here — *aquí*
    around here — *por aquí.*
    He spends a lot of time around here. *Pasa mucho tiempo por aquí.*

    here is — *aquí tiene.*
    Here is a copy. *Aquí tiene un ejemplar.*

    here is — *aquí viene.*
    Here's Mary. *Aquí viene María.*

    in here — *aquí dentro.*
    They're waiting in here. *Están esperando aquí dentro.*

    right here — *aquí mismo.*
    It happened right here. *Pasó aquí mismo.*

high — *alto*
    to act high and mighty — *darse mucha importancia.*
    He acts high and mighty. *Se da mucha importancia.*

    to leave high and dry — *dejar en seco (plantado).*
    He left her high and dry. *La dejó en seco (plantada).*

    to look high and low — *buscar por todas partes (de arriba abajo).*
    I looked high and low for it. *Lo busqué por todas partes (de arriba abajo).*

hint — *la indirecta*
    to take the hint — *darse por aludido.*
    He took the hint. *Se dio por aludido.*

    to throw out a hint — *lanzar una indirecta.*
    He threw out a hint. *Lanzó una indirecta.*

hit — *el éxito, el golpe*
    to make a big hit — *gustarles a todos.*
    Her new dress made a big hit. *Su nuevo vestido les gustó a todos.*

    to make a hit — *caerle en (la) gracia.*
    She made a hit with everyone. *Les cayó en (la) gracia a todos.*

to hit — *golpear*
    to hit it off well — *entenderse (llevarse) bien.*
    They hit it off well. *Se entienden (Se llevan) bien.*

   to hit on the idea of — *ocurrírsele.*
   He hit on the idea of traveling. *Se le ocurrió viajar.*

---

hold — *el agarro*
   to get hold of — *hacerse con (de).*
   I got hold of the passport. *Me hice con el (del) pasaporte.*

   to take hold of — *agarrar.*
   He took hold of the handle. *Agarró el asa.*

   to take hold of oneself — *dominarse; controlarse.*
   Try to take hold of yourself. *Trate de dominarse (controlarse).*

---

to hold — *tener (agarrado)*
   Hold it! — *¡Un momento!*

   to be held — *tener lugar.*
   We will hold the meeting (The meeting will be held) in my office. *La reunión tendrá lugar en mi oficina.*

   to hold good — *servir.*
   This rule doesn't hold good in this situation. *Esta regla no sirve en esta situación.*

   to hold on — *esperar.*
   Hold on a second. *Espere un segundo.*

   to hold on to — *agarrarse bien de.*
   Hold on to the saddle. *Agárrese bien de la silla.*

   to hold out — *resistir.*
   The enemy held out for two days. *El enemigo resistió dos días.*

   to hold out for — *insistir en.*
   He held out for ten dollars. *Insistió en diez dólares.*

   to hold over — *continuar (representando).*
   The play was held over for another week. *Continuaron (representando) la comedia otra semana.*

   to hold still — *estarse quieto.*
   The baby wouldn't hold still. *El nene no quiso estarse quieto.*

   to hold up — *asaltar.*
   They held up the bank. *Asaltaron el banco.*

to hold up — *detener.*
They held us up for a week. *Nos detuvieron una semana.*

to hold up — *suspender.*
We held up our work until the parts came. *Suspendimos nuestro trabajo hasta que llegaron los repuestos.*

hole — *el agujero*
to pick holes in — *hallar defectos.*
He picked holes in our proposal. *Halló defectos en nuestra propuesta.*

home — *la casa*
Make yourself at home. — *Está usted en su casa.*

to be (at) home — *estar en casa.*
He's not (at) home. *No está en casa.*

to come home — *venir a casa.*
He came home. *Vino a casa.*

to see someone home — *acompañar a casa.*
He'll see the babysitter home. *Acompañará a casa a la niñera.*

to strike home — *dar en lo vivo.*
My ideas struck home. *Mis ideas dieron en lo vivo.*

homesick — *nostálgico.*
to be homesick — *añorar su casa; sentir nostalgia de su casa.*
She's homesick. *Añora su casa (Siente nostalgia de su casa).*

to honor — *honrar*
to honor — *aceptar.*
They won't honor my check here. *No quieren aceptar mi cheque aquí.*

hook — *el gancho*
by hook or by crook — *por fas o por nefas.*
We're going to get it by hook or by crook. *Vamos a conseguirlo por fas o por nefas.*

to swallow hook, line, and sinker — *tragar el anzuelo.*
He swallowed it hook, line, and sinker. *Tragó el anzuelo.*

hooky

   to play hooky — *hacer novillos.*

   He was playing hooky. *Estaba haciendo novillos.*

to hop — *brincar, saltar*

   a hop, skip, and a jump from — *a un paso de.*

   He lives just a hop, skip, and a jump from the university. *Vive a un paso de la universidad.*

   to be hopping mad — *echar chispas.*

   She's hopping mad. *Está echando chispas.*

to hope — *esperar*

   I should hope so! — *¡No faltaría más!*

hopeless — *desesperado*

   to be hopeless at — *ser una desgracia para.*

   I'm hopeless at bridge. *Soy una desgracia para el bridge.*

horn — *la bocina, el claxon*

   to blow one's own horn — *alabarse a sí mismo.*

   He always blows his own horn. *Siempre se alaba a sí mismo.*

horse — *el caballo*

   That's a horse of a different (another) color. — *Eso es harina de otro costal.*

   to get on one's high horse — *ponerse muy arrogante.*

   He got on his high horse. *Se puso muy arrogante.*

horseback — *el lomo de caballo*

   on horseback — *montado a caballo.*

   They came on horseback. *Vinieron montados a caballo.*

hot — *caliente*

   to be hot (the weather) — *hacer calor.*

   It's hot today. *Hace calor hoy.*

   to be hot (a person) — *tener calor.*

I'm hot. *Tengo calor.*

to make it hot — *hacer la vida imposible.*
She makes it hot for everybody. *Hace la vida imposible a (para) todos.*

to sell like hot cakes — *venderse como pan bendito*
Perfume sells like hot cakes in France. *El perfume se vende como pan bendito en Francia.*

---

hour — *la hora*

at all hours — *a toda hora.*
It's open at all hours. *Está abierto a toda hora.*

rush hour(s) — *las horas de aglomeración.*
We don't leave during rush hour(s). *No salimos durante las horas de aglomeración.*

the wee hours of the morning — *las primeras horas de la mañana.*
He came in at the wee hours of the morning. *Entró en las primeras horas de la mañana.*

to keep late hours — *trasnochar.*
He keeps late hours. *Trasnocha.*

---

house — *la casa*

to be on the house — *ir por cuenta de la casa.*
The wine is on the house. *El vino va por cuenta de la casa.*

to have (hold) open house — *recibir amistades.*
We're having (holding) open house tomorrow at three. *Mañana recibimos amistades a las tres.*

to keep house — *hacer los quehaceres domésticos.*
She likes to keep house. *Le gusta hacer los quehaceres domésticos.*

---

how — *cómo*

How about that? — *¿Qué le parece?*

how else — *cómo, si no.*
How else can you do it? *¿Cómo, si no, se puede hacer?*

---

howl — *el aullido*

    to raise a big howl — *poner el grito en el cielo.*

    They raised a big howl. *Pusieron el grito en el cielo.*

Hoyle

    according to Hoyle — *como Dios manda.*

    They insist on having everything done according to Hoyle. *Insisten en que todo se haga como Dios manda.*

---

to humble — *humillar*

    to humble oneself — *rebajarse.*

    She humbled herself before him. *Se rebajó ante él.*

---

humor — *el humor*

    to be in a good (bad) humor — *estar de buen (mal) humor.*

    She's in a good (bad) humor today. *Está de buen (mal) humor hoy.*

---

hunger — *el hambre (f.)*

    to be hungry — *tener hambre.*

    He's not hungry. *No tiene hambre.*

---

hurry — *la prisa*

    Hurry back. — *Vuelva en seguida.*

    Hurry up. — *Apresúrese; Dese prisa.*

    to be in a hurry — *estar de (con) prisa; tener prisa; andar de prisa.*

    He's in a hurry. *Está de (Tiene) prisa (Anda de prisa).*

    to leave in a hurry — *salir en volandas.*

    He left in a hurry. *Salió en volandas.*

---

to hurt — *lastimar*

    to hurt someone — *hacerle daño (mal).*

    It hurt him. *Le hizo daño (mal).*

---

to hush — *callar*

    to hush up the scandal — *echar tierra al (acallar el) escándalo.*

    We hushed up the scandal. *Echamos tierra al (acallamos el) escándalo.*

I

i — *la i*

> **to dot every i and cross every t** — *poner los puntos sobre las íes.*
> He dots every i and crosses every t. *Pone los puntos sobre las íes.*

---

ice — *el hielo*

> **to break the ice** — *romper el hielo.*
> He broke the ice with his joke. *Rompió el hielo con su chiste.*

He broke the ice
with his joke.
*Rompió el hielo
con su chiste.*

> **to cut no ice** — *no pintar nada.*
> He cuts no ice with the manager. *No pinta nada con el gerente.*

> **to skate on thin ice** — *hallarse en una situación comprometida.*
> We're skating on thin ice. *Nos hallamos en una situación comprometida.*

---

idea — *la idea*

> **to have a bright idea** — *tener una ocurrencia.*
> He had the bright idea of inviting Alice. *Tuvo la ocurrencia de invitar a Alicia.*

> **What's the idea?** — *¿De qué se trata?; ¿Qué le pasa?*

---

ill — *enfermo*

> **to be very ill** — *estar de cuidado.*
> He's very ill. *Está de cuidado.*

to take ill — *caer enfermo; enfermarse.*
She took ill. *Cayó enferma (Se enfermó).*

to imagine — *imaginarse, figurarse*
Just imagine! — *¡Figúrese!*

impression — *la impresión*
    to make an impression — *dejar huella.*
    He's made an impression. *Ha dejado huella.*

in — *dentro*
    the ins and outs — *los recovecos.*
    You have to know all the ins and outs to work there. *Hay que conocer todos los recovecos para trabajar allí.*

    to be in — *estar de moda.*
    White shirts are in again. *Las camisas blancas están de moda de nuevo.*

    to be in for — *esperarle.*
    We're in for a cold night. *Nos espera una noche fría.*

inch — *la pulgada*
    Give him an inch and he'll take a mile. — *Le da la mano y se toma el brazo (pie).*

    inch by inch — *palmo a palmo.*
    They examined it inch by inch. *Lo examinaron palmo a palmo.*

    to be every inch a man — *ser un hombre hecho y derecho.*
    He's every inch a man. *Es un hombre hecho y derecho.*

to inch — *avanzar a poquitos*
    to inch along — *avanzar a paso de tortuga.*
    The convoy inched along. *El convoy avanzó a paso de tortuga.*

incredible — *increíble*
    to seem incredible — *parecer mentira.*
    It seems incredible. *Parece mentira.*

indeed — *de veras*
  No indeed. — *Eso sí que no.*
  Yes indeed. — *Ya lo creo; Eso sí.*

information — *los informes, la información*
  to give information about — *dar razón de.*
  She gave us information about her son. *Nos dio razón de su hijo.*

informed — *informado*
  to be informed about — *estar al corriente (al tanto) de*
  I'm not informed about politics. *No estoy al corriente (al tanto) de la política.*

to inquire — *averiguar, preguntar*
  to inquire about — *preguntar por.*
  He inquired about her. *Preguntó por ella.*

insane — *loco*
  to go insane — *perder la razón.*
  I think that she's going insane. *Creo que va a perder la razón.*

inside — *adentro*
  inside and out — *por dentro y por fuera.*
  They covered it inside and out with flowers. *Lo cubrieron por dentro y por fuera con flores.*
  inside (wrong side) out — *al revés.*
  The boy put his jacket on inside (wrong side) out. *El chico se puso la chaqueta al revés.*

installment — *la entrega*
  to pay by installments — *pagar a plazos.*
  He's paying by installments. *Está pagando a plazos.*

instrumental — *instrumental*
  to be instrumental in — *contribuir a.*
  He was instrumental in my getting it. *Contribuyó a que lo consiguiera.*

insult — *el insulto*
  to add insult to injury — *como si esto fuera poco.*
  To add insult to injury, he took two. *Como si esto fuera poco, se llevó dos.*

intention — *la intención*
  to have good (bad) intentions — *llevar buen (mal) fin.*
  He has good (bad) intentions. *Lleva buen (mal) fin.*

interest — *el interés*
  to draw interest — *devengar interés.*
  His money is drawing interest. *Su dinero devenga interés.*

  to take an interest in — *interesarse por.*
  He takes an interest in everything. *Se interesa por todo.*

interval — *el intervalo*
  at intervals — *de vez en cuando.*
  At intervals she stopped by to see her mother. *De vez en cuando pasaba a ver a su madre.*

to involve — *enredar, enmarañar*
  to be involved in — *estar metido en.*
  She's involved in so many things that she has no time for her family. *Está metida en tantas cosas que no tiene tiempo para su familia.*

iron — *el hierro; la plancha*
  to strike while the iron is hot — *aprovechar la oportunidad; a hierro caliente batir de repente.*
  We must strike while the iron is hot. *Tenemos que aprovechar la oportunidad (A hierro caliente batir de repente).*

to iron — *planchar*
  to iron out one's difficulties — *resolver las dificultades.*
  We ironed out our difficulties. *Resolvimos nuestras dificultades.*

J

jack — *el mozo*
   Jack of all trades, master of none. — *Aprendiz de todo, oficial de nada.*

---

to jack — *alzar*
   to jack up the prices — *aumentar los precios.*
   They jacked up the prices. *Aumentaron los precios.*

---

jam — *el aprieto*
   to be in a jam — *estar en un aprieto.*
   He's in a jam. *Está en un aprieto.*

   to get out of a jam — *salir de un apuro.*
   It's not always easy to get out of a jam. *No siempre es fácil salir de un apuro.*

   to get someone out of a jam — *sacar de un apuro.*
   I got him out of a jam. *Lo saqué de un apuro.*

---

jealous — *celoso*
   to be jealous — *tener celos.*
   He's jealous. *Tiene celos.*

   to guard something jealously — *guardar con solicitud (con vigilancia).*
   She guards her privacy jealously. *Guarda su retiro con solicitud (vigilancia).*

---

jewel — *la joya*
   to be a jewel (a treasure) — *ser una perla.*
   My aunt's gardener is a jewel (treasure). *El jardinero de mi tía es una perla.*

---

jiffy — *el periquete*
   in a jiffy — *en un santiamén; en un dos por tres.*
   It will be here in a jiffy. *Llegará en un santiamén (dos por tres).*

---

job — *el trabajo*
  to do a halfway job — *hacer un trabajo a medias.*
  They fired him because he always did a halfway job. *Lo despidieron porque siempre hacía su trabajo a medias.*

to join — *unir*
  to join — *acompañar.*
  He joined us on our trip. *Nos acompañó en nuestro viaje.*

  to join — *venir a sentarse con.*
  He joined us at our table. *Vino a sentarse con nosotros en nuestra mesa.*

  to join —*hacerse socio de.*
  He joined the club. *Se hizo socio del club.*

joke — *el chiste, la broma*
  as a joke (jokingly) — *en broma.*
  Don't get mad; I said it as a joke. *No te enojes, lo dije en broma.*

  to crack jokes — *hacer chistes.*
  He's always cracking jokes. *Siempre hace chistes.*

  to play a (practical) joke — *gastar (hacer) una broma (pesada).*
  They played a (practical) joke on him. *Le gastaron (hicieron) una broma (pesada).*

  to take a joke — *soportar una broma.*
  He can't take a joke. *No sabe soportar una broma.*

Joneses — *los Jones*
  to keep up with the Joneses — *hacer lo que hace el vecino.*
  It's useless to try to keep up with the Joneses. *Es inútil tratar de hacer lo que hace el vecino.*

to jot — *escribir a prisa*
  to jot down — *apuntar (tomar nota de).*
  I jotted down the address. *Apunté (tomé nota de) la dirección.*

joy — *la alegría*
  to be bursting with joy — *no caber en sí de gozo.*

She has received a letter from her mother, and she is bursting with joy. *Ha recibido una carta de su madre y no cabe en sí de gozo.*

---

to judge — *juzgar*
judging by — *a juzgar por.*
Judging by what is seen, it's luxurious. *A juzgar por lo que se ve, es de lujo.*

---

juice — *el jugo*
to stew in one's own juice — *freír en su aceite; cocer en su propia salsa.*
We left her to stew in her own juice. *La dejamos freír en su aceite (cocer en su propia salsa).*

---

jump — *el salto*
to get the jump on someone — *ganarle la acción.*
I got the jump on him. *Le gané la acción.*

---

to jump — *saltar*
to jump at the opportunity — *apresurarse a aceptar la oportunidad.*
I jumped at the opportunity. *Me apresuré a aceptar la oportunidad.*

---

just — *justo*
just about — *más o menos.*
It's just about two weeks. *Son más o menos dos semanas.*

just around the corner — *a la vuelta de la esquina.*
They live just around the corner. *Viven a la vuelta de la esquina.*

just as one thought — *tal como pensaba uno.*
She had it, just as I thought. *Lo tenía ella, tal como pensaba yo.*

just like — *lo mismo (igual) que.*
She's blonde, just like her mother. *Es rubia, lo mismo (igual) que su madre.*

to have just — *acabar de.*
He has just left. *Acaba de salir.*

---

keen — *agudo*
   to be keen about — *tener mucho entusiasmo por.*
   I'm not keen about the plan. *No tengo mucho entusiasmo por el plan.*

keep — *la manutención*
   to earn one's keep — *ganarse la vida.*
   He earns his keep. *Se gana la vida.*

   to play for keeps — *jugar de veras.*
   He is playing for keeps. *Está jugando de veras.*

to keep — *guardar; mantener*
   to keep abreast — *estar al corriente.*
   It's hard to keep abreast of the war. *Es difícil estar al corriente de la guerra.*

   to keep at — *perseverar.*
   He always keeps at what he is doing. *Siempre persevera.*

   to keep on — *seguir.*
   She keeps on driving despite her age. *Sigue manejando (conduciendo) a pesar de su edad.*

   to keep out of sight — *mantenerse fuera de vista.*
   He kept out of sight. *Se mantuvo fuera de vista.*

   to keep to oneself — *quedarse a solas.*
   He doesn't have much fun because he always keeps to himself. *Se divierte poco porque siempre se queda a solas.*

   to keep . . . to oneself — *no decirle a nadie.*
   I want you to keep this to yourself. *No quiero que le digas esto a nadie.*

   to keep up with — *mantener el mismo paso que.*
   The child can't keep up with his mother. *El niño no puede mantener el mismo paso que su mamá.*

---

kettle — *la caldera*
    to leave in a fine kettle of fish — *dejar en buen berenjenal.*
    They left us in a fine kettle of fish. *Nos dejaron en buen berenjenal.*

---

kick — *el puntapié, la coz*
    for kicks — *por gusto.*
    He does it just for kicks. *Lo hace por puro gusto.*

    to get a kick out of — *encantarle.*
    We get a kick out of traveling. *Nos encanta viajar.*

---

to kick — *dar puntapiés, dar coces, dar patadas*
    to kick (to chip) in — *contribuir.*
    We all kicked (chipped) in and bought him a book. *Todos contribuimos y le compramos un libro.*

    to kick out — *expulsar.*
    He got kicked out because of bad grades. *Lo expulsaron por sus malas notas.*

---

to kill — *matar*
    dressed fit to kill (all dressed up) — *vestido de veinticinco alfileres.*
    She came dressed fit to kill (all dressed up). *Vino vestida de veinticinco alfileres.*

---

killing — *la matanza*
    to make a killing — *hacer su agosto.*
    I made a killing on the stockmarket. *Hice mi agosto en la bolsa.*

---

kind — *la clase, la especie*
    a kind (sort) of (a) . . . — *una especie de.*
    He lives in a kind (sort) of (a) hut. *Vive en una especie de choza.*

    to be two of a kind — *ser tal para cual.*
    They are two of a kind. *Son tal para cual.*

    nothing of the kind — *nada de eso.*
    I said nothing of the kind. *No dije nada de eso.*

---

king — *el rey*
  fit for a king — *digno de un rey.*
  She served us a dinner fit for a king. *Nos sirvió una comida digna de un rey.*

kite — *la cometa*
  Go fly a kite. — *Váyase a freír espárragos.*

knee — *la rodilla*
  to walk on one's knees — *caminar de rodillas.*
  She walked on her knees. *Caminó de rodillas.*

to knock — *golpear*
  to knock at the door — *llamar a la puerta.*
  I knocked at the door. *Llamé a la puerta.*

  to knock down — *derribar.*
  He knocked down the door. *Derribó la puerta.*

  to knock off — *rebajar.*
  He knocked ten dollars off the price. *Rebajó el precio diez dólares.*

  to knock off — *suspender.*
  We knocked off the meeting at five. *Suspendimos la reunión a las cinco.*

  to knock out — *poner fuera de combate.*
  He knocked him out. *Lo puso fuera de combate.*

to know — *saber*
  before one knows it — *sin darse cuenta.*
  Before you know it, it's too late. *Sin darse cuenta es muy tarde.*

  How do I know? — *¿Qué sé yo?*

  to be in the know — *estar bien informado (enterado).*
  Because he's such a friend of the president, he's always in the know. *Por ser tan amigo del presidente, siempre está bien informado.*

  to know full well (only too well) — *saber de sobra.*
  He knows full well (only to well) that his wife doesn't love him. *Sabe de sobra que su esposa no lo quiere.*

  to make known — *dar a conocer.*
  It was made known today. *Se dio a conocer hoy.*

L

lack — *la falta*
for lack of — *por falta de.*
She failed for lack of experience. *Fracasó por falta de experiencia.*

---

to lag — *retrasarse*
to lag behind — *ir atrasado a.*
He is lagging behind the others. *Va atrasado a los otros.*

---

lake — *el lago*
to tell (someone) to go jump in the lake — *mandar al diablo.*
When she refused to go out with him, he told her to go jump in the lake.
   Cuando se negó a salir con él, la mandó al diablo.

---

lane — *la callejuela; la vía*
It's a long lane that has no turning. — *No hay bien ni mal que cien años
   dure.*

---

language — *el idioma, la lengua*
to use strong language — *expresarse en términos ofensivos.*
He used strong language. *Se expresó en términos ofensivos.*

---

large — *grande*
to be at large — *estar en libertad (suelto).*
The criminal is still at large. *El criminal todavía está en libertad (suelto).*

---

last — *último*
at last — *por (al) fin.*
He's here at last. *Por (Al) fin está aquí.*

last but not least — *último en orden pero no en importancia.*
Last but not least, the house must have three bedrooms. *Ultimo en orden
   pero no en importancia, la casa debe tener tres alcobas (dormitorios).*

to see the last of — *no volver a ver.*

He saw the last of us. *No nos volvió a ver*

to the last — *hasta el fin.*
We stayed to the last. *(Nos) quedamos hasta el fin.*

---

late — *tarde*
　late in life — *a una edad avanzada.*
　She got married late in life. *Se casó a una edad avanzada.*

　late in the morning — *a última hora de la mañana; muy entrada la mañana.*
　She has breakfast late in the morning. *Se desayuna a última hora de la mañana (muy entrada la mañana).*

　It's late. — *Es tarde.*

　later on — *más adelante.*
　Later on I'll explain it to you. *Más adelante te lo explicaré.*

　to be late — *hacérsele tarde.*
　I've got to leave because I'm late. *Tengo que marcharme porque se me hace tarde.*

　to be late — *llegar tarde.*
　I'm sorry I'm late. *Siento haber llegado tarde.*

---

latest — *último*
　at the latest — *a más tardar.*
　Come tomorrow at the latest. *Venga mañana a más tardar.*

　the latest gossip — *el chisme de la última hora.*
　The latest gossip is that she's divorced. *El chisme de la última hora es que está divorciada.*

---

to laugh — *reír*
　He laughs best who laughs last. — *Al freír será el reír.*

　to make one laugh — *causarle gracia.*
　It made me laugh. *Me causó gracia.*

　to laugh at — *reírse de.*
　She's laughing at me. *Se ríe de mí.*

　to laugh oneself sick — *tirarse al suelo de risa.*

I laughed myself sick. *Me tiré al suelo de risa.*

to laugh until one cries — *llorar de risa.*
They laughed until they cried. *Lloraron de risa.*

laurel — *el laurel*
to rest on one's laurels — *dormirse sobre sus laureles.*
He's resting on his laurels. *Se duerme sobre sus laureles.*

law — *la ley*
to lay down the law — *dar órdenes terminantes.*
Our professor laid down the law. *Nuestro profesor dio órdenes terminantes.*

to maintain law and order — *mantener la paz.*
They can't maintain law and order. *No pueden mantener la paz.*

to take the law into one's own hands — *hacerse justicia por sí mismo.*
The students took the law into their own hands. *Los estudiantes se hicieron justicia por sí mismos.*

to lay — *poner, colocar*
to lay off — *despedir; dejar cesante.*
They laid off ten men. *Despidieron (Dejaron cesantes) a diez hombres.*

lead — *la delantera*
to play the lead — *tener el papel principal.*
She plays the lead. *Tiene el papel principal.*

to take the lead — *tomar la delantera.*
She took the lead in deciding. *Tomó la delantera en decidir.*

to lead — *conducir*
to lead one to — *llevarle a.*
It led me to doubt it. *Me llevó a dudarlo.*

leader — *el jefe*
to be a born leader — *nacer para mandar.*
Mr. López was a born leader. *El señor López nació para mandar.*

leaf — *la hoja*
>   **to turn over a new leaf** — *enmendarse; cambiar su modo de vivir.*
>   He turned over a new leaf. *Se enmendó (Cambió su modo de vivir).*

---

to leak — *salirse (un fluido); gotear*
>   **to leak out** — *trascender; descubrirse.*
>   The secret leaked out. *El secreto trascendió (se descubrió).*

---

to lean — *inclinarse*
>   **to lean back** — *echarse hacia atrás.*
>   She leaned back. *Se echó hacia atrás.*

---

leap — *el salto*
>   **by leaps and bounds** — *a pasos agigantados.*
>   He's growing by leaps and bounds. *Está creciendo a pasos agigantados.*

---

least — *menos*
>   **at least** — *a lo menos; por lo menos; al menos; cuando menos.*
>   He has at least three. *Tiene a lo menos (por lo menos, al menos, cuando menos) tres.*
>
>   **in the least** — *en lo más mínimo.*
>   I didn't like it in the least. *No me gustó en lo más mínimo.*
>
>   **That's the least of it.** — *Eso es lo de menos.*

---

leave — *el permiso; la despedida*
>   **to take French leave** — *despedirse (irse) a la francesa.*
>   He took French leave. *Se despidió (Se fue) a la francesa.*
>
>   **to take leave of** — *despedirse de.*
>   He took leave of his friends. *Se despidió de sus amigos.*
>
>   **to take leave of one's senses** — *perder el juicio.*
>   She took leave of her senses. *Perdió el juicio.*

---

to leave — *salir, dejar*
>   **to be left** — *quedar.*
>   He was left crippled for life. *Quedó lisiado por toda la vida.*
>
>   **to have left** — *quedarle; restarle.*

I have a lot left to do. *Me queda (resta) mucho que hacer.*

to leave out — *omitir.*
We left out the first stanza. *Omitimos la primera estrofa.*

lecture — *la conferencia*
   to give a good lecture to — *reprender.*
   My father gave me a good lecture when he found out what I had done. *Mi
   padre me reprendió al saber lo que había hecho.*

leg — *la pierna*
   not to have a leg to stand on — *no tener disculpa alguna.*
   He doesn't have a leg to stand on. *No tiene disculpa alguna.*

   to be on its last legs — *andar de capa caída; estar en las últimas.*
   That company is on its last legs. *Esa compañía anda de capa caída (está
   en las últimas).*

   to pull someone's leg — *tomarle el pelo.*
   He likes to pull the public's leg. *Le gusta tomarle el pelo al público.*

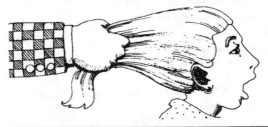

to lend — *prestar*
   to lend itself to — *prestarse a.*
   What he said lends itself to various interpretations. *Lo que dijo se presta a
   diversas interpretaciones.*

length — *el largo, la largura*
   at (great) length — *extensamente; por extenso.*
   He examined it at (great) length. *Lo examinó extensamente (por extenso).*

to go to any length — *ser capaz de todo.*
He'll go to any length to get ahead. *Es capaz de todo para adelantarse.*

---

leopard — *el leopardo*
You can't get a leopard to change his spots. — *Genio y figura hasta la sepultura.*

---

lesson — *la lección*
to teach someone a lesson — *darle una lección.*
By refusing to see her he taught her a lesson. *Negándose a verla le dio una lección.*

---

to let — *dejar*
let alone — *y mucho menos.*
He can't read Spanish, let alone speak it. *No sabe leer español y mucho menos hablarlo.*

let it go — *déjelo.*
Let it go. It's too late now. *Déjelo. Ya es demasiado tarde.*

Let's face it. — *No hay que darle vueltas.*

Let's see. — *Vamos a ver.*

to let alone — *dejar en paz.*
Let me alone. *Déjeme en paz.*

to let down — *desilusionar.*
She let him down. *Lo desilusionó.*

to let go — *despedir.*
The boss let him go. *El jefe lo despidió.*

to let go — *soltar.*
He let go of the rope. *Soltó la cuerda.*

to let on — *dejar saber.*
He didn't let on that he knew her. *No dejó saber que la conocía.*

to let out — *soltar.*
He let out a cry. *Soltó un grito.*

to let up — *disminuirse.*
The rain has let up a little. *La lluvia se ha disminuido un poco.*

to let up — *moderarse.*
The doctor told her to let up a little in her activities. *El médico le dijo que se moderara un poco en sus actividades.*

without letting up — *sin tregua.*
He studied all night without letting up. *Estudió toda la noche sin tregua.*

letter — *la letra*
to the letter — *al pie de la letra.*
He obeyed my instructions to the letter. *Obedeció mis instrucciones al pie de la letra.*

level — *el nivel*
on the level — *de buena fe.*
He told it to me on the level. *Me lo dijo de buena fe.*

liberty — *la libertad*
to take the liberty of — *tomarse la libertad de.*
He took the liberty of remaining. *Se tomó la libertad de quedarse.*

to lie — *echarse, acostarse*
to take it lying down — *aceptarlo con los brazos cruzados.*
He refused to take it lying down. *Se negó a aceptarlo con los brazos cruzados.*

life — *la vida*
never in one's life — *en su vida.*
Never in my life have I read so much. *En mi vida he leído tanto.*

not on your life — *bajo ninguna circunstancia.*
I'm not going to marry her — not on your life. *No me voy a casar con ella bajo ninguna circunstancia.*

the life of the party — *el alma de la fiesta.*
He's the life of the party. *Es el alma de la fiesta.*

to lay down one's life — *dar la vida.*
They laid down their lives for their country. *Dieron la vida por su patria.*

to lead a dog's life — *llevar una vida de perros.*

He leads a dog's life. *Lleva una vida de perros.*

to lead a . . . life — *hacer (llevar) una vida. . . .*
She leads a very secluded life. *Hace (Lleva) una vida muy solitaria.*

to make life miserable for — *amargarle la vida a.*
She made life miserable for her husband. *Le amargó la vida a su marido.*

to run for one's life — *salvarse por los pies.*
He ran for his life. *Se salvó por los pies.*

to take one's own life — *suicidarse.*
He took his own life. *Se suicidó.*

---

lifetime — *la vida; el curso de la vida.*
  in a single lifetime — *en una sola vida.*
In a single lifetime you can't see it all. *En una sola vida no se puede verlo todo.*

  in all of a lifetime — *en toda una vida.*
In all of a lifetime, he never saw Mexico. *En toda un vida no vio (a) México.*

---

light — *la luz*
  in the light of — *teniendo en cuenta.*
In the light of what he said, perhaps it would be better to stay home.
    Teniendo en cuenta lo que dijo, tal vez sea mejor quedarnos en casa.

  to bring to light — *sacar a luz.*

His investigations brought many new facts to life. *Sus investigaciones sacaron a luz muchos datos nuevos.*

to give someone a light — *darle fuego (lumbre).*
He gave me a light for my cigarette. *Me dio fuego (lumbre) para mi cigarrillo.*

to give someone the green light — *darle la autorización.*
We gave them the green light. *Les dimos la autorización.*

to make light of (to take lightly) — *tomar a broma.*
He made light of (took lightly) my problems. *Tomó a broma mis problemas.*

to see the light — *caer en la cuenta.*
After five explanations he saw the light. *Después de cinco explicaciones, cayó en la cuenta.*

to shed (throw) light on — *echar (arrojar) luz sobre.*
In his lecture he shed (threw) light on the mysteries of the universe. *En su conferencia echó (arrojó) luz sobre los misterios del universo.*

to turn (to switch) off the light — *apagar la luz.*
He turned (switched) off the light. *Apagó la luz.*

to turn (to switch) on the light — *encender (poner) la luz.*
Turn (switch) on the light. *Encienda (Ponga) la luz.*

---

like — *semejante*
    and the like — *y cosas por el estilo.*
He brought books, newspapers, magazines, and the like. *Trajo libros, periódicos, revistas y cosas por el estilo.*

    the likes of . . . — *otro semejante.*
I've never seen the likes of her. *Nunca he visto otra semejante.*

---

like — *como*
    like a — *hecho un.*
He roared like a wild beast. *Rugió hecho una fiera.*

---

to like — *gustar, agradar*
    how do you like . . . — *qué le parece. . . .*
How do you like Madrid? *¿Qué le parece Madrid?*

    to like — *caerle bien; gustarle.*

I don't like him. *No me cae bien (gusta).*

to like better — *gustarle más.*
He likes Spanish better. *Le gusta más el español.*

likely — *probable*
(as) like(ly) as not — *a lo mejor.*
As likely as not (Like as not) it will snow. *A lo mejor nevará.*

it's likely — *es fácil.*
It's likely that they've eaten. *Es fácil que hayan comido.*

the most likely is — *lo más fácil es.*
The most likely is that it's too late. *Lo más fácil es que sea muy tarde.*

liking — *el gusto*
to be to one's liking — *ser de su agrado (gusto).*
It's to my liking. *Es de mi agrado (gusto).*

to take a liking to — *caerle en gracia.*
I took a liking to her. *Me cayó en gracia.*

limelight — *el haz luminoso del proyector*
to be in the limelight — *estar a la vista del público.*
Right now, he's in the limelight. *Por el momento está a la vista del público.*

limit — *el límite*
That's the limit. — *Es el colmo.*

to exceed the limits — *rebasar los límites.*
He had exceeded the limits of his capabilities. *Había rebasado los límites de sus capacidades.*

to go to the limit — *no dejar piedra por mover.*
He went to the limit to please her. *No dejó piedra por mover para complacerla.*

line — *la línea*
to draw the line — *detenerse.*
He doesn't know where to draw the line. *No sabe dónde detenerse.*

to drop someone a few lines — *ponerle unas (cuatro) líneas (letras).*
I dropped her a few lines. *Le puse unas (cuatro) líneas (cuatro letras).*

to read between the lines — *leer entre líneas (renglones).*
You have to read between the lines. *Hay que leer entre líneas (renglones)*

to stand in line; to line up — *hacer cola.*
We stood in line (We lined up) outside the cinema. *Hicimos cola fuera del cine.*

---

to line — *alinear*
   to line up — *ponerse en fila; hacer cola.*
   We lined up. *Nos pusimos en fila (Hicimos cola).*

---

linen — *el lino*
   to wash one's dirty linen in public — *sacar a relucir sus asuntos personales.*
   She insists on washing her dirty linen in public. *Insiste en sacar a relucir sus asuntos personales.*

---

lip — *el labio*
   to keep a stiff upper lip — *no desanimarse.*
   It's hard to keep a stiff upper lip. *Es difícil no desanimarse.*

---

little — *poco; pequeño*
   a little — *un poco de.*
   He left her a little money. *Le dejó un poco de dinero.*

   a little of everything — *un poco de todo.*
   They have a little of everything. *Tienen un poco de todo.*

   little by little — *poco a poco.*
   Little by little he's growing. *Poco a poco está creciendo.*

---

to live — *vivir*
   to have to live with — *tener que aguantar.*
   She has an illness she'll have to live with. *Tiene una enfermedad que tendrá que aguantar.*

   to live and learn — *vivir para ver.*

We live and learn. *Vivimos para ver.*

To live and let live. — *Vivir y dejar vivir.*

to live it up — *darse buena vida.*
We spent the summer living it up. *Pasamos el verano dándonos buena vida.*

to live up to — *cumplir.*
He did not live up to his promises. *No cumplió sus promesas.*

---

living — *la vida*
  to earn (make) a living — *ganarse la vida.*
  He doesn't earn (make) a living. *No se gana la vida.*

---

load — *la carga*
  Take a load off your feet. — *Siéntate.*

  to take a load off one's mind — *quitarle un peso de encima.*
  What they said took a load off my mind. *Lo que dijeron me quitó un peso de encima.*

---

to lock — *cerrar con llave*
  to lock the door — *echar la llave.*
  He locked the door. *Echó la llave.*

  to lock up (in) — *encerrar con llave.*
  They locked him up (in). *Lo encerraron con llave.*

---

log — *el leño*
  It's as easy as falling off a log. — *Más fácil que beber un vaso de agua.*

  to sleep like a log — *dormir a pierna suelta.*
  They slept like a log. *Durmieron a pierna suelta.*

---

long — *largo; mucho tiempo*
  how long — *cuánto tiempo.*
  How long have you been here? *¿Cuánto tiempo lleva usted aquí?*

  long live — *viva.*
  Long live the party! *¡Viva el partido!*

  long since — *hace mucho (tiempo).*
  They left long since. *Salieron hace mucho (tiempo).*

not to be long for this world — *estar cercano a la muerte.*
He's not long for this world. *Está cercano a la muerte.*

So long. — *Hasta la vista.*

the long and the short of it is — *en resumidas cuentas.*
The long and the short of it is that she prefers Spain. *En resumidas cuentas, prefiere a España.*

to take long — *tardar mucho.*
It won't take him long. *No tardará mucho.*

---

longer — *más tiempo*
no longer — *ya no.*
He no longer lives here. *Ya no vive aquí.*

---

look — *la mirada*
to give someone a dirty look — *darle (dirigirle) una mirada despectiva.*
He gave me a dirty look. *Me dio (dirigió) una mirada despectiva.*

to take a look at — *echarle (dar) un vistazo (una ojeada) a.*
We took a look at his new car. *Le echamos (Dimos) un vistazo (una ojeada) a su coche nuevo.*

---

to look — *mirar*
look out — *cuidado.*
Look out for the train! *¡Cuidado con el tren!*

to be looking up — *ir mejorando.*
Things are looking up. *Las cosas van mejorando.*

to look after — *cuidar a.*
Look after my child. *Cuide a mi hijo.*

to look at — *mirar.*
They looked at our garden. *Miraron nuestro jardín.*

to look down on — *despreciar a.*
She looks down on her little sister. *Desprecia a su hermanita.*

to look for — *buscar.*
She's looking for her key. *Busca su llave.*

to look forward to — *esperar con ansia.*
I'm looking forward to Christmas. *Espero con ansia la Navidad.*

to look good (bad) — *tener buena (mala) cara; tener buen (mal) aspecto.*
She looks good (bad). *Tiene buena (mala) cara; Tiene buen (mal) aspecto.*

to look into — *investigar.*
I'll look into the matter. *Investigaré el asunto.*

to look like — *parecerse a.*
She looks like her mother. *Se parece a su madre.*

to look out — *asomarse a.*
She's looking out the window. *Está asomada al balcón.*

to look out for — *ocuparse de.*
She looked out for her mother. *Se ocupó de su madre.*

to look out for — *tener cuidado (mucho ojo) con.*
Look out for the pickpockets. *Tenga cuidado (mucho ojo) con los rateros.*

to look out on — *dar a.*
My window looks out on the square. *Mi balcón da a la plaza.*

to look over — *examinar.*
He looked over my report. *Examinó mi informe.*

to look someone up — *venir a verle.*
Look us up when you come to Madrid. *Venga a vernos cuando llegue a Madrid.*

to look up — *buscar.*
I looked up the date of his birth. *Busqué la fecha de su nacimiento.*

to look up — *levantar la mirada.*
When I spoke he looked up. *Cuando hablé, levantó la mirada.*

to look up to — *respetar (admirar) a.*
She looks up to her older sister. *Respeta (Admira) a su hermana mayor.*

---

lookout — *la vigilancia*
  to be on the lookout — *estar a la mira; estar alerta.*
  We've got to be on the lookout for their arrival. *Hay que estar a la mira de (estar alerta por) su llegada.*

---

loose — *flojo, suelto*
  to be on the loose — *andar suelto.*
  The children are always on the loose. *Los niños siempre andan sueltos.*

---

lord — *el señor*

   to be drunk as a lord — *estar hecho una cuba.*
   He arrived home drunk as a lord. *Llegó a casa hecho una cuba.*

---

to lose — *perder*

   Lost and found. — *Objetos perdidos.*

   to get lost — *perderse.*
   The child got lost. *El niño se perdió.*

   to tell someone to get lost — *decirle que se vaya a freír espárragos.*
   He told me to get lost. *Me dijo que me fuera a freír espárragos.*

---

lot — *la suerte*

   to throw in (to cast) one's lot with — *decidir compartir la suerte de.*
   I threw in (cast) my lot with John. *Decidí compartir la suerte de Juan.*

---

lot — *el lote*

   a lot — *en extremo.*
   I liked it a lot. *Me gustó en extremo.*

   a lot of — *mucho.*
   They sold a lot of wine. *Vendieron mucho vino.*

   a whole lot — *una gran cantidad.*
   I bought a whole lot. *Compré una gran cantidad.*

   what a lot of — *cuántos.*
   What a lot of fish! *¡Cuántos pescados!*

---

loud — *alto*
　　out loud — *en voz alta.*
　　She read the letter out loud. *Leyó la carta en voz alta.*

---

love — *el amor*
　　Love me, love my dog. — *Quien bien quiere a Beltrán, bien quiere a su can.*

　　not for love nor money — *ni a tiros.*
　　I won't do it for love nor money. *No lo haré ni a tiros.*

　　There is no love lost between them. — *La antipatía es mutua.*

　　to be in love with — *estar enamorado de.*
　　She's in love with Charles. *Está enamorada de Carlos.*

---

luck — *la suerte*
　　to try one's luck — *probar fortuna.*
　　I tried my luck. *Probé fortuna.*

---

lucky — *afortunado*
　　to be lucky — *tener suerte.*
　　He's lucky. *Tiene suerte.*

---

lump — *el terrón*
　　to have a lump in one's throat — *tener un nudo en la garganta.*
　　He had a lump in his throat. *Tenía un nudo en la garganta.*

---

lurch — *la sacudida*
　　to leave in the lurch — *dejar en la estacada.*
　　He left her in the lurch. *La dejó en la estacada.*

M

mad — *enfadado, enojado; loco*
　　like mad — *como loco.*
　　He drives like mad. *Maneja como loco.*

to be mad about — *tener locura por.*
He's mad about chess. *Tiene locura por el ajedrez.*

to get mad — *enfadarse.*
She got mad. *Se enfadó.*

to look mad — *tener cara de enfado.*
He looks mad. *Tiene cara de enfado.*

to make one mad — *darle rabia.*
It made us mad. *Nos dio rabia.*

---

mail — *el correo*
  by return mail — *por vuelta de correo.*
  Write me by return mail. *Escríbame por vuelta de correo.*

to mail — *echar al correo*
  to mail a letter — *echar una carta.*
  Mail this letter for me. *Écheme esta carta.*

main — *principal*
  in the main — *en general.*
  In the main she's a happy person. *En general es una persona feliz.*

---

to make — *hacer*
  Make yourself at home. — *Está usted en su casa.*

to be able to make it — *poder ir.*
They invited me but I can't make it. *Me invitaron pero no puedo ir.*

to be made for — *tener madera para.*
I'm not made for traveling. *No tengo madera para viajar.*

to make away (off) with — *escaparse con.*
They made away (off) with our money. *Se escaparon con nuestro dinero.*

to make believe — *fingir.*
She made believe that she was ill. *Fingió estar enferma.*

to make clear — *aclarar; explicar.*
She made it clear that she wasn't going. *Aclaró (Explicó) que no iba.*

to make for — *dirigirse a.*

He made for the door. *Se dirigió a la puerta.*

to make good — *tener éxito.*
It's hard to make good in Hollywood. *Es difícil tener éxito en Hollywood.*

to make it — *llegar.*
We won't make it by ten. *No llegaremos para las diez.*

to make it — *no morirse.*
He's so ill that I'm afraid that he won't make it. *Está tan enfermo que temo que se muera.*

to make (it) known — *dar a conocer.*
Yesterday they made that news known. *Ayer dieron a conocer esa noticia.*

to make off — *largarse.*
He made off. *Se largó.*

to make out — *entender; descifrar.*
I couldn't make out the signature. *No pude entender (descifrar) la firma.*

to make out — *fingir.*
He's trying to make out that he knows her. *Está fingiendo que la conoce.*

to make out — *irle.*
How did you make out? *¿Cómo le fue?*

to make out — *preparar.*
Make out his tourist card. *Prepare su tarjeta de turista.*

to make out a check — *hacer un cheque.*
Make out a check for ten dollars. *Haga un cheque por diez dólares.*

to make out a form — *llenar un formulario.*
He made out another form. *Llenó otro formulario.*

to make over — *reformar.*
She made over her coat. *Reformó su abrigo.*

to make up — *inventar.*
He made up a lot of lies. *Inventó muchas mentiras.*

to make up for — *compensar.*
I didn't help today but I'll make up for it tomorrow. *No ayudé hoy pero lo compensaré mañana.*

to make up with — *hacer las paces (reconciliarse) con.*
She made up with her husband. *Hizo las paces (se reconcilió) con su esposo.*

man — *el hombre*

  It's every man for himself. — *Cada cual se las arregle como pueda.*

  Man alive! — *¡Hombre!*

  Man overboard! — *¡Hombre al agua!*

  Man proposes, God disposes. — *El hombre propone, Dios dispone.*

  No man is an island. — *Nadie puede vivir aislado.*

  the man in the street — *el hombre de la calle (hombre corriente).*
  It's not for the man in the street. *No es para el hombre de la calle (hombre corriente).*

  to a man — *sin faltar uno solo.*
  They were there to a man. *Todos estaban sin faltar uno solo.*

  to be a man of his word — *ser un hombre de palabra.*
  He's a man of his word. *Es un hombre de palabra.*

  to be a reputable man — *ser un hombre de bien.*
  He's a reputable man. *Es un hombre de bien.*

  to be the man for the job — *ser el hombre indicado.*
  He's the man for the job. *Es el hombre indicado.*

manner — *la manera*

  in a manner of speaking — *en cierto modo; hasta cierto punto.*
  My sister was, in a manner of speaking, the cause of everything that happened. *Mi hermana fue en cierto modo (hasta cierto punto) la causa de todo lo ocurrido.*

  to be just a manner of speaking — *ser sólo un decir.*
  Don't get offended, it's just a manner of speaking. *No te ofendas, es sólo un decir.*

many — *muchos*

  and as many more — *y otros tantos.*
  He sold them five cows and as many more horses. *Les vendió cinco vacas y otros tantos caballos.*

marbles — *las canicas*

  not to have all one's marbles — *tener un tornillo suelto (flojo).*

It's obvious that he doesn't have all his marbles. *Se ve que tiene un tornillo suelto (flojo).*

---

march — *la marcha*
  Forward march! — *¡En marcha!*

  to steal a march on someone — *tomarle la delantera; ganarle por la mano.*
  I stole a march on him. *Yo le tomé la delantera (le gané por la mano).*

---

marine — *el soldado de infantería de marina.*
  Tell it to the marines. — *A otro perro con ese hueso.*

---

market — *el mercado*
  to play the market — *jugar a la bolsa.*
  He plays the market. *Juega a la bolsa.*

---

marriage — *el matrimonio*
  Marriages are made in heaven. — *Casamiento y mortaja, del cielo bajan.*

---

to marry — *casar*
  to marry — *casarse con.*
  He's going to marry Linda. *Va a casarse con Linda.*

---

master — *el amo*
  Like master like man. — *De tal palo tal astilla.*

---

match — *el igual*
  to meet one's match — *hallar la horma de su zapato.*
  He finally met his match. *Al fin halló la horma de su zapato.*

---

matter — *la materia*
  a laughing matter — *cosa de risa.*
  What they're demanding of us is not a (is no) laughing matter. *Lo que nos están exigiendo no es cosa de risa.*

  as a matter of course — *como cosa normal.*
  He accepted it as a matter of course. *Lo aceptó como cosa normal.*

as a matter of fact — *a decir verdad; en efecto; en realidad.*

As a matter of fact, I did it. *A decir verdad (En efecto, En realidad) lo hice yo.*

for that matter — *el caso es.*

For that matter, we didn't like it. *El caso es que no nos gustó.*

It doesn't matter. — *Es igual (No importa).*

to be a matter of — *ser cuestión de; consistir en.*

It's a matter of knowing how. *Es cuestión de (Consiste en) saber cómo.*

no matter how. . . . — *por más . . . que.*

No matter how cold it is, he goes swimming. *Por más frío que haga, va a nadar.*

no matter how — *sea como sea.*

No matter how, I'll do it. *Lo haré sea como sea.*

no matter when — *cuandoquiera que.*

No matter when we go there, they are watching television. *Cuandoquiera que vayamos allí están mirando (escuchando) la televisión.*

no matter where — *dondequiera que.*

No matter where he is, I'll find him. *Dondequiera que esté, lo encontraré.*

no matter who — *quienquiera que.*

No matter who tells you, don't believe it. *Quienquiera que se lo diga, no lo crea.*

that matter of — *eso (aquello) de.*

That matter of his accident is serious. *Eso (Aquello) de su accidente es grave.*

What's the matter? — *¿Qué hay?*

What's the matter with you? — *¿Qué tiene usted? (¿Qué le pasa)?*

maybe — *tal vez*

    Maybe so (not). — *Puede que sí (no).*

meal — *la comida*

    a square meal — *una comida abundante.*

He gets three square meals a day. *Tiene tres comidas abundantes al día.*

    Enjoy your meal. — *Que le aproveche; Buen provecho.*

means — *la manera, el modo; los bienes*

  beyond one's means — *por encima de sus posibilidades.*
  They are living beyond their means. *Viven por encima de sus posibilidades.*

  by all means — *sin falta.*
  By all means go to the dance. *Vaya al baile sin falta.*

  by means of — *mediante; por medio de.*
  He was convinced by means of persuasion. *Fue convencido mediante (por medio de) mucha persuasión.*

  by no means — *de (en) ningún modo; de (en) ninguna manera.*
  By no means will we accept it. *No lo aceptaremos de (en) ningún modo (ninguna manera).*

---

to mean — *querer decir, significar*

  to mean to — *pensar.*
  He didn't mean to hurt me. *No pensaba lastimarme.*

  to mean well — *tener buenas intenciones.*
  She means well. *Tiene buenas intenciones.*

  What do you mean? — *¿Qué quiere decir?*

  What do you mean you don't know? — *¡Cómo que no sabe!*

---

to measure — *medir*

  to measure up to one's expectations — *estar a la altura de sus esperanzas.*
  He didn't measure up to our expectations. *No estaba a la altura de nuestras esperanzas.*

---

meat — *la carne*

  One man's meat is another man's poison. — *Sobre gustos no hay nada escrito.*

---

to meet — *encontrar*

  to meet halfway — *partir(se) la diferencia con.*
  He always meets his friends halfway. *Siempre (se) parte la diferencia con sus amigos.*

---

meeting — *la reunión*
   to call a meeting — *convocar una junta.*
   We called a meeting. *Convocamos una junta.*

memory — *la memoria*
   from memory — *de memoria.*
   He knows all their names from memory. *Sabe todos los nombres de memoria.*

   if my memory serves me right — *si mal no recuerdo.*
   If my memory serves me right, it's tomorrow. *Si mal no recuerdo, es mañana.*

mend — *el remiendo*
   to be on the mend — *ir mejorando.*
   He was very sick, but now he is on the mend. *Estaba muy enfermo, pero ya va mejorando.*

to mention — *mencionar*
   Don't even mention it! — *¡Ni hablar!*

mercy — *la merced*
   at . . . 's mercy — *a la merced de. . . .*
   He's at his aunt's mercy. *Está a la merced de su tía.*

merit — *el mérito*
   on one's own merits — *por su justo valor.*
   He was judged on his own merits. *Lo juzgaron por su justo valor.*

mess — *el lío*
   to be (in) a mess — *estar en desorden.*
   His desk is (in) a mess. *Su escritorio está en desorden.*

   to get into a mess — *meterse en un lío.*
   We got into a mess. *Nos metimos en un lío.*

   to make a mess — *estropear.*
   They've made a mess of everything. *Lo han estropeado todo.*

149

method — *el método*
   There is method in his madness. — *Nadie da palos de balde; Es más cuerdo de lo que parece.*

middle — *el centro, el medio*
   about (around) the middle — *a mediados.*
   He was born about (around) the middle of May. *Nació a mediados de mayo.*

   in the middle of — *en medio de.*
   It stopped in the middle of the street. *Se paró en medio de la calle.*

   in the middle of — *en pleno.*
   We got there in the middle of summer. *Llegamos en pleno verano.*

mildly — *suavemente*
   to put it mildly — *sin exagerar.*
   He said, to put it mildly, that he should have stayed home. *Dijo, sin exagerar, que debió quedarse en casa.*

milk — *la leche*
   There's no use crying over spilt milk — *A lo hecho, pecho.*

mill — *el molino*
   to have been through the mill — *saber por experiencia.*
   I've been through the mill. *Lo sé por experiencia.*

mind — *la mente*
   to be in one's right mind — *estar en sus cabales (su juicio).*
   He's not in his right mind. *No está en sus cabales (su juicio).*

   to be out of one's mind — *haber perdido el juicio.*
   He's out of his mind. *Ha perdido el juicio.*

   to change one's mind — *cambiar (mudar; variar) de opinión.*
   She changed her mind. *Cambió (Mudó; Varió) de opinión.*

   to enter (cross) one's mind — *ocurrírsele.*
   It never entered (crossed) his mind. *Nunca se le ocurrió.*

   to have a one-track mind — *ser de un solo interés.*
   He has a one-track mind. *Es un hombre de un solo interés.*

to have in mind — *tener pensado (en la mente).*
I had in mind to go. *Tenía pensado (en la mente) ir.*

to have something on one's mind — *preocuparle algo.*
He's got something on his mind. *Algo le preocupa.*

to keep (to bear) in mind — *tener presente; tener en cuenta; recordar.*
Keep (Bear) in mind that I can't swim. *Tenga presente (Tenga en cuenta;
    Recuerde) que no sé nadar.*

to lose one's mind — *perder el seso.*
I'm losing my mind. *Estoy perdiendo el seso.*

to lose one's mind — *volverse loco.*
He lost his mind over Mary. *Se ha vuelto loco por María.*

to make up one's mind — *decidir; resolver.*
I made up my mind to stay. *Decidí (Resolví) quedarme.*

to slip one's mind — *olvidársele; pasársele de la memoria.*
It slipped my mind. *Se me olvidó (Se me pasó de la memoria).*

to speak one's mind freely — *hablar con toda franqueza.*
She spoke her mind freely to me. *Me habló con toda franqueza.*

---

to mind — *obedecer; tener inconveniente*
  Do you mind if I smoke? — *¿Le molesta si fumo?*

to mind — *tener inconveniente.*
I don't mind your staying. *No tengo inconveniente en que se quede.*

---

mint — *la casa de moneda*
  to cost a mint — *costar un ojo de la cara.*
  That car must have cost him a mint. *Ese coche debió de costarle un ojo de
    la cara.*

---

minute — *el minuto*
  at the last minute — *a última hora.*
  He refused to go at the last minute. *Se negó a ir a última hora.*

  Every minute counts. — *No hay tiempo que perder.*

---

miserable — *miserable*
  to make oneself miserable — *afligirse.*
  She makes herself miserable by crying so much. *Se aflige llorando tanto.*

miss — *el tiro errado, el malogro*
  A miss is as good as a mile. — *Lo mismo da librarse por poco que por mucho.*

to miss — *echar de menos; perder*
  to be missing — *faltar.*
  A book is missing from my shelf. *Falta un libro en mi estante.*

  to miss — *echar de menos (extrañar).*
  We miss her. *La echamos de menos (La extrañamos).*

  to miss — *escapársele.*
  They missed what I said to them. *Se les escapó lo que les dije.*

mistake — *el error*
  by mistake — *por equivocación.*
  I did it by mistake. *Lo hice por equivocación.*

  make no mistake about it — *no nos engañemos.*
  Make no mistake about it; it's true. *No nos engañemos; es verdad.*

  to mistake for — *confundir con; tomar por.*
  They mistook me for my brother. *Me confundieron con (Me tomaron por) mi hermano.*

to mix — *mezclar*
  to get mixed up — *confundirse.*
  I couldn't hear and got mixed up. *No pude oír y me confundí.*

moment — *el momento*
  at odd moments — *a (sus) ratos perdidos.*
  I read at odd moments. *Leo a (mis) ratos perdidos.*

  for the moment — *por el momento; de momento.*
  For the moment it's all we have. *Por el (De) momento es todo lo que tenemos.*

money — *el dinero*
  Money makes the mare go. — *Poderoso caballero es Don Dinero.*

  to be rolling in money — *rebosar en dinero.*
  We had a cousin who was rolling in money. *Teníamos un primo que
    rebosaba en dinero.*

  to have money to burn — *estar cargado de dinero.*
  That family has money to burn. *Esa familia está cargada de dinero.*

  to make good money — *ganar buen sueldo.*
  He's making good money. *Está ganando buen sueldo.*

mood — *el humor*
  to be in a good (bad) mood — *estar de buen (mal) humor (talante;
    genio)*
  He's in a good (bad) mood. *Está de buen (mal) humor (talante; genio).*

  to be in no mood for jokes — *no sentirse con humor para chistes.*
  I'm in no mood for jokes. *No me siento con humor para chistes.*

  to be in no mood to — *no estar en disposición de.*
  I'm in no mood to sing. *No estoy en disposición de cantar.*

  to be in the mood (feel inspired) (to) — *estar en vena (para).*
  Poets aren't always in the mood (don't always feel inspired) to write. *Los
    poetas no siempre están en vena para escribir.*

moon — *la luna*
  for the moon to shine — *hacer (haber) luna.*
  The moon is shining. *Hace (Hay) luna.*

  once in a blue moon — *muy de tarde en tarde.*
  We go to a movie once in a blue moon. *Vamos al cine muy de tarde en
    tarde.*

moonlight — *la luz de la luna*
  by moonlight — *a la luz de la luna.*
  It's better seen by moonlight. *Se ve mejor a la luz de la luna.*

more — *más*
  more and more — *cada vez más.*

They're getting more and more tired. *Se van cansando cada vez más.*

more often than not — *la mayoría de las veces.*

More often than not he doesn't eat breakfast. *La mayoría de las veces no se desayuna.*

the more . . . the more . . . — *cuanto más . . . , (tanto) más . . . ; mientras más . . . . , más . . . .*

The more one earns the more one spends. *Cuanto (Mientras) más se gana, (tanto) más se gasta.*

---

morning — *la mañana*

How are you this morning? — *¿Cómo amaneció?*

---

most — *más*

at most — *a lo sumo; cuando (a lo) más.*

We need five at most. *Nos hacen falta cinco a lo sumo (cuando más; a lo más).*

for the most part — *por lo general.*

For the most part, it's true. *Por lo general, es verdad.*

most — *la mayor parte de; los más.*

Most women marry. *La mayor parte de las (Las más) mujeres se casan.*

to make the most of — *sacar el mejor partido de.*

They make the most of their opportunities. *Sacan el mejor partido de sus oportunidades.*

---

motion — *el movimiento*

in slow motion — *a cámara lenta.*

They showed it in slow motion. *Lo proyectaron a cámara lenta.*

---

mountain — *la montaña*

to make a mountain out of a molehill — *hacer de una pulga un elefante (un camello).*

You're making a mountain out of a molehill. *Está haciendo de una pulga un elefante (un camello).*

---

mourning — *el luto*
    to be in mourning — *estar de luto.*
    The whole family is in mourning *Toda la familia está de luto.*

mouth — *la boca*
    for one's mouth to water — *hacérsele agua la boca.*
    His mouth waters. *Se le hace agua la boca.*

    It's straight from the horse's mouth. — *Lo sé de primera mano (de buena tinta).*

    not to open one's mouth — *no decir esta boca es mía.*
    He didn't open his mouth. *No dijo esta boca es mía.*

He didn't open his mouth.
No dijo esta boca es mía.

    to have a big mouth — *írsele demasiado la lengua.*
    He's got a big mouth. *Se le va demasiado la lengua.*

    to keep one's mouth shut (keep still) — *no despegar los labios.*
    No matter what they say, I'm going to keep my mouth shut (keep still).
    Digan lo que digan, no voy a despegar los labios.

    to melt in one's mouth — *hacérsele (un) agua en la boca.*
    It melts in my mouth. *Se me hace (un) agua en la boca.*

move — *el movimiento*
    to be on the move — *andar sin parar.*
    He's always on the move. *Siempre anda sin parar.*

    to be on the move — *estar en marcha.*

The enemy is on the move. *El enemigo está en marcha.*

to make a false move — *dar un paso en falso.*
He never makes a false move. *Nunca da un paso en falso.*

---

to move — *moverse*

to move (right) along — *ir a gran velocidad.*
They moved right along and arrived at ten. *Fueron a gran velocidad y llegaron a las diez.*

to move into — *instalarse en.*
A family just moved into that house. *Una familia acaba de instalarse en aquella casa.*

to move off — *alejarse.*
When he saw the policeman, the pickpocket moved off. *Al ver al policía el ratero se alejó.*

to move on — *marcharse.*
Move on! You can't park there. *¡Márchese! No se puede estacionar ahí.*

to move out (away) — *mudar(se) (de casa).*
Our neighbors moved out (away). *Nuestros vecinos (se) mudaron (de casa).*

---

much — *mucho*

How much does it sell for? — *¿A cómo se vende?*

not to think much of — *no tener un alto concepto de.*
He doesn't think much of our country. *No tiene un alto concepto de nuestro país.*

to make much of — *dar mucha importancia a.*
They made much of his performance. *Dieron mucha importancia a su actuación.*

---

mum — *callado*
Mum's the word! —*¡A callar!*

---

murder — *el asesinato*

to scream bloody murder — *gritar como si lo mataran.*
The victim was screaming bloody murder. *La víctima gritaba como si la mataran.*

---

music — *la música*
   to face the music — *arrostrar las consecuencias.*
   We had to face the music. *Tuvimos que arrostrar las consecuencias.*

---

must — *el deber*
   to be a must — *ser indispensable.*
   That play is a must. *Es indispensable ver esa comedia.*

N

nail (anat.) — *la uña*
   to bite one's nails — *comerse las uñas.*
   She bites her nails. *Se come las uñas.*

---

nail — *el clavo*
   to hit the nail on the head — *dar en el clavo.*
   You hit the nail on the head. *Dio en el clavo.*

---

name — *el nombre*
   in . . . 's name — *en (a) nombre de. . . .*
   He greeted us in the president's name. *Nos saludó en (a) nombre del
      presidente.*

   maiden name — *nombre de soltera.*
   She uses her maiden name. *Usa su nombre de soltera.*

   to call someone names — *injuriar (insultar) a.*
   She called her friend names. *Injurió (Insultó) a su amigo.*

   to go by . . . 's name — *conocérsele con el nombre de . . . .*
   He goes by his father's name. *Se le conoce con el nombre de su padre.*

   to make a name for oneself — *hacerse famoso.*
   He made a name for himself by studying hard. *Se hizo famoso estudiando
      mucho.*

   What's in a name? — *El nombre es lo de menos.*

---

to name — *llamar*

> **for one's name to be (to be named)** — *llamarse.*
> His name is (He is named) Peter. *Se llama Pedro.*

> **to be named after (for)** — *llevar el nombre de.*
> He's named after (for) his uncle. *Lleva el nombre de su tío.*

> **You name it and we've got it.** — *Lo que usted quiera lo tenemos.*

---

nap — *la siesta*

> **to catch napping** — *coger desprevenido.*
> We caught him napping. *Lo cogimos desprevenido.*

> **to take a nap** — *echar un sueño (una siesta).*
> If I get a chance, I'm going to take a nap. *Si tengo la oportunidad, voy a echar un sueño (una siesta).*

> **to take one's afternoon nap** — *dormir la (echar una) siesta.*
> She was taking her afternoon nap. *Estaba durmiendo la (echando una) siesta.*

---

necessity — *la necesidad*

> **of necessity** — *por fuerza.*
> I attended of necessity. *Asistí por fuerza.*

> **Necessity is the mother of invention.** — *La necesidad es la madre de la inventiva.*

---

neck — *el cuello*

> **to break one's neck** — *matarse.*
> He broke his neck studying. *Se mató estudiando.*

> **to breathe down one's neck** — *no dejar (ni) a sol ni a sombra.*
> His creditors were breathing down his neck. *Sus acreedores no lo dejaban (ni) a sol ni a sombra.*

> **to get it in the neck** — *recibir lo lindo.*
> He got it in the neck. *Recibió lo lindo.*

> **to stick one's neck out** — *arriesgarse.*
> He's afraid to stick his neck out. *Tiene miedo de arriesgarse.*

---

need — *la necesidad*
  There's no need to hurry. — *No corre prisa.*

to need — *necesitar*
  to need — *hacerle falta.*
  He needs help. *Le hace falta ayuda.*

needle — *la aguja*
  It's like looking for a needle in a haystack. — *Es como buscar una aguja en un pajar.*

neither — *ni; tampoco*
  neither is (does, etc.) . . . . — *ni . . . tampoco.*
  Neither is (does, etc.) he. *Ni él tampoco.*

  neither . . . nor . . . — *ni . . . ni. . . .*
  Neither the rain nor the snow stopped us. *Ni la lluvia ni la nieve nos pararon.*

nerve — *el nervio*
  the nerve of it! — *¡qué desvergüenza!*
  The nerve of it! He took it all! *¡Qué desvergüenza! ¡Se lo llevó todo!*

  to get on one's nerves — *crisparle los nervios.*
  He gets on my nerves. *Me crispa los nervios.*

nest — *el nido*

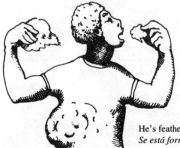

He's feathering his nest.
Se está forrando el riñón.

    to feather one's nest — *forrarse el riñón.*
    He's feathering his nest. *Se está forrando el riñón.*

    to stir up a hornet's nest — *provocar indignación general.*
    His action stirred up a hornet's nest. *Su acción provocó indignación general.*

---

never — *nunca; jamás*
    Never fear. — *No hay cuidado.*

    never mind — *no se moleste.*
    Never mind. I'll do it. *No se moleste. Lo haré yo.*

    never to have had it so good — *nunca haberlo pasado tan bien.*
    He's never had it so good. *Nunca lo ha pasado tan bien.*

---

news — *las noticias*
    to break the news — *ser el primero en dar la noticia.*
    He broke the news. *Fue el primero que dio la noticia.*

---

next — *siguiente; junto*
    next month (year, week, etc.) — *el mes (año, semana, etc.) que viene.*
    We're leaving next month (year, week, etc.). *Salimos el mes (año, semana, etc.) que viene.*

    next to — *junto a; al lado de.*
    They live next to the bakery. *Viven junto a (al lado de) la panadería.*

---

nick — *la mella*
    in the nick of time — *en el momento crítico (a última hora).*
    The ambulance arrived in the nick of time. *La ambulancia llegó en el momento crítico (a última hora).*

---

night — *la noche*
    at night — *de noche.*
    He works at night. *Trabaja de noche.*

    at nightfall — *al anochecer.*
    We'll stop at nightfall. *Nos pararemos al anochecer.*

    for night to fall — *cerrar la noche.*

Night has now fallen. *Ya ha cerrado la noche.*

overnight (unexpectedly) — *de la noche a la mañana.*
He became famous overnight. *De la noche a la mañana se hizo famoso.*

to make a night of it — *divertirse hasta muy entrada la noche.*
They made a night of it. *Se divirtieron hasta muy entrada la noche.*

to say good night (good evening) — *dar las buenas noches.*
We said good night (good evening) to her. *Le dimos las buenas noches.*

to stay out all night — *trasnochar.*
He stayed out all night. *Trasnochó.*

---

no — *ninguno*
  No parking (smoking, etc.). — *Se prohíbe estacionarse (fumar, etc.).*

  not to take no for an answer — *no aceptar negativas.*
  He doesn't take no for an answer. *No acepta negativas.*

  to be of no account — *ser un cero a la izquierda.*
  He's of no account. *Es un cero a la izquierda.*

---

to nod — *inclinar la cabeza*
  to nod — *dar cabezadas.*
  When he's sleepy, he nods. *Cuando tiene sueño, da cabezadas.*

  to nod (yes) — *afirmar con la cabeza.*
  I nodded (yes). *Afirmé con la cabeza.*

---

nonsense — *el disparate, la tontería*
  Enough nonsense. — *Ya basta de disparates.*

  What nonsense! — *¡Qué va!*

---

nook — *el rinconcito*
  in every nook and cranny — *por todos los rincones.*
  We looked in every nook and cranny. *Buscamos por todos los rincones.*

---

noon — *el mediodía*
  at noon — *a (al) mediodía.*
  We eat lightly at noon. *Comemos poco a (al) mediodía.*

---

nose — *la nariz*
   right under one's nose — *delante de las narices.*
   It's right under your nose. *Lo tiene delante de las narices.*

   to count noses — *contar personas.*
   The guide always counts noses before the tourists get on the bus. *El quía siempre cuenta los turistas antes que suban al autobús.*

   to lead by the nose — *tener agarrado por las narices.*
   She leads him by the nose. *Lo tiene agarrado por las narices.*

   to pay through the nose — *costarle un ojo de la cara.*
   Unfortunately, we had to pay through the nose. *Desafortunadamente, nos costó un ojo de la cara.*

   to stick one's nose in someone else's business — *meter la nariz en asuntos no suyos.*
   Don't stick your nose in my business. *No meta la nariz en asuntos míos.*

   to turn up one's nose — *mirar con desprecio.*
   She turned up her nose at my suggestion. *Miró con desprecio mi sugerencia.*

   to win by a nose — *ganar con poca ventaja.*
   He won by a nose. *Ganó con poca ventaja.*

   To cut off one's nose to spite one's face. — *Tirar piedras contra el propio tejado.*

---

not — *no*
   if not — *en caso contrario.*
   They want to go today; if not, they'll go tomorrow. *Quieren ir hoy; en caso contrario, irán mañana.*

   not at all — *de nada; no hay de qué.*
   Thank you. Not at all. *Gracias. De nada (No hay de qué).*

   Why not? — *¿Cómo no?*

---

notch — *el grado*
   to take someone down a notch — *bajarle los humos.*
   She had to take him down a notch. *Ella tuvo que bajarle los humos.*

---

note — *la nota, el apunte*

  to compare notes — *cambiar opiniones.*
  We were comparing notes. *Cambiábamos opiniones.*

  to make a note of — *tomar nota de; apuntar.*
  I made a note of the address. *Tomé nota de (Apunté) la dirección.*

  to take note of — *tomar nota de.*
  I took note of what she said. *Tomé nota de lo que dijo.*

---

nothing — *nada*

  for nothing — *gratis.*
  He gave it to me for nothing. *Me lo dio gratis.*

  not . . . for nothing — *por algo.*
  He's not the king for nothing. *Por algo es rey.*

  there's nothing to it — *es sencillísimo.*
  It's easy to do. There's nothing to it. *Es fácil de hacer. Es sencillísimo.*

  to be nothing to complain about — *no ser para quejarse.*
  It is nothing to complain about. *No es para quejarse.*

  to be nothing to it — *carecer de fundamento.*
  It's a rumor, but there's nothing to it. *Es un rumor, pero carece de fundamento.*

  to be nothing to one — *no afectarle.*
  That's nothing to me. *Eso a mí no me afecta.*

  to be nothing to speak of — *no merecer la pena.*
  The speech was nothing to speak of. *El discurso no merecía la pena.*

  to be nothing to write home about — *no ser nada extraordinario.*
  It's nothing to write home about. *No es nada extraordinario.*

  to have nothing to do with — *no tener nada que ver con.*
  He has nothing to do with the matter. *No tiene nada que ver con el asunto.*

  to make nothing of it — *no concederle importancia.*
  He found out but made nothing of it. *Lo supo pero no le concedió importancia.*

  to sell for almost nothing — *vender regalado.*
  I sold it for almost nothing. *Lo vendí, regalado.*

---

notice — *el aviso*
   to escape one's notice — *escapársele.*
   It escaped my notice. *Se me escapó.*

   to serve notice — *hacer saber; notificar.*
   He served notice that our rent was due tomorrow. *Nos hizo saber
     (notificó) que la renta vencía mañana.*

   to sit up and take notice — *parar la oreja.*
   What she told me made me sit up and take notice. *Lo que me dijo me hizo
     parar la oreja.*

---

notion — *la noción*
   to take a notion to — *antojársele.*
   We took a notion to sell it. *Se nos antojó venderlo.*

---

now — *ahora*
   from now on — *de ahora (aquí) en adelante.*
   From now on, she'll stay home. *De ahora (aquí) en adelante se quedará
     en casa.*

   just now — *por ahora.*
   Just now, I can't go. *Por ahora, no puedo ir.*

   now and again (then) — *de vez en cuando.*
   I tell it to him now and again (then). *Se lo digo de vez en cuando.*

   now then — *ahora bien.*
   Now then, tell me the truth. *Ahora bien, dígame la verdad.*

   only now — *apenas ahora.*
   Only now did he receive the news. *Apenas ahora recibió las noticias.*

   right now — *ahora mismo.*
   Do it right now. *Hágalo ahora mismo.*

---

nuisance — *la molestia*
   to make a nuisance of oneself — *molestar.*
   That boy is always making a nuisance of himself. *Ese chico siempre está
     molestando.*

---

null — *nulo*
  null and void — *sin efecto.*
  The agreement is null and void. *El acuerdo está sin efecto.*

number — *el número*
  in round numbers — *en números redondos.*
  They prefer us to express it in round numbers. *Prefieren que lo expresemos en números redondos.*

  to have someone's number — *saber de qué pie cojea.*
  I've got his number. *Sé de qué pie cojea.*

nutshell — *la cáscara (de nuez)*
  in a nutshell — *en pocas palabras.*
  He told us in a nutshell. *Nos lo dijo en pocas palabras.*

O

oar — *el remo*
  to put one's oar in — *meter su cuchara.*
  In every conversation he has to put his oar in. *En cualquier conversación tiene que meter su cuchara.*

In every conversation
he has to put his oar in.
*En cualquier conversación
tiene que meter su cuchara.*

oats — *la avena*
  to sow one's wild oats — *pasar las mocedades.*
  He's sowing his wild oats. *Está pasando las mocedades.*

objection — *la objeción*
  to raise objections to — *hacer objeciones (poner reparo) a.*
  He is raising objections to the speech. *Está haciendo objeciones (poniendo reparo) al discurso.*

  to see no objection — *no ver ningún inconveniente.*
  We saw no objection. *No vimos ningún inconveniente.*

obligated — *obligado*
  to be obligated to — *estar en el caso de.*
  We're obligated to work there. *Estamos en el caso de trabajar allí.*

obvious — *obvio*
  it's obvious — *se conoce; salta a la vista.*
  It's obvious that he knows it. *Se conoce (Salta a la vista) que lo sabe.*

occasion — *la ocasión*
  on other occasions — *otras veces.*
  On other occasions we would paint. *Otras veces pintábamos.*

  on the occasion of — *con motivo de.*
  They invited us on the occasion of their daughter's wedding. *Nos invitaron con motivo de la boda de su hija.*

  to leave for another occasion — *dejar para otra vez.*
  We left it for another occasion. *Lo dejamos para otra vez.*

  to rise to the occasion — *mostrarse a la altura de las circunstancias.*
  He will rise to the occasion. *Se mostrará a la altura de las circunstancias.*

to occur — *ocurrir*
  to occur to one — *ocurrírsele.*
  It doesn't occur to me now. *No se me ocurre ahora.*

odds — *la ventaja*
  for the odds to be against one — *no tener ventajas.*

He'll lose because the odds are against him. *Perderá porque no tiene ventajas.*

the odds are — *lo probable es.*
The odds are that he'll lose. *Lo probable es que perderá.*

to be at odds with — *andar a la greña con.*
He's at odds with his father. *Anda a la greña con su padre.*

---

off — *de, desde; lejos, fuera*
off and on — *de vez en cuando.*
We skate off and on. *Patinamos de vez en cuando.*

to be off — *haber salido; haberse marchado.*
Are they off yet? *¿Han salido (¿Se han marchado)?*

to live off — *vivir a expensas de.*
He lives off his parents. *Vive a expensas de sus padres.*

---

offhand — *de improviso*
(right) offhand — *a primera vista; sin pensarlo.*
(Right) offhand, I'd say no. *A primera vista (Sin pensarlo), diría que no.*

---

offense — *la ofensa*
No offense meant. — *Lo dije sin mala intención.*

to take offense at — *ofenderse de.*
He took offense at what I said. *Se ofendió de lo que dije.*

---

office — *la oficina*
to take office — *tomar posesión de su cargo.*
He takes office tomorrow. *Toma posesión de su cargo mañana.*

---

offing — *la lontananza*
to be in the offing — *estar en perspectiva.*
It's in the offing. *Está en perspectiva.*

---

often — *a menudo*
how often — *cada cuánto (tiempo).*
How often does it rain? *¿Cada cuánto (tiempo) llueve?*

167

    so often — *tantas veces.*

    He so often sleeps late. *Tantas veces duerme tarde.*

oil — *el aceite*

    to burn the midnight oil — *quemarse las cejas.*

    We burned the midnight oil. *Nos quemamos las cejas.*

We burned the midnight oil.
Nos quemamos las cejas.

    to pour oil on the flames — *echar leña al fuego.*

    He only poured oil on the flames. *Sólo echó leña al fuego.*

    to strike oil (to strike it rich) — *enriquecerse de súbito.*

    They struck oil (struck it rich). *Se enriquecieron de súbito.*

old — *viejo*

    to be . . . years old — *tener . . . años.*

    She's sixteen years old. *Tiene dieciséis años.*

omelette — *la tortilla (de huevos)*

    You can't make an omelette without breaking eggs. — *Lo que algo vale, algo cuesta.*

on — *en, sobre*

    from . . . on — *desde . . . .*

    From 1960 on, she's been in Spain. *Desde 1960, está en España.*

    to be on to someone — *conocerle el juego.*

I'm on to him. *Le conozco el juego.*

to have on one — *llevar encima.*
I haven't any change on me. *No llevo suelto encima.*

---

once — *una vez*
   at once — *inmediatamente; en seguida.*
   He called at once. *Llamó inmediatamente (en seguida).*

   at once (at the same time) — *a la vez; al mismo tiempo.*
   How do you expect them to do five things at once (at the same time)?
      ¿Cómo quieres que hagan cinco cosas a la vez (al mismo tiempo)?

   not even once — *ni una sola vez.*
   Not even once did I receive it. *Ni una sola vez lo recibí.*

   once and for all — *por última vez; de una vez por todas (y para siempre)*
   He told them once and for all to shut up. *Les dijo por última vez (de una vez por todas; de una vez y para siempre) que se callaran.*

---

once-over — *el vistazo*
   to give the once-over — *dar un vistazo.*
   He gave her the once-over. *Le echó un vistazo.*

---

one — *uno*
   it's either one or the other — *una de dos.*
   It's either one or the other: eat or leave the table. *Una de dos: o coma o deje la mesa.*

   one by one — *uno a uno; de uno en uno.*
   They passed one by one. *Pasaron uno a uno (de uno en uno).*

   to pull a fast one — *engañar.*
   He pulled a fast one on us. *Nos engañó.*

---

one-way — *de una sola dirección*
   a one-way street — *una calle de dirección única.*
   It's a one-way street. *Es una calle de dirección única.*

---

only — *sólo, solamente*
   not only . . . but also . . . . — *no sólo . . . sino también . . . .*

He reads not only Spanish but also French. *Lee no sólo el español sino también el francés.*

open — *abierto*

in the open — *al descubierto.*
They were playing in the open. *Jugaban al descubierto.*

out in the open — *al aire libre.*
They like to be out in the open. *Les gusta estar al aire libre.*

wide open — *abierto de par en par.*
The door was wide open. *La puerta estaba abierta de par en par.*

to open — *abrir*

to open — *estrenarse.*
The play will open tomorrow. *La comedia se estrenará mañana.*

to open with — *dar principio con.*
The program opened with a song. *Se dio principio al programa con una canción.*

opinion — *la opinión*

in one's opinion — *a su parecer (entender).*
In my opinion he's too young. *A mi parecer (entender) es muy joven.*

opposite — *opuesto*

just the opposite — *en sentido contrario.*
I understood just the opposite. *Lo entendí, en sentido contrario.*

opposition — *la oposición*

in opposition to — *en contra de.*
He spoke in opposition to the revolution. *Habló en contra de la revolución.*

order — *el (la) orden*

in apple-pie order — *en perfecto orden.*
They left the room in apple-pie order. *Dejaron la habitación en perfecto orden.*

in order — *en regla.*
Everything seems to be in order. *Todo parece estar en regla.*

in order to — *para*.
We're here in order to learn. *Estamos aquí para aprender.*

in short order — *en breve plazo*.
They finished in short order. *Terminaron en breve plazo.*

on order — *por encargo*.
They sell only on order. *Venden sólo por encargo.*

That's a tall order. — *Eso es mucho pedir.*

to be made to order — *estar hecho a la medida; ser de encargo*.
It's made to order. *Está hecho a la medida (Es de encargo).*

to be out of order — *no funcionar*.
The elevator is out of order. *El ascensor no funciona.*

to call to order — *abrir; llamar al orden*.
The meeting was called to order. *Abrieron (Llamaron al orden) la reunión.*

to get out of order — *descomponerse*.
The motor got out of order. *El motor se descompuso.*

---

out — *fuera*
Get out! (Scram!) — *¡Largo de aquí!*

---

outset — *el principio*
at the outset — *al principio*.
At the outset I didn't like the idea. *Al principio no me gustó la idea.*

---

outside — *fuera*
at the outside — *cuando más; a lo más*.
It's going to cost us thirty dollars at the outside. *Nos va a costar treinta dólares cuando más (a lo más).*

on the outside — *por fuera*.
He dried it on the outside. *Lo secó por fuera.*

---

over — *de nuevo; excesivo*
all over (anywhere) — *por todas partes*.
You can get them all over (anywhere). *Se consiguen por todas partes.*

left over — *de sobra*.

171

They have money left over. *Tienen dinero de sobra.*

over and over (again) — *una y otra vez.*
He called over and over (again). *Llamó una y otra vez.*

over there — *por allá.*
They're over there. *Están por allá.*

to be over — *pasar; acabarse*
It's over now. *Ya pasó (se acabó).*

---

overboard — *al agua*
   to go overboard — *excederse.*
   What a dinner! This time they have really gone overboard. *¡Qué cena!
      Esta vez se han excedido.*

---

overdue — *atrasado*
   to be overdue — *estar retrasado.*
   The train is overdue. *El tren está retrasado.*

---

own — *propio*
   on one's own — *por (sus) puños.*
   He achieved it on his own. *Lo realizó por (sus) puños.*

   to be on one's own — *vivir por su propia cuenta.*
   He's on his own. *Vive por su propia cuenta.*

   to hold one's own — *mantenerse firme.*
   He held his own. *Se mantuvo firme.*

---

to own — *poseer*
   to own up to the truth — *confesar la verdad.*
   He won't own up to the truth. *No quiere confesar la verdad.*

---

ox — *el buey*
   to be as strong as an ox — *tener salud de piedra; ser fuerte como un
      roble.*
   He's as strong as an ox. *Tiene salud de piedra (Es fuerte como un roble).*

P

p — *la p*
  to mind one's p's and q's — *andar con cuidado con lo que dice (hace).*
  She minds her p's and q's. *Anda con cuidado con lo que dice (hace).*

pace — *el paso*
  to set the pace — *dar ejemplo.*
  She set the pace for the rest. *Dio ejemplo para los demás.*

  to set the pace — *establecer el paso.*
  John set the pace for the other runners. *Juan estableció el paso para los otros corredores.*

to pack — *empaquetar*
  to pack off — *despachar.*
  He packed his family off to the country. *Despachó a su familia al campo.*

  to pack suitcases (bags) — *hacer las maletas (equipaje).*
  We packed our suitcases (bags). *Hicimos las maletas (el equipaje).*

pain — *el dolor*
  to be a pain in the neck — *ser una persona antipática.*
  She's a pain in the neck. *Es una persona antipática.*

  to take pains — *poner mucho cuidado (esmerarse) en.*
  She took pains in writing the letter. *Puso mucho cuidado (Se esmeró) en escribir la carta.*

pan — *la cacerola*
  Out of the frying pan into the fire. — *Huir del fuego y caer en las brasas.*

pants — *los pantalones*
  to wear the pants — *llevar los pantalones en; mandar en.*
  She wears the pants in that family. *Es ella quien lleva los pantalones (manda) en esa familia.*

pardon — *el perdón*

  I beg your pardon — *Dispénseme (perdóneme).*

  I beg your pardon — *¿qué (cómo) dice usted?*

  I beg your pardon. I didn't hear you. *¿Qué (Cómo) dice usted? No lo oí.*

---

parole — *la palabra de honor*

  to be out on parole — *estar libre bajo palabra.*

  He's out on parole. *Está libre bajo palabra.*

---

part — *la parte*

  in part — *en parte.*

  We liked it in part. *Nos gustó en parte.*

  to be a part of — *formar parte de.*

  He's a part of our group. *Forma parte de nuestro grupo.*

  to take part in — *tomar parte (participar) en.*

  They took part in the rebellion. *Tomaron parte (Participaron) en la rebelión.*

---

particular — *particular, especial*

  in particular — *en especial.*

  I like the last chapter in particular. *Me gusta el último capítulo en especial.*

---

party — *la fiesta*

  to throw a party — *dar una fiesta.*

  We threw a party. *Dimos una fiesta.*

---

pass — *el paso*

  to make a pass at — *hacer una propuesta amorosa.*

  He made a pass at her. *Le hizo una propuesta amorosa.*

---

to pass — *pasar*

  in passing — *de paso.*

  He called to say goodbye and in passing told us that he would return in six months. *Llamó para despedirse y de paso nos dijo que volvería dentro de seis meses.*

  to pass an exam — *aprobar (salir bien en) un examen.*

I passed my exam. *Aprobé (Salí bien en) mi examen.*

to pass as — *pasar por.*
He passed as an American. *Pasó por americano.*

to pass away — *morir(se).*
She passed away last night. *(Se) murió anoche.*

to pass by (without stopping) — *pasar de largo.*
He passed by (without stopping). *Pasó de largo.*

to pass out — *desmayarse.*
He passed out. *Se desmayó.*

to pass out — *distribuir.*
The teacher passed out the paper. *El maestro distribuyó el papel.*

to pass through — *pasar por.*
They passed through Madrid. *Pasaron por Madrid.*

---

to pat — *dar golpecitos a*
to pat on the back — *darle palmadas en la espalda.*
He patted him gently on the back. *Le dio unas palmadas suavemente en la espalda.*

to pat on the back — *elogiar a.*
He patted his class on the back for its intelligence. *Elogió a su clase por su penetración.*

---

to patch — *remendar*
to patch up a quarrel — *hacer las paces.*
They patched up their quarrel. *Hicieron las paces.*

---

path — *la senda*
to beat a path — *asediar.*
He keeps beating a path to my office. *Sigue asediando mi despacho.*

---

peace — *la paz*
May he (she) rest in peace. *Que en paz descanse.*

peace of mind — *tranquilidad de espíritu.*
With more rest you'll have peace of mind. *Con un poco de descanso tendrá tranquilidad de espíritu.*

to be left in peace — *quedar en paz.*
We were left in peace. *Quedamos en paz.*

to disturb the peace — *perturbar (alterar) el orden público.*
They disturbed the peace. *Perturbaron (Alteraron) el orden público.*

to keep the peace — *mantener el orden público.*
They sent the soldiers to keep the peace. *Mandaron a los soldados para mantener el orden público.*

to make peace — *hacer las paces.*
We made peace. *Hicimos las paces.*

---

peak — *la cima*
  to reach its peak — *llegar a su punto cumbre.*
  It has reached its peak. *Ha llegado a su punto cumbre.*

---

pearl — *la perla*
  to cast pearls before swine — *echar margaritas a los cerdos.*
  This is casting pearls before swine. *Esto es echar margaritas a los cerdos.*

---

penchant — *la afición*
  to have a penchant for — *ser atraído por.*
  I have a penchant for languages. *Las lenguas me atraen.*

---

pencil — *el lápiz*
  to sharpen a pencil — *sacar punta a un lápiz.*
  I sharpened the pencils. *Saqué punta a los lápices.*

---

penniless — *sin dinero*
  to be left penniless — *quedarse con el día y la noche.*
  She was left penniless. *Se quedó con el día y la noche.*

---

penny — *el centavo*
  A penny saved is a penny earned. — *Alquimia probada, tener renta y no gastar nada.*

  to cost one a pretty penny — *costarle un ojo de la cara (un dineral).*
  It cost him a pretty penny. *Le costó un ojo de la cara (un dineral).*

---

person — *la persona*
  in person — *en persona.*
  He went in person. *Fue en persona.*

Peter — *Pedro*

He robs Peter
  to pay Paul.
*Desnuda a un santo
  para vestir a otro.*

  to rob Peter to pay Paul — *desnudar a un santo para vestir a otro.*
  He robs Peter to pay Paul. *Desnuda a un santo para vestir a otro.*

---

to pick — *escoger*
  to pick and choose — *ser quisquilloso al escoger.*
  There is no time to pick and choose. *No hay tiempo para ser quisquilloso al escoger.*

---

picnic — *la jira*
  to be no picnic — *no ser cosa fácil.*
  It's no picnic to organize a team. *Organizar un equipo no es cosa fácil.*

---

picture — *el cuadro*
  Get the picture? — *¿Entiende?*

  to fit into the picture — *venir a.*
  I don't see how that fits into the picture. *No veo a qué viene eso.*

  to present a gloomy picture — *hablar en términos muy pesimistas.*
  He presented a gloomy picture of the war. *Habló de la guerra en términos muy pesimistas.*

to take a picture — *sacar una foto*.
He took a picture of the tree. *Sacó una foto del árbol.*

---

piece — *el pedazo*
   to break into pieces — *hacer añicos*.
   I broke the pitcher into pieces. *Hice añicos la jarra.*

   to fall to pieces — *venirse abajo*.
   The government is falling to pieces. *El gobierno se viene abajo.*

   to give someone a piece of one's mind — *decirle cuántas son cinco*.
   She gave me a piece of her mind. *Me dijo cuántas son cinco.*

   to speak one's piece — *decir todo lo que quiere decir*.
   He spoke his piece. *Dijo todo lo que quería decir.*

---

pig — *el cerdo, el puerco*
   to buy a pig in a poke — *comprar a ciegas*.
   We bought a pig in a poke. *Lo compramos a ciegas.*

---

pill — *la píldora*
   to sugarcoat the pill — *dorar la píldora*.
   Tell me the truth and don't sugarcoat the pill. *Dígame la verdad y no dore la píldora.*

---

pin — *el alfiler*
   to be on pins and needles — *estar en ascuas (espinas)*.
   They're all on pins and needles. *Todos están en ascuas (espinas).*

---

to pin — *prender con un alfiler*
   to pin down — *precisar*.
   We couldn't pin down who it was who started the fire. *No pudimos precisar quién fue el que empezó el incendio.*

   to pin someone down — *obligarle a decirlo*.
   They tried to pin him down but he refused to explain. *Trataron de obligarle a decirlo pero él no quiso explicar.*

---

to pinch — *pellizcar*
   in a pinch — *en un aprieto*.

In a pinch you can use our car. *En un aprieto pueden usar nuestro coche.*

to feel the pinch — *pasar estrecheces.*
He's been out of work for six months and is beginning to feel the pinch.
Lleva seis meses sin trabajo y ya empieza a pasar estrecheces.

---

piper — *el flautista*
He who pays the piper calls the tune. — *Quien paga, manda.*

---

to pitch — *lanzar*
to pitch in — *cooperar.*
If we all pitch in, we'll finish by five. *Si todos cooperamos, lo terminaremos para las cinco.*

---

pitchfork — *la horca*
to rain pitchforks — *llover a cántaros.*
It's raining pitchforks. *Está lloviendo a cántaros.*

---

pity — *la piedad, la lástima*
It's a pity (too bad). — *Es (una) lástima.*

to take pity on — *tenerle lástima.*
They took pity on us. *Nos tuvieron lástima.*

---

place — *el lugar*
in place of — *en lugar de.*
He came in place of his sister. *Vino en lugar de su hermana.*

in the first place — *en primer lugar.*
In the first place, it's not mine. *En primer lugar, no es mío.*

to be going places — *llegar lejos.*
He's going places. *Llegará lejos.*

to be out of place — *estar de más.*
Will it be out of place to invite her? *¿Estará de más invitarla?*

to know one's place — *saber cuál es su sitio.*
Our maid knows her place. *Nuestra criada sabe cuál es su sitio.*

to take first place — *quedar primero.*
This horse took first place. *Este caballo quedó primero.*

to take place — *celebrarse; tener lugar.*
The meeting will take place in my office. *La reunión se celebrará (tendrá lugar) en mi oficina.*

---

plague — *la peste*
   to avoid someone like the plague — *huir de alguien como de la peste.*
   We avoid him like the plague. *Huimos de él como de la peste.*

play — *el juego*
   foul play — *un hecho delictivo.*
   It failed because of foul play. *Fracasó a causa de un hecho delictivo.*

---

to play — *jugar*
   to play down the merit of — *darle poca importancia.*
   He played down its merit. *Le dio poca importancia.*

   to play dumb — *hacerse el tonto.*
   He won't gain anything by playing dumb. *No gana nada con hacerse el tonto.*

   to play up to — *bailarle el agua a.*
   She played up to her professor. *Le bailó el agua al profesor.*

---

to please — *gustar*
   please — *haga el favor de; tenga la bondad de.*
   Please come in. *Haga el favor (Tenga la bondad) de pasar.*

---

pleasure — *el gusto*
   to be a pleasure — *dar gusto.*
   It's a pleasure to hear it. *Me da gusto oírlo.*

---

plenty — *suficiente*
   to go through plenty — *pasar grandes apuros.*
   They went through plenty in the beginning. *Pasaron grandes apuros al principio.*

---

plot — *la trama.*
   The plot thickens. — *La madeja se enreda.*

---

point — *el punto*

a turning point — *un punto crucial.*
Her marriage was a turning point in her life. *Su matrimonio fue un punto crucial en su vida.*

at this point — *a estas alturas.*
Why stop studying at this point? *¿Para qué dejar de estudiar a estas alturas?*

It's beside the point. — *No viene al caso.*

point blank — *a quemarropa.*
He fired at him point blank. *Disparó contra él a quemarropa.*

That's not the point. — *No se trata de eso.*

to be on (at) the point of — *estar a punto de.*
We're on (at) the point of moving. *Estamos a punto de mudarnos.*

to get (come) to the point — *ir al grano.*
He talks a lot but doesn't get (come) to the point. *Habla mucho pero no va al grano.*

to make a point of — *dar mucha importancia a.*
She made a point of her beauty. *Dio mucha importancia a su belleza.*

to make one's point — *hacerse entender.*
He made his point. *Se hizo entender.*

to miss the point — *no caer en la cuenta.*
He missed the point. *No cayó en la cuenta.*

to press one's point — *insistir en su argumento.*
No need to press your point. *No vale la pena insistir en su argumento.*

to see the point — *ver el objeto.*
I don't see the point of buying two. *No veo el objeto de comprar dos.*

to speak to the point — *hablar al caso.*
He spoke to the point. *Habló al caso.*

to stretch a point — *hacer una concesión.*
They stretched a point and hired her. *Hicieron una concesión y la emplearon.*

up to a point — *hasta cierto punto.*

Up to a point I agree with you. *Hasta cierto punto estoy de acuerdo contigo.*

---

to polish — *pulir*

to polish off — *acabar con.*

He polished off two bottles of beer. *Acabó con dos botellas de cerveza.*

---

poll — *la encuesta*

to take a poll — *hacer una encuesta.*

They took a poll to find out which program was the most popular.
Hicieron una encuesta para saber cuál programa era el más popular.

---

poor — *pobre*

Poor me! — *¡Pobre (Ay) de mí!*

---

possible — *posible*

as far as possible — *en cuanto sea posible; en lo posible.*

I'll follow it as far as possible. *Lo seguiré en cuanto sea posible (en lo posible).*

as soon as possible — *lo más pronto posible; lo antes posible; cuanto antes.*

Come as soon as possible. *Vengan lo más pronto posible (lo antes posible; cuanto antes).*

---

posted — *enterado*

to keep posted — *tener al corriente.*

Keep us posted on the outcome. *Ténganos al corriente de los resultados.*

---

pot — *la caldera*

A watched pot never boils. — *Quien espera desespera.*

It's the pot calling the kettle black. — *Dijo la sartén al cazo: quítate allá que me tiznas.*

to hit the jackpot — *ponerse las botas; sacar el gordo.*

We hit the jackpot. *Nos pusimos las botas (Sacamos el gordo).*

---

premium — *el premio*
   to be at a premium — *estar muy solicitado.*
   It's at a premium. *Está muy solicitado.*

present — *el presente*
   at present — *en el momento actual.*
   At present it's open. *En el momento actual está abierto.*

prevention — *la prevención*
   An ounce of prevention is worth a pound of cure. — *Más vale prevenir que curar.*

price — *el precio*
   to set a price — *poner un precio.*
   They set a very low price. *Pusieron un precio muy bajo.*

pride — *el orgullo*
   to swallow one's pride — *tragarse el orgullo.*
   Sometimes it's best to swallow your pride. *A veces es mejor tragarse el orgullo.*

prime — *el estado de mayor perfección*
   in the prime of life — *en la flor de la vida (de edad).*
   He died in the prime of life. *Murió en la flor de la vida (de edad).*

print — *la impresión, la estampa*
   to be out of print — *estar agotado.*
   The book is out of print. *El libro está agotado.*

prize — *el premio*
   to win the grand prize — *sacar el (premio) gordo.*
   She won the grand prize. *Sacó el (premio) gordo.*

problem — *el problema*
   That's your problem. — *Eso es cosa suya (Allá usted).*

production — *la producción*
    to step up production — *incrementar la producción.*
    The factory stepped up production during the war. *La fábrica incrementó la producción durante la guerra.*

to profit — *aprovechar*
    to profit from — *sacar provecho de.*
    He profits from her advice. *Saca provecho de su consejo.*

promise — *la promesa*
    to have a lot of promise — *prometer mucho.*
    She's got a lot of promise. *Promete mucho.*

provocation — *la provocación*
    on the slightest provocation — *por cualquier cosa.*
    He gets mad on the slightest provocation. *Se enoja por cualquier cosa.*

proxy — *el poder*
    by proxy — *por poder.*
    He voted by proxy. *Votó por poder.*

pudding — *el pudín*
    The proof of the pudding is in the eating. — *Al freír será el reír.*

pull — *el tirón, el estirón*
    to have lots of pull — *tener buenas aldabas.*
    He has lots of pull. *Tiene buenas aldabas.*

to pull — *tirar*
    to pull oneself together — *componerse.*
    She pulled herself together. *Se compuso.*

    to pull through — *salir de sus apuros (su enfermedad).*
    I think he'll pull through. *Creo que saldrá de sus apuros (su enfermedad).*

    to pull up — *arrimar.*
    Pull up a chair. *Arrime una silla.*

purpose — *el propósito*
   on purpose — *adrede; intencionadamente.*
   He did it on purpose. *Lo hizo adrede (intencionadamente).*

   to talk at cross purposes — *hablar sin comprenderse uno a otro.*
   They are talking at cross purposes. *Están hablando sin comprenderse uno a otro.*

purse — *la bolsa*
   You can't make a silk purse out of a sow's ear. — *Aunque la mona se vista de seda, mona se queda.*

pursuit — *la busca, la persecución*
   to be in pursuit of — *ir en pos de.*
   He's in pursuit of the enemy. *Va en pos del enemigo.*

to push — *empujar*
   to push one's way through — *abrir paso a empujones (empellones).*
   He pushed his way through. *Se abrió paso a empujones (empellones).*

to put — *poner, colocar*
   to be hard put — *verse apurado.*
   He's very hard put. *Se ve muy apurado.*

   to put across — *hacer entender.*
   He can't put across his ideas to us. *No puede hacernos entender sus ideas.*

   to put away — *guardar.*
   He put away his toys. *Guardó sus juguetes.*

   to put down — *sofocar.*
   They put down the insurrection. *Sofocaron la insurrección.*

   to put off — *aplazar.*
   We put off our trip. *Aplazamos nuestro viaje.*

   to put on — *ponerse.*
   He put on his jacket. *Se puso la chaqueta.*

   to put oneself out — *deshacerse.*
   She put herself out to please us. *Se deshizo por complacernos.*

   to put out — *apagar.*

They put out the fire (light). *Apagaron el fuego (la luz).*

to put someone up — *darle cama; dar donde pasar . . . .*
They put us up for the night. *Nos dieron cama para pasar la noche (Nos dieron donde pasar la noche).*

to put together — *armar.*
They put together the motor. *Armaron el motor.*

to put up — *construir.*
They put up the building in two months. *Construyeron el edificio en dos meses.*

to put up with — *aguantar (soportar).*
She put up with a lot. *Aguantó (Soportó) mucho.*

---

quandary — *la incertidumbre*
   to be in a quandary — *verse ante un dilema.*
   We're in a quandary. *Nos vemos ante un dilema.*

---

quarrel — *la disputa*
   to pick fights (quarrels) — *tomarse (meterse) con.*
   He likes to pick a fight (quarrel) with his wife. *Le gusta tomarse (meterse) con su esposa.*

---

quarters — *la morada*
   at (in) close quarters — *muy pegados.*
   They work at (in) close quarters. *Trabajan muy pegados.*

---

question — *la pregunta, la cuestión*
   beyond all question — *indudable.*
   He's beyond all question a rebel. *Es un rebelde indudable.*

   It's out of the question. — *¡Eso ni pensarlo (Es imposible)!*

   That's beside the question. — *Eso no viene al caso.*

   to ask a question — *hacer una pregunta.*

I asked a question. *Hice una pregunta.*

to be a question of — *tratarse de.*
It's a question of money. *Se trata de dinero.*

to be an open question — *ser una cuestión discutible.*
It's an open question. *Es una cuestión discutible.*

to call into question — *poner en tela de juicio.*
He called into question his colleague's conclusions. *Puso en tela de juicio las conclusiones de su colega.*

without question — *sin más vueltas.*
It was John, without question. *Fue Juan, sin más vueltas.*

---

quick — *la carne viva*
  to cut to the quick — *herir en lo vivo.*
  His criticism cut me to the quick. *Su crítica me hirió en lo vivo.*

---

quite — *completamente, bastante*
  quite a few — *bastantes.*
  Quite a few came. *Vinieron bastantes.*

  to be quite a woman — *ser toda una mujer.*
  She's quite a woman. *Es toda una mujer.*

---

quits — *la tregua*
  to call it quits — *abandonar la partida.*
  We called it quits. *Abandonamos la partida.*

R

rag — *el trapo*
  to be in rags — *andar en andrajos.*
  He's in rags. *Anda en andrajos.*

  to go from rags to riches — *pasar de la miseria a la riqueza.*
  He's gone from rags to riches. *Ha pasado de la miseria a la riqueza.*

---

rage — *la rabia*
  to be all the rage — *hacer furor.*
  Those hats were all the rage last year. *Esos sombreros hicieron furor el año pasado.*

rain — *la lluvia*
  in the rain — *bajo la lluvia.*
  They worked in the rain. *Trabajaron bajo la lluvia.*

  rain or shine — *con buen o mal tiempo.*
  We're going to work there rain or shine. *Vamos a trabajar allí con buen o mal tiempo.*

to rain — *llover*
  It never rains but it pours. — *Siempre llueve sobre mojado; Las desgracias nunca vienen solas.*

random — *casual*
  at random — *al azar.*
  They were chosen at random. *Se les escogió al azar.*

range — *la escala*
  at close range — *de cerca.*
  I want to see it at close range. *Deseo verlo de cerca.*

  to be within range — *estar a tiro.*
  The animal is within range. *El animal está a tiro.*

rank — *la fila*
  the rank and file — *las masas; el pueblo.*
  We must educate the rank and file. *Debemos educar a las masas (al pueblo).*

  to join the ranks — *darse de alta.*
  He joined the ranks. *Se dio de alta.*

to rank — *tener posición*
  to rank high — *ocupar una alta posición.*
  Our city ranks high. *Nuestra ciudad ocupa una alta posición.*

rap — *golpecito*
  to take the rap — *sufrir las consecuencias.*
  I took the rap for his negligence. *Sufrí yo las consecuencias de su descuido.*

---

rascal — *el pícaro*
  You old rascal! — *¡Mala pieza!*

---

rat — *la rata*
  to smell a rat — *olerle mal el asunto.*
  I smell a rat. *Me huele mal el asunto.*

---

rate — *la razón; el paso*
  at any rate — *de todos modos; de todas maneras.*
  At any rate, he's the one who has it. *De todos modos (De todas maneras) es él quien lo tiene.*

  at the rate of — *a razón de.*
  We were traveling at the rate of 100 kilometers an hour. *Viajábamos a razón de cien kilómetros la hora.*

  at this rate — *a este paso.*
  At this rate we won't get there. *A este paso no llegaremos.*

---

rather — *más bien*
  would rather — *preferir.*
  I would rather go. *Preferiría ir.*

---

to rave — *delirar*
  to rave about — *deshacerse en elogios de.*
  He raved about his children. *Se deshizo en elogios de sus hijos.*

---

reach — *el alcance*
  to be out of (within) one's reach — *estar fuera de (estar a) su alcance.*
  It's out of (within) our reach. *Está fuera de (está a) nuestro alcance.*

---

to reach — *alcanzar*
  to reach — *darle a.*

His hair reached his neck. *El cabello le daba al cuello.*

to reach an understanding — *llegar a una inteligencia (un acuerdo).*
We've reached an understanding. *Hemos llegado a una inteligencia (un acuerdo).*

to reach for — *esforzarse por coger.*
He reached for the bread. *Se esforzó por coger el pan.*

to read — *leer*

to read over — *echar una ojeada a.*
I read over his exam. *Eché una ojeada a su examen.*

to read up on — *leer sobre; informarse de.*
I'm reading up on Pérez Galdós. *Estoy leyendo sobre (Me estoy informando de) Pérez Galdós.*

ready — *listo*

to get ready to — *disponerse (prepararse) a.*
I'm getting ready to study. *Me dispongo (Me preparo) a estudiar.*

reason — *la razón*

for no reason — *sin ningún motivo.*
He insulted her for no reason. *La insultó sin ningún motivo.*

it stands to reason — *es lógico.*
It stands to reason that he must go. *Es lógico que tenga que ir.*

to have reason to — *tener por qué.*
You have no reason to criticize. *No tiene por qué criticar.*

to listen to reason — *entrar en razón.*
She refused to listen to reason. *No quiso entrar en razón.*

to lose one's reason — *perder la razón.*
She lost her reason. *Perdió la razón.*

record — *el registro*

for the record — *para que conste en acta.*
He said it for the record. *Lo dijo para que constara en acta.*

off the record — *en confianza.*
What he said is off the record. *Lo que dijo lo dijo en confianza.*

to keep a record — *llevar cuenta.*

She keeps a record of all the family expenses. *Lleva cuenta de todos los gastos de familia.*

receipt — *el recibo*

to acknowledge receipt — *acusar recibo.*

He acknowledged receipt of the money order. *Acusó recibo del giro.*

red — *rojo*

in the red — *en déficit; endeudado.*

His business is always in the red. *Su negocio está siempre en déficit (endeudado).*

to see red — *encolerizarse.*

I see red when he beats her. *Me encolerizo cuando él le pega.*

red-handed (in the act) — *con las manos ensangrentadas; con las manos en la masa.*

He was caught red-handed (in the act). *Lo cogieron con las manos ensangrentadas (en la masa).*

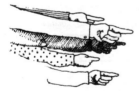

He was caught red-handed (in the act).
Lo cogieron con las manos ensangrentadas (en la masa).

red-hot — *calentado al rojo*

red-hot — *al rojo (vivo) (al rojo blanco).*

The iron was red-hot. *El hierro estaba al rojo (vivo) (al rojo blanco).*

to refuse — *rehusar*

to refuse flatly — *negarse rotundamente.*

He flatly refused to accept it. *Se negó rotundamente a aceptarlo.*

to refuse to — *resistirse a.*
She refused to get old. *Se resistía a envejecer.*

regalia — *atavío de gala*
   in full regalia (all dressed up) — *de punta en blanco.*
   At the banquet everybody was in full regalia. *En el banquete todos
      estaban de punta en blanco.*

rein — *la rienda*
   to give free rein to — *dar rienda suelta a.*
   He always gives free rein to his feelings. *Siempre da rienda suelta a sus
      sentimientos.*

rent — *el alquiler*
   to pay the rent — *pagar la casa.*
   I can't pay the rent. *No puedo pagar la casa.*

repair — *la reparación*
   to be beyond repair — *no poder repararse (componerse).*
   This car is beyond repair. *Este coche no puede repararse (componerse).*

   to be in bad (good) repair — *estar en malas (buenas) condiciones.*
   The roads are always in bad (good) repair. *Los caminos siempre están en
      malas (buenas) condiciones.*

to report — *hacer informe, informar*
   to report for — *presentarse para.*
   He reported for work on Monday. *Se presentó para trabajar el lunes.*

   to report on — *dar cuenta de.*
   He always reports on his trips. *Siempre da cuenta de sus viajes.*

reputation — *la reputación, la fama*
   to have the reputation of — *tener fama de.*
   They have the reputation of being honest. *Tienen fama de ser honrados.*

   to live up to one's reputation — *hacer honor a su fama.*
   He'll have to live up to his reputation. *Tendrá que hacer honor a su fama.*

request — *la petición*
   at . . . 's request — *a petición (instancia) de. . . .*
   We sent it at John's request. *Lo mandamos a petición (instancia) de Juan.*

requirement — *la exigencia*
   to meet all the requirements — *reunir (llenar) todos los requisitos.*
   He met all the requirements for his doctorate. *Reunió (Llenó) todos los
      requisitos para su doctorado.*

to resign — *resignar*
   to resign oneself to — *conformarse con.*
   I have resigned myself to staying. *Me he conformado con quedarme.*

resort — *el recurso*
   as a last resort — *en último caso; como último recurso.*
   As a last resort, use this one. *En último caso (Como último recurso),
      sírvase de éste.*

to rest — *descansar*
   to come to rest — *venir a parar.*
   It came to rest in front of our house. *Vino a parar en frente de nuestra
      casa.*
   to rest assured — *tener la seguridad.*
   Rest assured that we'll come. *Tenga la seguridad de que vendremos.*

respect — *el respecto, el respeto*
   with respect to — *(con) respecto a.*
   He wrote with respect to the earthquake. *Escribió (con) respecto al
      terremoto.*

result — *el resultado*
   as a result of — *por (de) resultas de.*
   As a result of the snow, there's no class. *Por (De) resultas de la nevada,
      no hay clase.*

to result — *resultar*
  to result in — *terminar en.*
  It has resulted in a serious quarrel. *Terminó en una disputa seria.*

returns — *los provechos*
  to wish someone many happy returns of the day — *felicitarle el cumpleaños.*
  They wished him many happy returns of the day. *Le felicitaron el cumpleaños.*

to revert — *revertir*
  to revert to — *recaer en.*
  After his wife died, he reverted to his old vices. *Después de la muerte de su esposa, recayó en sus antiguos vicios.*

rhyme — *la rima*
  without rhyme or reason — *sin ton ni son.*
  His statement was without rhyme or reason. *Su declaración fue sin ton ni son.*

rich — *rico*
  to be rich in — *tener mucho . . .*
  This medicine is rich in vitamin C. *Este medicamento tiene mucha vitamina C.*

to rid — *librar*
  to get rid of — *deshacerse (librarse) de.*
  I got rid of my car. *Me deshice (libré) de mi coche.*

ride — *el paseo*
  to go for a ride — *dar un paseo (en coche).*
  They went out for a ride. *Salieron a dar un paseo (en coche).*

  to take for a ride — *llevar de paseo (en coche).*
  He took us for a ride. *Nos llevó de paseo (en coche).*

riduculous — *ridículo*
  to make look ridiculous — *poner en ridículo.*
  He made me look ridiculous. *Me puso en ridículo.*

right — *el derecho; la derecha; la razón*
  right and left — *a diestra y siniestra.*
  Snow was falling right and left. *Caía la nieve a diestra y siniestra.*

  to be in the right — *estar en lo firme (tener razón).*
  He told me I was in the right when I wouldn't accept the money. *Me dijo
    que estaba en lo firme (tenía razón) al no querer aceptar el dinero.*

  to be right — *tener razón.*
  He's right. *Tiene razón.*

  to have a right to — *tener derecho a.*
  He has a right to talk. *Tiene derecho a hablar.*

  to (on) the right — *a la derecha.*
  It's to (on) the right. *Está a la derecha.*

right — *correcto; bien; mismo*
  right away (off) — *en seguida.*
  He refused right away (off) *Rehusó en seguida.*

  right here — *aquí mismo.*
  It's right here. *Está aquí mismo.*

  right now — *ahora mismo.*
  Come right now. *Venga ahora mismo.*

  right then and there — *en el acto.*
  I bought it right then and there. *Lo compré en el acto.*

  right there — *allá mismo.*
  It's right there. *Está allá mismo.*

  That's right. — *Así es; Eso es.*

  to be all right with — *con el permiso de.*
  If it's all right with you, I won't stay. *Con su permiso no me quedaré.*

  to be right back — *volver en seguida.*
  I'll be right back. *Vuelvo en seguida.*

  to serve one right — *estarle bien empleado; merecérselo.*

John thinks it serves me right. *A Juan le parece que me está bien
empleado (que me lo merezco).*

---

rightly — *correctamente*
  rightly or wrongly — *mal que bien; con razón o sin ella.*
  Rightly or wrongly, they won. *Mal que bien (Con razón o sin ella),
  ganaron.*

  rightly so — *a justo título.*
  He said no, and rightly so. *Dijo que no y a justo título.*

---

ring — *la llamada*
  to give someone a ring — *llamarle por teléfono (darle un telefonazo).*
  He gave me a ring. *Me llamó por teléfono (Me dio un telefonazo).*

  to have a familiar ring — *sonarle a algo conocido.*
  It has a familiar ring. *Me suena a algo conocido.*

---

rise — *la subida*
  to give rise to — *dar lugar (origen) a.*
  It gave rise to many problems. *Dio lugar (origen) a muchos problemas.*

---

risk — *el riesgo*
  to run the risk — *correr el riesgo (peligro).*
  We ran the risk of being discovered. *Corrimos el riesgo (peligro) de ser
  descubiertos.*

---

river — *el río*
  to sell someone down the river — *traicionarle.*
  We've been sold down the river. *Nos han traicionado.*

---

road — *el camino*
  The road to hell is paved with good intentions. — *El infierno está lleno
  de buenos propósitos, y el cielo de buenas obras.*

  to be on the road — *estar de viaje.*
  My work forces me to be on the road almost all the time. *Mi trabajo me
  obliga a estar de viaje casi todo el tiempo.*

to hit the road — *ponerse en camino.*
It's time for us to hit the road. *Ya es hora de ponernos en camino.*

rock — *la piedra*
  on the rocks — *solo con hielo.*
  He took his rum on the rocks. *Tomó su ron solo con hielo.*

  to be on the rocks — *andar mal.*
  Their friendship is on the rocks. *Su amistad anda mal.*

role — *el papel*
  to play one's role — *representar su papel.*
  He plays his role well. *Representa bien su papel.*

  to play the role — *desempeñar (hacer) el papel.*
  He plays the role of the uncle. *Desempeña (Hace) el papel del tío.*

Rome — *Roma*
  Rome was not built in a day. — *No se ganó Zamora en una hora.*

  When in Rome do as the Romans do. — *Donde fueres, haz lo que vieres.*

room — *el cuarto; el espacio*
  room and board — *pensión completa.*
  We'd like to have room and board. *Nos gustaría tener pensión completa.*

  There's always room for one more. — *Donde comen seis comen siete.*

  to make room for — *dejar sitio.*
  They made room for us in the car. *Nos dejaron sitio en el coche.*

  to make room for — *hacer espacio.*
  We made room for the box. *Hicimos espacio para la caja.*

  to take up room — *ocupar espacio.*
  This table takes up too much room. *La mesa ocupa demasiado espacio.*

roost — *la percha de gallinero*
  to rule the roost — *mandar.*
  In that house the mother rules the roost. *En esa casa manda la madre.*

root — *la raíz*
  to take root — *echar raíces; arraigar.*
  It's taking root. *Está echando raíces (arraigando).*

rope — *la cuerda*
  to give someone too much rope — *darle demasiada libertad.*
  His parents gave him too much rope. *Sus padres le dieron demasiada libertad.*

  to know the ropes — *saber cuántas son cinco; estar al tanto de las cosas.*
  He knows the ropes. *Sabe cuántas son cinco (Está al tanto de las cosas).*

  to reach the end of one's rope — *no poder más.*
  He had reached the end of his rope. *No podía más.*

rough — *agitado*
  to have a rough idea — *tener una idea aproximada.*
  I have a rough idea. *Tengo una idea aproximada.*

  to have a rough time of it — *pasarlas muy duras.*
  We had a rough time of it. *Las pasamos muy duras.*

row — *la pelea*
  to have a row — *armarse un bochinche.*
  There was quite a row near our house. *Se armó un bochinche bastante grande cerca de nuestra casa.*

row — *la fila*
  in a row — *seguidos.*
  We went two days in a row. *Fuimos dos días seguidos.*

rub — *el busilis*
  to be the rub — *ser lo malo.*
  The rub is that he can't speak it. *Lo malo es que no sabe hablarlo.*

to rub — *frotar*
  to rub it in — *machacar.*

When I'm wrong, he always rubs it in. *Cuando estoy equivocado, siempre machaca.*

---

to ruin — *arruinar*
  to ruin — *echar a perder.*
  It was ruined. *Se echó a perder.*

rule — *la regla*
  a hard and fast rule — *una regla inflexible.*
  It's a hard and fast rule. *Es una regla inflexible.*

  as a rule — *por lo regular.*
  As a rule they don't get here before ten. *Por lo regular no llegan antes de las diez.*

  as a general rule — *por regla general.*
  As a general rule, I walk. *Por regla general voy a pie.*

---

to rule — *gobernar*
  to rule out — *excluir, descartar.*
  They have ruled out that possibility. *Han excluido (Han descartado) esa posibilidad.*

---

to rumor — *rumorearse*
  it is rumored — *es fama.*
  It is rumored that she poisoned her husband. *Es fama que envenenó a su esposo.*

---

run — *el curso, la carrera*
  in the long run — *a la larga; a largo plazo; a la postre.*
  In the long run it will cost less. *A la larga (A largo plazo; A la postre) costará menos.*

  on the run — *a la carrera.*
  If I don't want to be late, I'll have to eat on the run. *Si no quiero llegar tarde, tendré que comer a la carrera.*

  to give someone a run for his money — *darle una competencia fuerte.*
  I gave him a run for his money. *Le di una competencia fuerte.*

---

to run — *correr*

  to run across — *tropezar (dar) con.*
  I ran across an old friend. *Tropecé (Di) con un viejo amigo.*

  to run after — *ir detrás.*
  He runs after blondes. *Va detrás de las rubias.*

  to run around with — *asociarse con.*
  He runs around with young people. *Se asocia con los jóvenes.*

  to run away — *escaparse; huirse.*
  The thief ran away. *El ladrón se escapó (huyó).*

  to run down — *dar con.*
  The parents finally ran her down and brought her home. *Sus padres por fin dieron con ella y la trajeron a casa.*

  to run down — *desacreditar; hablar mal de.*
  She runs down all her friends. *Desacredita a (Habla mal de) todos sus amigos.*

  to run down — *parar.*
  My watch has run down. *Mi reloj ha parado.*

  to run dry — *secarse.*
  The well ran dry. *El pozo se secó.*

  to run into — *tropezar (encontrarse) con.*
  I ran into him. *Tropecé (Me encontré) con él.*

  to run low on (short of) — *írsele acabando.*
  We're running low on (short of) paper. *Se nos va acabando el papel.*

  to run off — *fugarse.*
  She ran off with a bachelor. *Se fugó con un soltero.*

  to run out — *acabársele.*
  I've run out of money. *Se me acabó el dinero.*

  to run over (down) — *atropellar (derribar) a.*
  He ran over (down) a pedestrian. *Atropelló (Derribó) a un peatón.*

  to run smoothly — *ir sobre ruedas.*
  The business is running smoothly. *El negocio va sobre ruedas.*

  to run up (down) to — *correr a.*

Run up (down) to the corner and get a paper. *Corra a la esquina y compre un periódico.*

---

to rush — *darse prisa*
  for blood to rush to one's face — *ponerse colorado (sonrojarse).*
  Blood rushed to his face. *Se puso colorado (Se sonrojó).*

  to rush things — *precipitar las cosas.*
  You're rushing things. *Está precipitando las cosas.*

  to rush through — *hacer de prisa.*
  He rushed through his work. *Hizo de prisa su trabajo.*

rush — *la prisa*
  in a mad rush — *precipitadamente.*
  He left me in a mad rush. *Me dejó precipitadamente.*

---

sack — *el saco*
  to be left holding the sack (bag) — *quedarse con la carga en las costillas.*
  I was left holding the sack (bag). *Me quedé con la carga en las costillas.*

  to give someone the sack (to sack someone) — *despedirlo.*
  They gave him the sack (They sacked him). *Lo despidieron.*

---

safe — *salvo, seguro*
  safe and sound — *sano y salvo.*
  They arrived safe and sound. *Llegaron sanos y salvos.*

  to be on the safe side — *para mayor seguridad.*
  To be on the safe side, let's take ten. *Para mayor seguridad tomemos diez.*

  to be safe — *estar a salvo.*
  He's safe. *Está a salvo.*

  to play it safe — *andar con precaución.*
  He tried to play it safe. *Trató de andar con precaución.*

---

safety — *la seguridad*
  safety first — *la seguridad ante todo.*
  Our motto is "Safety First." *Nuestro lema es "La seguridad ante todo."*

  to reach safety — *ponerse a salvo.*
  They reached safety. *Se pusieron a salvo.*

saintly — *santo*
  to act saintly — *hacerse el santo.*
  He acts so saintly. *Se hace el santo.*

sake — *el motivo*
  For Heaven's sake! — *¡Por Dios!*

  for one's sake — *para su propio bien.*
  It's for your sake. *Es para su propio bien.*

  for the sake of — *por ganas (motivo) de.*
  He argues for the sake of arguing. *Disputa por ganas (motivo) de disputar.*

sale — *la venta*
  on sale — *a la venta.*
  They put them on sale. *Los pusieron a la venta.*

salt — *la sal*
  to be worth one's salt — *valer el pan que come.*
  He's not worth his salt. *No vale el pan que come.*

  to take with a grain of salt — *acoger con reserva(s).*
  You have to take what he says with a grain of salt. *Hay que acoger con reserva(s) todo lo que dice.*

to salt — *salar*
  to salt away — *ahorrar.*
  He salts away all he earns. *Ahorra todo lo que gana.*

same — *mismo*
  It's all the same. — *Es lo mismo (Lo mismo da).*

  The same to you. — *Igualmente (Lo mismo digo).*

to be all the same — *ser igual.*
It's all the same to me. *A mí me es igual.*

---

say — *el decir*
  to have one's say — *decir su parecer; dar su opinión.*
  He had his say. *Dijo su parecer (Dio su opinión).*

---

to say — *decir*
  It is easier said than done. — *Una cosa es decirlo y otra hacerlo.*

  It's no sooner said than done. — *Dicho y hecho.*

  that is to say — *es decir.*
  Our friends, that is to say, the Joneses, came. *Nuestros amigos, es decir
    los Jones, vinieron.*

  to go without saying — *holgar decir; entenderse.*
  It goes without saying that she's intelligent. *Huelga decir (Se entiende)
    que es inteligente.*

  to say the least — *por lo menos.*
  It's interesting, to say the least. *Es interesante, por lo menos.*

  when all is said and done — *al fin y al cabo.*
  When all is said and done, it's an excellent university. *Al fin y al cabo es
    una universidad excelente.*

  You can say that again. — *Bien puede usted decirlo.*

---

saying — *el dicho*
  as the saying goes (as they say) — *como dijo el otro.*
  Well, Rome wasn't built in a day, as the saying goes (as they say). *Bueno,
    no se ganó Zamora en una hora, como dijo el otro.*

---

scale — *la escala; la balanza*
  on a large scale — *en gran escala; en grande.*
  They're bought on a large scale. *Se compran en gran escala (en grande).*

  to tip the scales — *decidirlo.*
  His recommendation tipped the scales in my favor. *Su recomendación lo
    decidió a mi favor.*

to scale — *escalar*
   to scale down — *reducir.*
   He scaled down his prices. *Redujo sus precios.*

scapegoat — *víctima propiciatoria*
   to be made the scapegoat — *pagar los vidrios rotos.*
   He's going to have to be made the scapegoat, even though we know he's
      not the guilty one. *Va a tener que pagar los vidrios rotos, aunque
      sabemos que no es el culpable.*

scarce — *escaso*
   to make oneself scarce — *irse; no dejarse ver.*
   Make yourself scarce. *Váyase (No se deje ver).*

scene — *la escena*
   behind the scenes — *entre bastidores.*
   It was decided behind the scenes. *Se decidió entre bastidores.*

   to make a scene — *armar (causar) un escándalo.*
   She made a scene when her husband didn't return. *Armó (Causó) un
      escándalo cuando no volvió su esposo.*

schedule — *el horario*
   to be behind schedule — *traer (llevar) retraso.*
   That train is an hour behind schedule. *Ese tren trae (lleva) una hora de
      retraso.*

to scrape — *raspar*
   to scrape along — *ir tirando.*
   She scrapes along on five dollars a week. *Va tirando con cinco dólares a
      la semana.*

   to scrape together — *reunir (dinero).*
   He scraped together enough (money) to buy bread and milk. *Reunió
      (dinero) para comprar pan y leche.*

scratch — *el arañazo, el rasguño*
   to start from scratch — *empezar desde el principio.*

He started from scratch in his profession. *Empezó desde el principio en su profesión.*

---

screw — *el tornillo*
  to have a screw loose — *faltarle un tornillo.*
  Sometimes I think that Ricardo has a screw loose. *A veces me parece que a Ricardo le falta un tornillo.*

sea — *el (la) mar*
  on the high seas — *en alta mar.*
  They collided on the high seas. *Se chocaron en alta mar.*

  to be at sea about — *tenerle en un mar de dudas.*
  We're at sea about it. *Nos tiene en un mar de dudas.*

---

search — *la busca*
  to go out in search of — *salir a la (en) busca de.*
  We went out in search of our cat. *Salimos a la (en) busca de nuestro gato.*

---

season — *la estación*
  off season — *fuera de temporada.*
  We were in Acapulco off season. *Estuvimos en Acapulco fuera de temporada.*

---

seat — *el asiento*
  to take a back seat — *perder mucha influencia.*
  After losing the championship, he had to take a back seat. *Después de perder el campeonato, perdió mucha influencia.*

  to take a seat — *tomar asiento.*
  Take a seat. *Tome asiento.*

---

second — *segundo*
  to be second to none — *no tener rival.*
  As a teacher he's second to none. *Como maestro no tiene rival.*

  to permit second helpings — *permitir repetir.*
  They permit second helpings here. *Se permite repetir aquí.*

---

secret — *el secreto*

  an open secret — *un secreto conocido de todos.*

  Her bad conduct is an open secret. *Su mala conducta es un secreto conocido de todos.*

  to let someone in on the secret — *decirle el secreto.*

  He let me in on the secret. *Me dijo el secreto.*

---

security — *la seguridad*

  to give security — *dar fianza.*

  They couldn't give security. *No pudieron dar fianza.*

---

to see — *ver*

  as one sees it — *a su modo de ver.*

  As I see it, it's a mistake. *A mi modo de ver, es un error.*

  let's see — *a ver.*

  Let's see. Which is yours? *A ver. ¿Cuál es el suyo?*

  See you later. — *Hasta luego.*

  Seeing is believing. — *Santo Tomás, ver y creer.*

  to see military service — *hacer su servicio militar.*

  He saw military service in Vietnam. *Hizo su servicio militar en Vietnam.*

  to see off — *despedirse de.*

  We went to the station to see him off. *Fuimos a la estación para despedirnos de él.*

  to see to it — *encargarse de.*

  I'll see to it that she knows it. *Me encargaré de que lo sepa.*

  to see to the door — *acompañar a la puerta.*

  She saw me to the door. *Me acompañó a la puerta.*

  We'll see about that! — *¡Ya lo veremos!*

---

to sell — *vender*

  to be sold out — *estar agotado.*

  The tickets are sold out. *Las entradas están agotadas.*

  to sell out — *liquidar.*

  They sold out all their stock. *Liquidaron todas sus existencias.*

to sell someone out — *traicionarle.*
He sold us out. *Nos traicionó.*

---

to send — *mandar*
    to send for — *hacer venir.*
    He sent for his parents. *Hizo venir a sus padres.*

    to send out — *enviar.*
    He has not sent out the monthly invoices yet. *Todavía no ha enviado las facturas mensuales.*

---

send-off — *la despedida*
    to give a big send-off — *dar una despedida suntuosa.*
    We gave my aunt a big send-off. *Dimos a mi tía una despedida suntuosa.*

---

sense — *el sentido*
    horse sense — *buen sentido común.*
    He's got horse sense. *Tiene buen sentido común.*

    in a sense — *en cierto sentido.*
    In a sense it's your own fault. *En cierto sentido tú mismo tienes la culpa.*

    to come to one's senses — *entrar en razon.*
    Some day he'll come to his senses. *Algún día entrará en razón.*

    to make sense — *tener sentido.*
    It doesn't make sense. *No tiene sentido.*

---

seriously — *seriamente*
    to take seriously — *tomar en serio (a pecho).*
    He takes his work seriously. *Toma en serio (a pecho) su trabajo.*

---

service — *el servicio*
    At your service. — *Para servirle a usted (Servidor de usted).*

    I'm at your service. — *Estoy a sus órdenes.*

    to be of service — *ser útil (servir).*
    This book is of no service to me. *Este libro no me es útil (no me sirve).*

    to pay lip service to — *fingir respetar.*
    We paid lip service to his rules. *Fingimos respetar sus reglas.*

---

set — *la colección*

    a set of teeth — *dentadura.*
    She has a new set of teeth. *Tiene dentadura nueva.*

to set — *poner, colocar*

    to be set — *estar listo.*
    They are set to travel to Mexico. *Están listos para viajar a México.*

    to set (the sun) — *ponerse (el sol).*
    The sun sets early. *El sol se pone temprano.*

    to set about — *ponerse a.*
    He set about organizing a new company. *Se puso a organizar una nueva compañía.*

    to set aside — *poner a un lado.*
    I put my work aside. *Puse a un lado mi trabajo.*

    to set back — *aplazar.*
    Her illness caused her to set back the date of her wedding. *Su enfermedad le hizo aplazar la fecha de su boda.*

    to set forth — *presentar.*
    He set forth some interesting ideas. *Presentó unas ideas interesantes.*

    to set forth — *salir.*
    We set forth on our trip. *Salimos de viaje.*

    to set forward (ahead) — *hacer adelantar.*
    I set my watch forward (ahead). *Hice adelantar mi reloj.*

    to set off — *hacer estallar.*
    They set off the bomb. *Hicieron estallar la bomba.*

    to set off (out) — *ponerse en camino.*
    They set off (out) after breakfast. *Se pusieron en camino después del desayuno.*

    to set out — *salir.*
    We set out for the mountains. *Salimos para las montañas.*

    to set right — *aclarar.*
    In his speech he set things right. *En su discurso aclaró las cosas.*

    to set straight — *poner en su punto.*
    We set things straight. *Pusimos las cosas en su punto.*

   to set up — *establecer.*

   My father set me up in business. *Mi padre me estableció en un negocio.*

   to set up — *formar.*

   They set up a group to sell magazines. *Formaron un grupo para vender revistas.*

   to set up — *levantar.*

   They set up their equipment in the park. *Levantaron su equipo en el parque.*

to settle — *establecer; solucionar*

   to settle — *ir a cuentas.*

   Let's settle this! *¡Vamos a cuentas!*

   to settle down — *arraigar; establecerse.*

   My father settled down in the U.S. *Mi padre arraigó (se estableció) en los Estados Unidos.*

   to settle down — *ponerse a.*

   He settled down to study. *Se puso a estudiar.*

   to settle down — *sentar la cabeza.*

   My son refuses to settle down. *Mi hijo se niega a sentar la cabeza.*

   to settle for — *conformarse con.*

   He settled for fifty dollars. *Se conformó con cincuenta dólares.*

   to settle on — *ponerse de acuerdo.*

   They settled on how much to charge. *Se pusieron de acuerdo sobre cuánto cobrar.*

shame — *la vergüenza*

   It's a crying shame. — *Es una verdadera vergüenza.*

   It's a shame. — *Es una lástima (¡Qué pena!).*

shape — *la forma*

   to be in the shape of — *tener la forma de.*

   It's in the shape of a bird. *Tiene la forma de un pájaro.*

   to be in tip-top shape — *estar en excelentes condiciones.*

   It's in tip-top shape. *Está en excelentes condiciones.*

to put in final shape — *darle forma a.*
It took them a long time to put their plans in final shape. *Tardaron mucho en darle forma a sus planes.*

to take shape — *comenzar a formarse.*
His plans for the future were taking shape. *Sus planes para el futuro comenzaban a formarse.*

share — *la parte*
one's share — *lo que le corresponde.*
They always receive more than their share. *Siempre reciben más de lo que les corresponde.*

the lion's share — *la parte del léon.*
He got the lion's share. *El recibió la parte del león.*

sharp — *agudo*
at . . . sharp — *a la(s) . . . en punto.*
Come at four o'clock sharp. *Venga a las cuatro en punto.*

to be sharp — *cortar.*
The wind is very sharp today. *El viento corta mucho hoy.*

shave — *el afeitado*
to have a close shave — *salvarse por los pelos.*
We had a close shave. *Nos salvamos por los pelos.*

to shave — *afeitarse*
to be old enough to shave — *haberle salido la barba.*
He is old enough to shave. *Le ha salido la barba.*

sheep — *la oveja*
the black sheep of the family — *la oveja negra de la familia; el garbanzo negro de la familia.*
He's the black sheep of the family. *Es la oveja negra (el garbanzo negro) de la familia.*

to separate the sheep from the goats — *distinguir entre los buenos y los malos.*

Our boss separated the sheep from the goats. *Nuestro jefe distinguió entre los buenos y los malos.*

---

to shift — *ayudarse, cambiar*
    to shift for oneself — *arreglárselas (por sí) solo.*
    He left home to shift for himself. *Abandonó su casa para arreglárselas (por sí) solo.*

---

shirt — *la camisa*
    to keep one's shirt on — *no perder la paciencia.*
    Keep your shirt on. *No pierda la paciencia.*

    to lose one's shirt — *perder hasta la camisa.*
    He lost his shirt in that deal. *Perdió hasta la camisa en ese negocio.*

---

shoe — *el zapato*
    to be in someone else's shoes — *estar (hallarse) en su lugar (pellejo).*
    If I were in your shoes, I'd stay. *Si estuviera (Si me hallara) en su lugar (pellejo), me quedaría.*

    to get along on a shoe string — *vivir con muy poco dinero.*
    He gets along on a shoe string. *Vive con muy poco dinero.*

---

to shoot — *disparar*
    to shoot — *pegar (dar) un tiro.*
    He shot it. *Le pegó (dio) un tiro.*

    to shoot someone — *matarlo a bala (a tiros).*
    They shot him. *Lo mataron a bala (a tiros).*

---

shop — *la tienda*
    to go shopping — *ir de compras (tiendas).*
    Let's go shopping. *Vamos de compras (tiendas).*

    to talk shop — *hablar de su trabajo.*
    He always talks shop. *Siempre habla de su trabajo.*

---

shore — *la costa*
    to be . . . off shore — *estar a . . . de la costa.*
    It's two miles off shore. *Está a dos millas de la costa.*

---

short — *corto*
  in short — *en resumen; en fin.*
  In short, we spent it all. *En resumen (En fin), lo gastamos todo.*

  There is no shortcut to success. — *No hay atajo sin trabajo.*

  to be short of — *andar escaso de.*
  I am short of cash. *Ando escaso de efectivo (dinero).*

shortly — *en breve*
  shortly after — *a poco de.*
  Shortly after seeing her, he fell. *A poco de verla, se cayó.*

  shortly before (after) — *poco antes (después).*
  I had received it shortly before (after). *Lo había recibido poco antes (después).*

shot — *el tiro*
  not by a long shot — *ni con (por) mucho.*
  Our team didn't win. Not by a long shot. *Nuestro equipo no ganó. Ni con (por) mucho.*

  to be a big shot — *ser un pez gordo.*
  He's a big shot. *Es un pez gordo.*

  to be a good shot — *ser buen tirador.*
  He's a good shot. *Es buen tirador.*

  to call all the shots — *hacer todas las decisiones.*
  He's calling all the shots. *Está haciendo todas las decisiones.*

  to take a shot at — *hacer una tentativa (un intento) de.*
  He took a shot at solving the problem. *Hizo una tentativa (un intento) de resolver el problema.*

shoulder — *el hombro*
  straight from the shoulder — *con toda franqueza; sin rodeos.*
  She let us have it straight from the shoulder. *Nos lo dijo con toda franqueza (sin rodeos).*

  to give someone the cold shoulder — *volverle las espaldas; tratarle con frialdad.*

She gave him the cold shoulder. *Le volvió las espaldas (Le trató con frialdad).*

to put one's shoulder to the wheel — *arrimar el hombro.*
He put his shoulder to the wheel. *Arrimó el hombro.*

to shrug one's shoulders — *encogerse de hombros.*
He shrugged his shoulders. *Se encogió de hombros.*

show — *el espectáculo*
a one-man show — *una exposición individual.*
We saw her sketches at her one-man show. *Vimos sus dibujos en su exposición individual.*

to make a great show of — *hacer alarde (ostentación) de.*
He made a great show of his knowledge. *Hizo alarde (ostentación) de sus conocimientos.*

to steal the show — *ser la sensación de la fiesta.*
The baby stole the show. *El nene fue la sensación de la fiesta.*

to show — *mostrar*
to show around — *mostrar.*
He showed us around town. *Nos mostró la ciudad.*

to show into — *hacer pasar a.*
He showed us into his office. *Nos hizo pasar a su oficina.*

to show off — *presumir.*
She likes to show off. *Le gusta presumir.*

to show up — *presentarse.*
He showed up late. *Se presentó tarde.*

showing — *la demostración*
to make a good (poor) showing — *hacer buen (mal) papel.*
They made a good (poor) showing in the contest. *Hicieron buen (mal) papel en el concurso.*

shrift — *la confesión*
to give short shrift — *despachar de prisa.*
He gave it short shrift. *Lo despachó de prisa.*

to shut — *cerrar*

to shut down — *clausurar.*
They have shut down the university. *Han clausurado la universidad.*

to shut (up) in — *encerrar en.*
They shut him (up) in the garage. *Lo encerraron en el garage.*

to shut off — *cerrar; cortar.*
They shut off the water. *Cerraron (Cortaron) el agua.*

to shut out — *cerrar la puerta a.*
He shut out the cat. *Le cerró la puerta al gato.*

to shut up — *callarse.*
He refused to shut up. *No quiso callarse.*

---

sick — *enfermo*

to be sick and tired of — *estar harto y cansado.*
I'm sick and tired of this place. *Estoy harto y cansado de este lugar.*

to get sick — *enfermar(se).*
He gets sick when he eats too much. *(Se) enferma cuando come demasiado.*

to make one sick — *hacerle mal.*
That fruit will make you sick. *Esa fruta le hará mal.*

to make one sick (fig.) — *reventarle.*
Her ideas make me sick. *Sus ideas me revientan.*

---

side — *el lado*

at (to) one side — *al lado.*
At (To) one side is the church. *Al lado está la iglesia.*

from one side to the other — *de un lado a otro.*
He ran from one side to the other. *Corrió de un lado a otro.*

on all sides — *por todas partes.*
It's surrounded by mountains on all sides. *Está rodeado de montañas por todas partes.*

on the other side — *al otro lado.*
On the other side it's red. *Al otro lado es rojo.*

on the other side of — *más allá de.*
It's on the other side of the station. *Está más allá de la estación.*

right side up — *boca arriba.*
Put the trunk right side up. *Ponga el baúl boca arriba.*

to get up on the wrong side of the bed — *levantarse por los pies de la cama (del lado izquierdo).*
I don't know what's the matter with him today. He must have gotten up on the wrong side of the bed. *No sé qué tiene hoy. Se habrá levantado por los pies de la cama (del lado izquierdo).*

to take sides — *tomar partido.*
I decided not to take sides. *Decidí no tomar partido.*

---

sight — *la vista*

at first sight — *a primera vista.*
They recognized each other at first sight. *Se reconocieron a primera vista.*

Out of sight, out of mind. — *Ojos que no ven, corazón que no siente.*

sight unseen — *sin verlo.*
I bought it sight unseen. *Lo compré sin verlo.*

to be in sight — *estar a la vista.*
It's in sight. *Está a la vista.*

to get out of sight — *perderse de vista.*
He wants us to get out of his sight. *Quiere que nos perdamos de vista.*

to know by sight — *conocer de vista.*
I know him by sight. *Lo conozco de vista.*

to lose sight of — *perder de vista.*
I lost sight of them. *Los perdí de vista.*

to lower one's sights — *moderar las aspiraciones.*
We had to lower our sights. *Tuvimos que moderar nuestras aspiraciones.*

to see the sights — *ver los puntos de interés.*
We went out to see the sights. *Salimos para ver los puntos de interés.*

---

sign — *el signo; la señal*

to give a sign — *hacer seña.*
He gave me a sign to come in. *Me hizo seña para que entrara.*

to show signs of — *dar muestras de.*
He showed signs of uneasiness. *Dio muestras de inquietud.*

to sign — *firmar*
    to sign off — *terminar las emisiones.*
    The station signed off. *La estación terminó sus emisiones.*

    to sign up — *alistarse.*
    He signed up for the trip. *Se alistó para el viaje.*

silence — *el silencio*
    Silence is consent. — *Quien calla otorga.*

    Silence is golden. — *En boca cerrada no entran moscas.*

silent — *silencioso*
    to remain silent — *guardar silencio.*
    He's remaining silent. *Guarda silencio.*

to sit — *sentarse*
    to sit back — *recostarse.*
    He sat back in his chair. *Se recostó en su silla.*

    to sit down — *sentarse; tomar asiento.*
    He sat down. *Se sentó (tomó asiento).*

    to sit out — *pasar por alto.*
    Let's sit this one out. *Pasemos éste por alto.*

    to sit up — *incorporarse.*
    I can hardly sit up. *Apenas puedo incorporarme.*

sitting — *la sentada*
    at a sitting — *de una sentada.*
    He used to eat a kilo of meat at a sitting. *Comía un kilo de carne de una
       sentada.*

six — *seis*
    It's six of one and half a dozen of the other. — *Lo mismo da.*

to size — *medir el tamaño*
    to size up — *medir con la vista.*

He sized us up and then invited us in. *Nos midió con la vista y luego nos invitó a pasar.*

sketch — *el boceto*
  a thumb-nail sketch — *un resumen muy breve.*
  He gave us a thumb-nail sketch of the plot. *Nos dio un resumen muy breve de la trama.*

skin — *la piel*
  by the skin of one's teeth — *por los pelos.*
  I got here by the skin of my teeth. *Llegué por los pelos.*

  to be nothing but skin and bones — *estar en los huesos.*
  I almost didn't recognize John; he was nothing but skin and bones. *Por poco no reconozco a Juan; estaba en los huesos.*

  to be soaked to the skin — *estar calado (mojado) hasta los huesos.*
  We're soaked to the skin. *Estamos calados (mojados) hasta los huesos.*

  to get under one's skin — *irritarle.*
  The noise got under our skin. *El ruido nos irritó.*

  to nearly jump out of one's skin — *por poco morirse de susto.*
  He nearly jumped out of his skin when he heard it. *Por poco se muere de susto al oírlo.*

sky — *el cielo*
  to go sky high — *ponerse por las nubes.*
  Prices went sky high. *Los precios se pusieron por las nubes.*

  to praise to the skies — *poner por (sobre) las nubes.*
  We praised him to the skies. *Lo pusimos por (sobre) las nubes.*

to slap — *dar una palmada*
  to slap someone — *arrimarle una bofetada.*
  She slapped me. *Me arrimó una bofetada.*

  to slap someone on the back — *palmotearle la espalda.*
  He slapped me on the back. *Me palmoteó la espalda.*

slate — *la pizarra*

    to have a clean slate — *tener las manos limpias.*
    We have a clean slate. *Tenemos las manos limpias.*

    to wipe the slate clean — *empezar de nuevo.*
    They wiped the slate clean. *Empezaron de nuevo.*

to sleep — *dormir*

    to sleep away — *pasarse durmiendo.*
    He slept the afternoon away. *Se pasó la tarde durmiendo.*

    to sleep it off — *dormir la mona.*
    He's sleeping it off. *Está durmiendo la mona.*

    to sleep on it — *consultarlo con la almohada.*
    I'll sleep on it. *Lo consultaré con la almohada.*

I'll sleep on it.
Lo consultaré con la almohada

sleepy — *soñoliento*

    to be sleepy — *tener sueño.*
    He's sleepy. *Tiene sueño.*

sleeve — *la manga*

    in (one's) shirtsleeves — *en mangas de camisa.*
    He went out in the garden in (his) shirtsleeves. *Salió al jardín en mangas de camisa.*

    to have something up one's sleeve — *tener algo en reserva (tramado).*
    He's got something up his sleeve. *Tiene algo en reserva (tramado).*

to laugh up one's sleeve — *reír para sí (para sus adentros)*.
He's laughing up his sleeve. *Está riéndose para sí (para sus adentros)*.

slip — *la falta, el error, el desliz*
  a slip of the tongue — *error de lengua (lapsus linguae)*.
  If she said it, it was just a slip of the tongue. *Si lo dijo, fue sólo un error de lengua (lapsus linguae)*.

  There's many a slip twixt the cup and the lip. — *De la mano a la boca se pierde la sopa.*

  to give someone the slip — *escaparse de*.
  She gave them the slip. *Se escapó de ellos.*

to slip — *escapar*
  to slip away — *escurrirse*.
  It slipped away. *Se escurrió.*

to slip — *deslizar*
  to slip one over on — *jugar una mala pasada*.
  She won by slipping one over on her opponent. *Ganó jugándole una mala pasada a su contrario.*

  to slip through one's fingers — *írsele (escurrirse) de entre las manos*.
  Money just slips through my fingers. *El dinero se me va (se me escurre) de entre las manos.*

to slow — *ir más despacio*
  to slow down (up) — *tomar las cosas con más calma*.
  The doctor told me to slow down (up). *El médico me dijo que tomara las cosas con más calma.*

sly — *secreto, astuto*
  on the sly — *a escondidas*.
  She would visit him on the sly. *Lo visitaba a escondidas.*

to smell — *oler*
  to smell like — *oler a*.
  It smells like brandy. *Huele a aguardiente.*

smile — *la sonrisa*
  to give someone a smile — *hacerle una sonrisa.*
  I gave her a pitying smile. *Le hice una sonrisa de lástima.*

smoke — *el humo*
  Where there's smoke there's fire. — *Cuando el río suena, agua lleva.*

  to go up in smoke — *quedar en nada.*
  His plans went up in smoke. *Sus planes quedaron en nada.*

  to have a smoke — *echar un cigarrillo (cigarro).*
  We went out and had a smoke. *Salimos y echamos un cigarrillo (cigarro).*

smoker — *fumador*
  to be a chain-smoker — *fumar un cigarrillo tras otro.*
  He's a chain-smoker. *Fuma un cigarrillo tras otro.*

snag — *el tropiezo*
  to hit (strike) a snag — *tropezar con un obstáculo.*
  We hit (struck) a snag in our plans. *Tropezamos con un obstáculo con nuestros planes.*

snail — *el caracol*
  at a snail's pace — *a paso de tortuga.*
  The procession was advancing at a snail's pace. *La procesión avanzaba a paso de tortuga.*

snappy — *enérgico*
  Make it snappy. — *Dese prisa.*

to sneak — *mover(se) a hurtadillas*
  to sneak into — *entrar sin pagar.*
  He sneaked into the movie. *Entró en el (al) cine sin pagar.*

  to sneak off (away, out) — *irse a hurtadillas.*
  He sneaked off (away, out). *Se fue a hurtadillas.*

so — *así*
  and so — *y así es que; de modo que; por lo cual.*

He went, and so I have to remain. *El fue, y así es que (de modo que, por lo cual) yo tengo que quedarme.*

and so on — *y así sucesivamente; y así por el estilo.*

They discussed economics, politics, money, and so on. *Discutieron la economía, la política, el dinero y así sucesivamente (y así por el estilo).*

so as to — *para.*

So as not to waste time, let's begin right now. *Para no perder tiempo, empecemos ahora mismo.*

so be it — *así sea.*

If that is really what you want, so be it. *Si de veras es lo que tú quieres, así sea.*

So do (did, will, etc.) I. — *Yo también.*

so far — *hasta ahora.*

So far no one has called. *Hasta ahora, no ha llamado nadie.*

So far so good. — *Hasta ahora todo va bien.*

So much for that. — *Asunto concluido.*

so much so — *hasta tal punto; tanto es así.*

She likes the movies, so much so that she goes every week. *Le gusta el cine, hasta tal punto (tanto es así) que va todas las semanas.*

So much the better (worse). — *Tanto mejor (peor).*

so-so — *así así.*

She feels so-so. *Se siente así así.*

---

so-and-so — *fulano*

  so-and-so — *fulano de tal.*

  So-and-so called. *Fulano de tal llamó.*

---

some — *algún*

  some . . . (some . . . -odd) — *. . . y tantos; y pico.*

  Some fifty (Some fifty-odd) students came. *Vinieron cincuenta y tantos (y pico) alumnos.*

  some . . . or other — *no sé qué. . . .*

He gave me some book or other on bullfighting. *Me dio no sé qué libro sobre el toreo.*

---

something — *algo*

for there to be something . . . about it — *tener algo de. . . .*
There was something boring about it. *Tenía algo de aburrido.*

for there to be something . . . about someone — *tener un no sé qué. . . .*
There's something likeable about her. *Tiene un no sé qué simpático.*

something else — *otra cosa.*
I want something else. *Deseo otra cosa.*

something like that — *algo por el estilo.*
He said that she was his cousin, or something like that. *Dijo que era su prima, o algo por el estilo.*

to be something of — *tener algo de.*
He's something of a painter. *Tiene algo de pintor.*

to give something to drink (to eat) — *dar a (de) beber (comer).*
He gave us something to drink (to eat). *Nos dio a (de) beber (comer).*

You can't get something for nothing. — *Lo que algo vale, algo cuesta.*

---

song — *la canción*

swan song — *el canto del cisne.*
Yesterday's class was his swan song. *La clase de ayer fue su canto del cisne.*

to buy for a song — *comprar regalado.*
They bought it for a song. *Lo compraron regalado.*

---

soon — *pronto*

as soon as — *en cuanto; así que.*
As soon as we eat, we'll go. *En cuanto (Así que) comamos, iremos.*

as soon as possible — *con la mayor brevedad; cuanto antes.*
She informed us as soon as possible. *Nos avisó con la mayor brevedad (cuanto antes).*

soon after — *poco después.*
Soon after, he left for Europe. *Poco después, salió para Europa.*

---

sooner — *más pronto*

  no sooner — *no bien.*

  He no sooner got the money than be bought the car. *No bien recibió el dinero, compró el coche.*

  No sooner said than done. — *Dicho y hecho.*

  sooner or later — *tarde o temprano.*

  Sooner or later he'll know. *Tarde o temprano sabrá.*

---

sorrow — *el dolor*

  to drown one's sorrows — *ahogar las penas.*

  He drowned his sorrows in drink. *Ahogó sus penas en vino.*

---

sorry — *apenado*

  to feel sorry for — *tenerle lástima.*

  He feels sorry for her. *Le tiene lástima.*

---

sort — *la clase, la especie*

  something of the sort — *algo por el estilo.*

  She said something of the sort. *Dijo algo por el estilo.*

  sort of — *un poco.*

  He's sort of stupid. *Es un poco estúpido.*

  to be out of sorts — *estar de mal humor.*

  He's out of sorts. *Está de mal humor.*

---

soul — *el alma*

  every living soul — *todo bicho viviente.*

  I imagine every living soul knows about it by now. *Supongo que ya lo sabe todo bicho viviente.*

  not a living soul — *no . . . alma nacida (viviente).*

  There's not a living soul who's capable of doing that. *No hay alma nacida (viviente) que sea capaz de hacer eso.*

---

to sound — *sonar*

  to sound like — *sonar a.*

  It sounds like a woman's voice. *Suena a voz de mujer.*

---

spade — *la pala*
   to call a spade a spade — *llamar al pan, pan y al vino, vino.*
   He calls a spade a spade. *Llama al pan, pan, y al vino, vino.*

to spare — *pasar sin*
   to have time to spare — *tener tiempo que perder.*
   I have no time to spare. *No tengo tiempo que perder.*

   to have . . . to spare — *sobrarle. . . .*
   I have two to spare. *Me sobran dos.*

to speak — *hablar*
   so to speak — *por decirlo así.*
   He's a rabble rouser, so to speak. *Es un alborotapueblos, por decirlo así.*

   to be speaking to each other (to be on speaking terms) — *hablarse.*
   They aren't speaking to each other (on speaking terms). *No se hablan.*

   to be spoken for — *estar comprometido.*
   The car is already spoken for. *El coche ya está comprometido.*

   to speak highly of — *decir mil bienes de.*
   He spoke highly of my daughter. *Dijo mil bienes de mi hija.*

   to speak out — *hablar.*
   He didn't dare speak out. *No se atrevió a hablar.*

   to speak up — *hablar más alto.*
   Please speak up. *Haga el favor de hablar más alto.*

   to speak up for — *salir en defensa de.*
   He always spoke up for me. *Siempre salía en mi defensa.*

speed — *la velocidad*
   at breakneck speed — *a todo correr (a mata caballo).*
   The rider was traveling at breakneck speed. *El jinete iba a todo correr (a mata caballo).*

   at full speed — *a toda carrera (vela; prisa).*
   He came running at full speed. *Vino a toda carrera (vela; prisa).*

   to travel at a speed of — *llevar una velocidad de.*

He often travels at a speed of 90 miles an hour. *A menudo lleva una velocidad de 90 millas la hora.*

spic-and-span — *nuevo, bien arreglado*
  spic-and-span — *limpio como una patena.*
  They left the house spic-and-span. *Dejaron la casa limpia como una patena.*

spirit — *el espíritu*
  in high spirits — *de muy buen humor.*
  They arrived in high spirits. *Llegaron de muy buen humor.*

spite — *el despecho*
  in spite of — *a pesar de; a despecho de.*
  They came in spite of the rain. *Vinieron a pesar de (a despecho de) la lluvia.*

  in spite of the fact that — *y eso que.*
  She's tired in spite of the fact that she slept 10 hours. *Está cansada, y eso que durmió diez horas.*

sponge — *la esponja*
  to throw in the sponge — *darse por vencido.*
  Toward the end, he decided to throw in the sponge. *Hacia el final, decidió darse por vencido.*

to sponge — *limpiar con esponja*
  to sponge off someone — *vivir de gorra; vivir a costa de alguien.*
  He sponges off his friends. *Vive de gorra (Vive a costa de sus amigos).*

spoon — *la cuchara*
  To be born with a silver spoon in one's mouth. — *Nacer en la opulencia; Nacer de pie.*

spot — *la mancha*
  on the spot — *en el acto.*
  He sold it to me on the spot. *Me lo vendió en el acto.*

to have a soft spot in one's heart for — *tenerle mucho cariño.*
I have a soft spot in my heart for her. *Le tengo mucho cariño.*

to put someone on the spot — *ponerle en un aprieto (una situación comprometida).*
He put us all on the spot. *Nos puso a todos en un aprieto (una situación comprometida).*

to touch a sore spot — *poner el dedo en la llaga.*
He touched a sore spot. *Puso el dedo en la llaga.*

spree — *la juerga*
   to go out on a spree — *irse de juerga (parranda).*
   We went out on a spree. *Nos fuimos de juerga (parranda).*

spur — *la espuela*
   on the spur of the moment — *impulsivamente.*
   I decided on the spur of the moment. *Decidí impulsivamente.*

stab — *la puñalada*
   a stab in the back — *una puñalada trapera.*
   His comment was a stab in the back. *Su comentario fue una puñalada trapera.*

stake — *la estaca; la (a)puesta*
   to be at stake — *estar en juego.*
   His life is at stake. *Su vida está en juego.*

   to die at the stake — *morir en la hoguera.*
   They died at the stake. *Murieron en la hoguera.*

   to pull up stakes — *mudar(se de casa).*
   They pulled up stakes. *(Se) Mudaron (de casa).*

stand — *la opinión, el puesto*
   to take a stand — *adoptar una actitud.*
   Our club refused to take a stand. *Nuestro club no quiso adoptar una actitud.*

to stand — *poner derecho; estar; soportar*
   not to be able to stand the sight of — *no poder ver ni en pintura.*

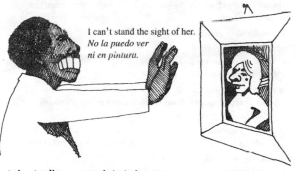

I can't stand the sight of her. *No la puedo ver ni en pintura.*

to be standing — *estar de (en) pie*
She's standing. *Está de (en) pie.*

to know where one stands — *saber a qué atenerse.*
I wish we knew where we stand. *Ojalá que supiéramos a qué atenernos.*

to stand aside — *mantenerse apartado.*
He stood aside. *Se mantuvo apartado.*

to stand back — *retirarse (al fondo).*
He asked us to stand back. *Nos pidió que nos retiráramos (al fondo).*

to stand behind (back of) — *garantizar.*
He stood behind (back of) his offer. *Garantizó su oferta.*

to stand behind (back of) — *respaldar a.*
He stood behind (back of) his son in the argument. *Respaldó a su hijo en la discusión.*

to stand for — *significar; representar.*
What does that symbol stand for? *¿Qué significa (representa) ese símbolo?*

to stand for — *tolerar.*
He won't stand for her foolishness. *No quiere tolerar sus tonterías.*

to stand on one's own two feet — *valerse de sí mismo.*
He stands on his own two feet. *Se vale de sí mismo.*

to stand out — *ser prominente.*

227

His red hair stands out in any crowd. *Su pelo rojo es prominente en cualquier grupo*

to stand still — *estarse quieto.*
Stand still! *¡Estése quieto!*

to stand up — *ponerse de pie; pararse.*
They stood up. *Se pusieron de pie (Se pararon).*

to stand . . . up — *dejar plantado.*
We had an appointment for four but they stood me up. *Estábamos citados para las cuatro pero me dejaron plantado.*

to stand up against — *resistir.*
The wall has stood up against the flood. *El muro ha resistido la inundación.*

to stand up for — *defender.*
He stood up for his rights. *Defendió sus derechos.*

to stand up for — *salir en defensa de.*
He stood up for his accused son. *Salió en defensa de su hijo acusado.*

to stand up to — *enfrentarse con.*
She stands up to her husband. *Se enfrenta con su esposo.*

to stand up to — *hacer frente a.*
He stood up to his accusers. *Hizo frente a sus acusadores.*

---

standard — *la norma*
  by any standard — *en modo alguno.*
  They're not as good as these by any standard. *No son tan buenos como éstos en modo alguno.*

  to meet the standards — *estar al nivel deseado.*
  His work doesn't meet the standards. *Su trabajo no está al nivel deseado.*

---

standing — *la reputación*
  to be in good standing — *estar al corriente de sus obligaciones.*
  He's not in good standing. *No está al corriente de sus obligaciones.*

---

standstill — *la parada*
  to come to a standstill — *pararse.*
  Traffic has come to a standstill. *El tránsito se ha parado.*

---

to stare — *mirar fijamente*
    to stare at — *mirar de hito en hito.*
    She's staring at him. *La está mirando de hito en hito.*

start — *el principio; el sobresalto*
    right from the start — *desde un principio.*
    We realized his intentions right from the start. *Nos dimos cuenta de sus
        intenciones desde un principio.*

    to get one's start — *empezar.*
    He got his start in his father's store. *Empezó en la tienda de su padre.*

    to give one a start — *darle un susto.*
    The noise gave me a start. *El ruido me dio un susto.*

to start — *empezar*
    to start — *poner en marcha.*
    She started the motor. *Puso en marcha el motor.*

    to start down (up) stairs — *tomar por la escalera abajo (arriba).*
    He started down (up) stairs. *Tomó por la escalera abajo (arriba).*

    to start out — *ponerse en camino.*
    We started out. *Nos pusimos en camino.*

to stay — *quedar(se)*
    to be here to stay — *estar destinado a perdurar.*
    Football is here to stay. *El futbol está destinado a perdurar.*

    to stay in — *quedarse en casa.*
    The doctor told him to stay in. *El médico le dijo que se quedara en casa.*

    to stay out — *quedarse fuera (de casa).*
    They stayed out all night. *Se quedaron fuera (de casa) toda la noche.*

    to stay (to keep) out of someone's business — *no meterse en sus
        asuntos.*
    He stayed (kept) out of my business. *No se metió en mis asuntos.*

    to stay up — *no acostarse.*
    I stayed up all night. *No me acosté en toda la noche.*

stead — *el lugar*
   to stand one in good stead — *serle muy útil.*
   It will stand you in good stead. *Le será muy útil.*

steam — *el vapor*
   to blow off steam — *desahogarse.*
   He blew off steam. *Se desahogó.*

   under one's own steam — *por sí mismo; por sus propias fuerzas.*
   He was able to do the work under his own steam. *Pudo llevar a cabo el trabajo por sí mismo (por sus propias fuerzas) .*

step — *el paso*
   step by step — *paso a paso.*
   He described it step by step. *Lo describió paso a paso.*

   to be a step away from — *estar a un paso de.*
   He's a step away from death. *Está a un paso de la muerte.*

   to retrace one's steps — *volver sobre sus pasos.*
   We retraced our steps. *Volvimos sobre nuestros pasos.*

   to take a step — *dar un paso.*
   The child took two steps. *El niño dio dos pasos.*

   Watch your step. — *Tenga usted cuidado.*

to step — *dar un paso*
   to step down — *renunciar.*
   The manager is going to step down. *El gerente va a renunciar.*

   to step in — *pasar.*
   Step in. *Pase.*

   to step out — *salir.*
   He stepped out. *Salió.*

   to step out on — *engañar a.*
   He was stepping out on his wife. *Engañaba a su esposa.*

   to step up — *acelerar.*
   They stepped up their activities. *Aceleraron sus actividades.*

to step up — *acercarse.*
Step up when your name is called. *Acérquese cuando llamen su nombre.*

to stick — *pegar*
  Stick 'em up! *¡Manos arriba!*

  to be stuck-up — *ser muy presuntuosa.*
  She's stuck-up. *Es muy presuntuosa.*

  to be stuck with — *no poder deshacerse.*
  I'm stuck with these five copies. *No puedo deshacerme de estos cinco ejemplares.*

  to stick by — *ser fiel a.*
  He'll stick by us forever. *Nos será fiel para siempre.*

  to get stuck — *ser engañado (estafado).*
  I paid five dollars and got stuck. *Pagué cinco dólares y me engañaron (estafaron).*

  to stick it out (till the end) — *perseverar hasta el final.*
  He stuck it out (till the end). *Perseveró hasta el final.*

  to stick one's head out — *asomarse.*
  He stuck his head out the window. *Se asomó a la ventana.*

  to stick out one's tongue — *sacar la lengua.*
  He stuck out his tongue. *Sacó la lengua.*

  to stick to — *andar pegado a.*
  She sticks to her mother all the time. *Anda pegada a su madre todo el tiempo.*

  to stick to — *atenerse a.*
  Stick to the book. *Aténgase al libro.*

  to stick to — *ceñirse a.*
  He sticks to the rules. *Se ciñe a las reglas.*

  to stick to — *pegársele a.*
  It sticks to my fingers. *Se me pega a los dedos.*

  to stick to — *perseverar en.*
  He sticks to his studies. *Persevera en sus estudios.*

stir — *la agitación*
  to cause a stir — *llamar la atención.*
  He entered without causing a stir. *Entró sin llamar la atención.*

to stir — *agitar*
  to stir up — *incitar.*
  He's always stirring up his colleagues. *Siempre está incitando a sus colegas.*

  to stir up — *provocar.*
  Her death stirred up a lot of rumors. *Su muerte provocó muchos rumores.*

stock — *el surtido*
  to be out of stock — *estar agotado.*
  The book is out of stock. *El libro está agotado.*

  to have in stock — *tener en existencia.*
  We don't have hammers in stock. *No tenemos martillos en existencia.*

  to take stock — *hacer inventario.*
  The store is closed because they are taking stock. *La tienda está cerrada porque están haciendo inventario.*

  to take stock in — *confiar en.*
  I take no stock in his ideas. *No confío en sus ideas.*

  to take stock of — *hacer un estudio de.*
  Take stock of what his capabilities are. *Haga un estudio de sus capacidades.*

to stomach — *tragar*
  not to be able to stomach — *no poder soportar.*
  I can't stomach him. *No lo puedo soportar.*

stone — *la piedra*
  A rolling stone gathers no moss. —*Hombre de muchos oficios, pobre seguro.*

  It's a stone's throw from here. — *Está a un tiro de piedra de aquí.*

to stoop — *inclinarse, encorvarse.*
  to stoop to — *rebajarse a.*

She would never stoop to (lower herself to) begging on the street. *Nunca se rebajaría a pedir limosna por la calle.*

---

stop — *la parada; el fin*

to put a stop to — *poner fin (término) a.*

He put a stop to the shouting. *Puso fin (término) a los gritos.*

---

to stop — *parar*

to stop at nothing — *ser capaz de todo.*

He'll stop at nothing to get what he wants. *Es capaz de todo para conseguir lo que quiere.*

to stop dead — *detenerse repentinamente (de repente).*

They stopped dead when they saw the tiger. *Su detuvieron repentinamente al ver al tigre.*

to stop over — *hacer escala.*

He stopped over in Madrid to see us. *Hizo escala en Madrid para vernos.*

---

store — *la tienda*

to have . . . in store for one — *tener . . . que le espera.*

He's got a lot of work in store for him. *Tiene mucho trabajo que le espera.*

---

storm — *la tormenta*

to take by storm — *asaltar.*

The students took the bookstore by storm. *Los estudiantes asaltaron la librería.*

to take one by storm — *cautivarle.*

Her voice took us by storm. *Su voz nos cautivó.*

---

story — *el cuento*

a cock-and-bull story — *un cuento chino.*

He told us a cock-and-bull story. *Nos contó un cuento chino.*

That's another story. — *Es cosa aparte.*

to make a long story short — *en resumidas cuentas.*

To make a long story short, he died. *En resumidas cuentas, murió.*

---

straight — *derecho*
  to get it straight — *entenderlo bien.*
  I never got it straight. *Nunca lo entendí bien.*

  to go straight — *enmendarse.*
  He got out of jail and went straight. *Salió de la cárcel y se enmendó.*

strategist — *el estratega*
  arm-chair strategist — *estadista de café.*
  For the arm-chair strategists, all problems can be solved. *Para los estadistas de café todos los problemas se pueden resolver.*

straw — *la paja*
  It's the last straw. — *¡Es el colmo (No faltaba más)!*

  It's the straw that breaks the camel's back. — *La última gota es la que hace rebosar el vaso.*

streak — *la raya, la lista.*
  to swear (cuss) a blue streak — *echar sapos y culebras.*
  Since he couldn't find his wallet, he was swearing (cussing) a blue streak. *Por no poder encontrar su cartera, estaba echando sapos y culebras.*

street — *la calle*
  across the street — *enfrente.*
  The building across the street is new. *El edificio de enfrente es nuevo.*

  to go down a street — *tomar por una calle.*
  I went down that street. *Tomé por esa calle.*

  to go down (up) the street — *seguir calle abajo (arriba).*
  He went down (up) the street. *Siguió calle abajo (arriba).*

  to live on easy street — *estar en buena situación económica.*
  They are living on easy street. *Están en buena situación económica.*

strike — *la huelga*
  to go on strike — *declararse en huelga.*
  They went on strike. *Se declararon en huelga.*

to strike — *golpear*
   to strike — *dar.*
   It struck five. *Dieron las cinco.*

   to strike back — *defenderse.*
   The accused struck back with new evidence. *El acusado se defendió con nueva evidencia.*

   to strike it rich — *tener un golpe de fortuna.*
   Have you seen his new car? He must have struck it rich. *¿Has visto su coche nuevo? Habrá tenido un golpe de fortuna.*

   to strike out — *suprimir; tachar.*
   We had to strike out the last word. *Tuvimos que suprimir (tachar) la última palabra.*

   to strike up — *empezar a tocar.*
   The band struck up a march. *La banda empezó a tocar una marcha.*

string — *la cuerda*
   to be tied to one's mother's apron strings — *estar pegado a las faldas de su madre.*
   She's been tied to her mother's apron strings all her life. *Ha estado pegada a las faldas de su madre toda la vida.*

   to have on the string — *tener pretendiente.*
   She has two men on the string. *Tiene dos pretendientes.*

   to pull strings — *tocar todos los resortes.*
   I had to pull strings to get it. *Tuve que tocar todos los resortes para conseguirlo.*

   with no strings attached — *sin compromiso.*
   He gave it to us with no strings attached. *Nos lo dio sin compromiso.*

stroke — *el golpe*
   a stroke of luck — *un golpe de suerte.*
   He won by a sheer stroke of luck. *Ganó a puro golpe de suerte.*

stuff — *la materia*
   to know one's stuff — *ser experto.*
   He really knows his stuff. *Es muy experto.*

style — *el estilo*
   in a modern style — *a lo moderno.*
   She dresses in a modern style. *Se viste a lo moderno.*

   . . . style — *a la . . . .*
   Love, Italian style. *Amor a la italiana.*

   to be in style — *estar de moda.*
   It's not in style any more. *Ya no está de moda.*

   to go out of style — *pasarse de moda.*
   They've gone out of style. *Se han pasado de moda.*

---

subject — *el tema*
   to change the subject — *cambiar de tema.*
   All of a sudden he changed the subject. *De repente cambió de tema.*

---

success — *el éxito.*
   to be a howling success — *tener un éxito clamoroso.*
   The play was a howling success. *La comedia tuvo un éxito clamoroso.*

---

successful — *exitoso*
   to be successful — *tener (buen) éxito.*
   He went into business but he wasn't successful. *Se dedicó a los negocios
      pero no tuvo (buen) éxito.*

---

sudden — *súbito*
   all of a sudden — *de repente; de pronto, de golpe.*
   All of a sudden he fell. *De repente (De pronto; De golpe) se cayó.*

---

suit — *el palo (de la baraja)*
   to follow suit — *seguir el ejemplo.*
   He refused to follow suit. *Se negó a seguir el ejemplo.*

---

to suit — *satisfacer*
   Suit yourself. — *Haga lo que quiera.*

---

suitcase — *la maleta*
   to live out of a suitcase — *vivir con la maleta hecha.*

236

For nine months we lived out of a suitcase. *Por nueve meses vivimos con la maleta hecha.*

---

to sum — *sumar*
  to sum up — *para resumir.*
  To sum up, the trip was too short. *Para resumir, el viaje fue demasiado corto.*

---

summer — *el verano*
  Indian summer — *el veranillo de San Martín.*
  We like to travel in Indian summer. *Nos gusta viajar en el veranillo de San Martín.*

---

sun — *el sol*
  to be (right) out in the sun — *estar al (a pleno) sol.*
  They're (right) out in the sun. *Están al (a pleno) sol.*

---

to sun — *asolear*
  to sun oneself — *tomar el sol.*
  They're sunning themselves. *Están tomando el sol.*

---

sure — *seguro*
  as sure as two and two are four — *como dos y dos son cuatro.*
  As sure as two and two are four, they'll not arrive on time. *Como dos y dos son cuatro, no van a llegar a tiempo.*

  for sure — *a punto fijo.*
  I don't know for sure. *No sé a punto fijo.*

  to make sure — *no dejar de.*
  Make sure that you sign it. *No deje de firmarlo.*

  sure enough — *efectivamente.*
  I thought she was going to buy the car and sure enough she did. *Creía que iba a comprar el coche y efectivamente lo compró.*

---

surprise — *la sorpresa*
  to take by surprise — *sorprender.*
  The news took me by surprise. *La noticia me sorprendió.*

---

swallow — *el trago; la golondrina*

  One swallow does not make a summer. — *Una golondrina no hace verano.*

  to down in one swallow — *tomar de un golpe.*
  He downed it in one swallow. *Lo tomó de un golpe.*

---

to swallow — *tragar*

  to swallow — *tragarse.*
  He swallowed the insult. *Se tragó el insulto.*

---

to swear — *jurar*

  to swear by — *tener una fe ciega en; poner toda su confianza en.*
  She swears by this medicine. *Tiene una fe ciega (Pone toda su confianza) en esta medicina.*

  to swear off — *renunciar a.*
  He swore off smoking. *Renunció a fumar.*

---

to swim — *nadar*

  to swim (across) — *cruzar (atravesar) a nado (nadando).*
  He swam (across) the river. *Cruzó (Atravesó) el río a nado (nadando) .*

---

swing — *la oscilación*

  to be in full swing — *estar en plena actividad.*
  Things are in full swing. *Las cosas están en plena actividad.*

---

to sympathize — *compadecer*

  to sympathize with — *compadecer (se de).*
  I sympathize with your bad luck. *(Me) compadezco (de) su mala fortuna.*

---

sympathy — *la compasión, la condolencia*

  to extend one's sympathy — *dar el pésame.*
  He extended me his sympathy. *Me dio el pésame.*

T

t — *la t*

    to suit to a T — *satisfacer a la perfección.*

    Our new home suits us to a T. *Nuestra casa nueva nos satisface a la perfección.*

---

tab — *la cuenta*

    to keep tabs on — *tener a la vista.*

    She keeps tabs on her husband. *Tiene a la vista a su esposo.*

    to pick up the tab — *pagar la cuenta.*

    My friend picked up the tab. *Mi amigo pagó la cuenta.*

---

table — *la mesa*

    to chat at the table — *estar de sobremesa.*

    We were chatting at the table. *Estábamos de sobremesa.*

    to clear the table — *levantar (quitar) la mesa.*

    I cleared the table. *Levanté (Quité) la mesa.*

    to end up under the table — *acabar borracho.*

    He drank so much that he ended up under the table. *Tomó tanto que acabó borracho.*

    to set the table — *poner la mesa.*

    She set the table. *Puso la mesa.*

    to turn the tables — *volver las tornas.*

    He turned the tables on us. *Nos volvió las tornas.*

    to wait on tables — *servir (a) la mesa.*

    They wait on tables. *Sirven (a) la mesa.*

---

to table — *poner sobre la mesa*

    to table the motion — *aplazar la discusión de la moción.*

    We tabled the motion. *Aplazamos la discusión de la moción.*

---

tack — *la tachuela*
   to get down to brass tacks — *ir al grano.*
   Let's get down to brass tacks. *Vamos al grano.*

---

to take — *tomar; llevar*
   to be taken aback — *quedarse asombrado.*
   He was taken aback. *Se quedó asombrado.*

   to be taken in — *ser engañado.*
   He got taken in by the salesman. *Fue engañado por el vendedor.*

   to take after — *parecerse a; ser de la pasta de.*
   He takes after his father. *Se parece a (Es de la pasta de) su padre.*

   to take amiss — *tomar (llevar) a mal.*
   He took what I said amiss. *Tomó (Llevó) a mal lo que dije.*

   to take apart — *desarmar.*
   He took the toy apart. *Desarmó el juguete.*

   to take aside — *llevar aparte.*
   He took us aside. *Nos llevó aparte.*

   to take away — *llevarse.*
   He took away the desk. *Se llevó la mesa.*

   to take back — *llevarse.*
   He took back what he gave me. *Se llevó lo que me dio.*

   to take back — *retractarse de.*
   He took back what he said. *Se retractó de lo que dijo.*

   to take down — *bajar.*
   He took the picture down to the lobby. *Bajó el cuadro al vestíbulo.*

   to take down — *descolgar.*
   He took down the picture. *Descolgó el cuadro.*

   to take down — *tomar nota de; apuntar.*
   He took down what I said. *Tomó nota de (Apuntó) lo que dije.*

   to take for — *tomar por.*
   She took him for a doctor. *Lo tomó por médico.*

   to take in — *ir a ver.*
   We took in a play. *Fuimos a ver una comedia.*

to take it — *tener entendido.*
I take it that you're leaving. *Tengo entendido que sale.*

to take it out of one — *agotar.*
This work really takes it out of me. *Este trabajo me agota.*

to take it out on — *desquitarse a costa de.*
He lost his job and is taking it out on his boss. *Perdió su trabajo y se está
    desquitando a costa de su jefe.*

to take off — *despegar.*
The plane took off in the snow. *El avión despegó en la nieve.*

to take off — *marcharse.*
They took off at dawn. *Se marcharon al amanecer.*

to take off — *quitarse.*
He took off his hat. *Se quitó el sombrero.*

to take on — *echarse encima; tomar sobre sí.*
He took on more work. *Se echó encima (Tomó sobre sí) más trabajo.*

to take on — *emplear.*
They took on a new secretary. *Emplearon a una nueva secretaria.*

to take on — *luchar con.*
He took me on single-handed. *Luchó conmigo mano a mano.*

to take out — *sacar.*
He took it out of the box. *Lo sacó de la caja.*

to take over — *asumir cargo de.*
He took over my job. *Asumió cargo de mi puesto (trabajo).*

to take over — *hacer cargo.*
He took over when she became ill. *El se hizo cargo cuando ella (se)
    enfermó.*

to take to — *entregarse a; darle por.*
He took to gambling. *Se entregó al juego (Le dio por jugar).*

to take to — *lanzarse a.*
We all took to the streets. *Todos nos lanzamos a la calle.*

to take to — *tomarle cariño.*
He took to my sister immediately. *Le tomó cariño a mi hermana en seguida.*

to take up — *acortar.*

He took up the sleeves of the coat a little. *Acortó las mangas del saco.*

to take up — *discutir; preocuparse de.*

He took up the matter of the flights. *Discutió el (Se preocupó del) asunto de los vuelos.*

to take up — *estudiar; dedicarse a.*

She's taking up music. *Estudia (Se dedica a) la música.*

to take up — *reanudar.*

We'll take up our conversation later. *Reanudaremos nuestra conversación más tarde.*

to take up with — *ir con; relacionarse con.*

He's taken up with a group of doctors. *Va (Se ha relacionado) con un grupo de médicos.*

to take wrong — *interpretar mal.*

She took him wrong. *Lo interpretó mal.*

---

tale — *el cuento*

    to tell tales out of school — *írsele la lengua.*

    He's always telling tales out of school. *Siempre se le va la lengua.*

---

talk — *la charla*

    to be all talk — *ser puras palabras.*

    His promises are all talk. *Sus promesas son puras palabras.*

    to engage in small talk — *hablar de trivialidades.*

    They engaged in small talk to kill time. *Hablaron de trivialidades para matar el tiempo.*

---

to talk — *hablar*

    to be all talked out — *haber hablado hasta no poder más.*

    By evening I was all talked out. *Para la noche había hablado hasta no poder más.*

    to talk back to — *replicar a.*

    He talked back to his mother. *Replicó a su madre.*

    to talk big — *exagerar.*

    He likes to talk big. *Le gusta exagerar.*

to talk into — *persuadir a.*
He talked her into going. *La persuadió a que fuera.*

to talk out of — *disuadir de.*
He talked me out of buying it. *Me disuadió de comprarlo.*

to talk over — *discutir.*
We talked over our plans. *Discutimos nuestros planes.*

---

talker — *el hablador*
  to be a loose talker — *ser muy ligero de palabra.*
She's a very loose talker. *Es muy ligera de palabra.*

---

talking-to — *la represión*
  to give a (good) talking-to — *dar un rapapolvo.*
When she arrived home late, her father gave her a (good) talking-to.
    Cuando llegó tarde a casa, su padre le dio un rapapolvo.

---

tape — *la cinta*
  red tape — *papeleo.*
There's a lot of red tape. *Hay mucho papeleo.*

---

target — *el blanco*
  to hit the target — *dar en el blanco.*
She hit the target. *Dio en el blanco.*

---

task — *la tarea*
  to take to task — *reprender.*
He took them to task for being lazy. *Los reprendió por ser perezosos.*

  to undertake the task — *darse a la tarea.*
She undertook the task of learning Russian. *Se dio a la tarea de aprender
    ruso.*

---

taste — *el gusto*
  to acquire a taste for — *aficionarse a; tomar gusto a.*
I have acquired a taste for ballet. *Me he aficionado (He tomado gusto) al
    ballet.*

to be a matter of taste — *ir en gustos.*
It's a matter of taste. *Va en gustos.*

to be in poor taste — *ser de mal gusto.*
What he said was in very poor taste. *Lo que dijo fue de muy mal gusto.*

to leave a bad taste in one's mouth — *dejarlo con mal sabor de boca.*
It has left a bad taste in his mouth. *Lo dejó con mal sabor de boca.*

---

to taste — *gustar*
to taste like (of) — *saber a.*
It tastes like (of) garlic. *Sabe a ajo.*

---

to team — *enyugar*
to team up with — *aliarse con.*
They teamed up with our president. *Se aliaron con nuestro presidente.*

---

tear — *la lágrima*
to move to tears — *conmover a (mover a) lágrimas.*
His story moved me to tears. *Su relato me conmovió (movió) a lágrimas.*

to shed bitter tears — *llorar a lágrima viva.*
She's shedding bitter tears. *Está llorando a lágrima viva.*

to shed crocodile tears — *llorar lágrimas de cocodrilo.*
She shed crocodile tears. *Lloró lágrimas de cocodrilo.*

---

to tear — *romper*
to tear down — *derribar.*
They are tearing down the building. *Están derribando el edificio.*

to tear up — *romper.*
He tore up the contract. *Rompió el contrato.*

---

telegram — *el telegrama*
to send a telegram — *poner un telegrama.*
He sent them a telegram. *Les puso un telegrama.*

---

to tell — *decir*
Tell me! — *¡Cuénteme a ver!*

to tell apart — *distinguir entre.*
I can't tell the two apart. *No puedo distinguir entre los dos.*

to tell it like it is — *hablar sin rodeos.*
He likes to tell it like it is. *Le gusta hablar sin rodeos.*

to tell . . . off — *decirle cuántas son cinco.*
If he keeps bothering me I'm going to tell him off. *Si me sigue molestando le voy a decir cuántas son cinco.*

to tell on — *denunciar.*
He always tells on his sister. *Siempre denuncia a su hermana.*

---

temper — *el temple, el humor, la condición*
  to keep one's temper — *no perder la paciencia (calma).*
  Try to keep your temper. *Trate de no perder la paciencia (calma).*

  to lose one's temper — *perder la paciencia; encolerizarse.*
  He lost his temper. *Perdió la paciencia (Se encolerizó).*

tempest — *la tempestad*
  It's a tempest in a teapot. — *Es una tempestad en un vaso de agua.*

---

term — *el término*
  to be on good terms — *estar en buenas relaciones.*
  They are on good terms. *Están en buenas relaciones.*

  to come to terms — *llegar a (concertar) un acuerdo.*
  They came to terms. *Llegaron a (Concertaron) un acuerdo.*

  to serve a term — *cumplir condena.*
  He served a term in jail. *Cumplió condena en la cárcel.*

---

test — *la prueba*
  to put to a test — *poner a prueba(s).*
  I put her to a test. *La puse a prueba(s).*

---

that — *eso*
  that is — *es decir.*
  She is living in the capital of Venezuela, that is, in Caracas. *Vive en la capital de Venezuela, es decir, en Caracas.*

That'll do. — *Ya está bien.*

That's it! — *¡Eso es!*

That's that. — *Así es. Fin.*

to be as bad as (all) that — *ser para tanto.*
It wasn't as bad as (all) that. *No fue para tanto.*

---

there — *allí*
to be all there — *estar en sus cabales.*
She's not all there. *No está en sus cabales.*

---

thick — *grueso*
through thick and thin — *por las buenas y las malas.*
She stuck with him through thick and thin. *Se quedó con él por las buenas y las malas.*

---

to thin — *adelgazar*
to thin out — *ponérsele ralo.*
His hair is thinning out. *Su pelo se le está poniendo ralo.*

to thin out — *reducir el número.*
We thinned out our employees. *Redujimos el número de empleados.*

---

thing — *la cosa*
for one thing — *en primer lugar.*
For one thing, I don't have any. *En primer lugar, no tengo ninguno.*

It's a good thing! — *¡Menos mal!*

It's (just) one of those things. — *Son cosas de la vida.*

It's the same old thing. — *Es lo de siempre.*

not to know the first thing about — *no saber nada de.*
He doesn't know the first thing about chemistry. *No sabe nada de química.*

not to understand a thing — *no entender ni papa (jota).*
They didn't understand a thing! *¡No entendieron ni papa (jota)!*

Of all things! — *¡Qué sorpresa!*

such a thing — *tal cosa.*
I can't believe such a thing. *No puedo creer tal cosa.*

that very thing — *eso mismo.*
That very thing disturbs us. *Eso mismo nos molesta.*

the first thing in the morning — *a primera hora.*
Let's leave the first thing in the morning. *Salgamos mañana a primera hora.*

the only thing — *lo único.*
It's the only thing he said. *Es lo único que dijo.*

Things are humming around here. — *Hay mucha actividad por aquí.*

Things are not what they used to be. — *Los tiempos han cambiado.*

to be seeing things — *ver visiones.*
She's seeing things. *Ve visiones.*

to be the real thing — *ser auténtico.*
This diamond isn't false; it's the real thing. *Este diamante no es falso; es auténtico.*

to know a thing or two about — *saber algo de.*
I know a thing or two about Spain. *Sé algo de España.*

to manage things all right — *arreglárselas.*
He managed things all right. *Se las arregló.*

to take things in one's stride — *tomarse todo con calma.*
He takes things in his stride. *Se toma todo con calma.*

to talk about things Spanish — *hablar de lo español.*
We talked about things Spanish. *Hablamos de lo español.*

to tell someone a thing or two — *decirle cuántos son cinco.*
I told her a thing or two. *Le dije cuántos son cinco.*

You can't have too much of a good thing. — *Lo que abunda no daña.*

---

to think — *pensar*
  I should think so! — *¡Así lo creo!*

  not to think much of — *tener en poco.*
  He didn't think much of his son's friends. *Tenía en poco a los amigos de su hijo.*

to think a lot of oneself — *estar muy pagado (tener buena opinión) de sí mismo.*

He thinks a lot of himself. *Está muy pagado (Tiene buena opinión) de sí mismo.*

to think about — *pensar en.*

He's thinking about (of) his future. *Está pensando en su porvenir.*

to think highly of — *tener un alto concepto de.*

She thinks highly of her teacher. *Tiene un alto concepto de su maestro.*

to think it over — *pensarlo.*

I was thinking it over when he entered. *Lo estaba pensando cuando entró.*

to think twice — *pensar dos veces.*

I thought twice before I did it. *Pensé dos veces antes de hacerlo.*

to think up — *inventar.*

I have to think up an excuse. *Tengo que inventar una excusa.*

What do you think of it? — *¿Qué le parece?*

Who would have thought it! — *¡Quién había de creerlo!*

---

thinking — *el pensamiento*
wishful thinking — *castillos en el aire.*

He does too much wishful thinking. *Pasa mucho tiempo construyendo castillos en el aire.*

---

thirst — *la sed*
to be thirsty — *tener sed.*
He's thirsty. *Tiene sed.*

to make one thirsty — *darle sed.*
It makes us thirsty. *Nos da sed.*

---

this — *esto; tan*
this — *así de.*
They have a son this tall. *Tienen un hijo así de alto.*

---

thought — *el pensamiento*
on second thought — *pensándolo bien.*

On second thought he decided to go. *Pensándolo bien, decidió ir.*

the very thought of it — *sólo pensarlo.*
They very thought of it made her cry. *Sólo pensarlo la hizo llorar.*

to be lost in thought — *estar abstraído.*
He couldn't answer because he was deeply lost in thought. *No supo contestar porque estaba muy abstraído.*

without a thought — *sin pensarlo.*
They did it without a thought. *Lo hicieron sin pensarlo.*

---

thread — *el hilo*
   to break the thread — *cortar el hilo.*
   He broke the thread of my story. *Me cortó el hilo del cuento.*

   to lose the thread — *perder el hilo.*
   He lost the thread of the conversation. *Perdió el hilo de la conversación.*

---

through — *a través*
   through and through — *de pies a cabeza.*
   He's a patriot through and through. *Es un patriota de pies a cabeza.*

   to be through with — *haber terminado con.*
   I'm through with your book. *He terminado con su libro.*

---

to throw — *echar*
   to throw a party — *dar una fiesta.*
   They threw a party for us. *Nos dieron una fiesta.*

   to throw away — *botar; tirar.*
   He threw away the rest. *Botó (Tiró) lo demás.*

   to throw it up to someone — *echárselo en cara.*
   She keeps throwing it up to me. *Sigue echándomelo en cara.*

   to throw out — *echar; expulsar.*
   He was thrown out of the club. *Lo echaron (expulsaron) del club.*

   to throw up — *vomitar.*
   He threw up. *Vomitó.*

   to throw up one's hands — *desesperarse.*

When he told me to wait five hours, I threw up my hands. *Cuando me dijo que esperara cinco horas, me desesperé.*

to throw up one's hands — *levantar (rápidamente) las manos.*
He threw up his hands. *Levantó (rápidamente) las manos.*

thumb — *el dedo pulgar*
to be all thumbs — *tener manos torpes; caérsele todo de las manos.*
He's all thumbs. *Tiene manos torpes (Todo se le cae de las manos).*

to have a green thumb — *tener don de jardinería.*
He's got a green thumb. *Tiene don de jardinería.*

to have under one's thumb — *tener dominado.*
She has him under her thumb. *Lo tiene dominado.*

to twiddle one's thumbs — *estar ocioso.*
He's twiddling his thumbs. *Está ocioso.*

to thumb — *hojear*
to thumb through — *hojear.*
I only had time to thumb through the book. *Sólo tuve el tiempo para hojear el libro.*

ticket — *la entrada, el boleto, el billete*
a one-way ticket — *un billete (boleto) de ida.*
We have a one-way ticket. *Tenemos un billete (boleto) de ida.*

a round-trip ticket — *un billete (boleto) de ida y vuelta.*
He has a round-trip ticket. *Tiene un billete (boleto) de ida y vuelta.*

to buy a ticket — *sacar la entrada (el boleto).*
We bought the tickets here. *Sacamos las entradas (los boletos) aquí.*

tidings — *las noticias*
the glad tidings — *las buenas noticias.*
They announced the glad tidings. *Anunciaron (Dieron) las buenas noticias.*

tight — *apretado*
Hold tight. — *Agárrese bien.*

to sit tight — *no hacer nada.*
Let's sit tight for awhile. *No hagamos nada por un rato.*

---

time — *el tiempo; la hora*

   a long time — *mucho tiempo.*
   She worked a long time. *Trabajó mucho tiempo.*

   a long time before — *desde mucho antes.*
   They had gone to Spain a long time before. *Se habían ido a España desde mucho antes.*

   a short time ago — *hace poco.*
   He entered a short time ago. *Entró hace poco.*

   ahead of time — *con anticipación; con anterioridad; de antemano.*
   It came ahead of time. *Vino con anticipación (con anterioridad, de antemano).*

   any time (now) — *de un momento a otro; de hoy a mañana.*
   It will start any time (now). *Comenzará de un momento a otro (de hoy a mañana).*

   around that time — *por esos días; por esa época.*
   Around that time she got married. *Por eso días (esa época) se casó.*

   at a set time — *a hora fija.*
   We eat at a set time. *Comemos a hora fija.*

   at all times — *en todo tiempo.*
   We were helping them at all times. *Los ayudábamos en todo tiempo.*

   at one time — *en algún tiempo; un tiempo.*
   At one time I had ten. *En algún (Un) tiempo tenía diez.*

   at that time — *en aquel momento (tiempo; entonces).*
   At that time he was sixteen. *En aquel momento (tiempo; entonces) tenía diez y seis años.*

   at the present time — *en la actualidad.*
   At the present time we haven't any. *En la actualidad no tenemos ninguno.*

   at the same time — *a la vez; al mismo tiempo.*

She was laughing and crying at the same time. *(Se) reía y lloraba a la vez (al mismo tiempo).*

at the same time — *al par; a la par*

He was reading and at the same time listening to (the) music. *Leía y al par (a la par) escuchaba la música.*

at the same time — *de paso.*

She went out to buy bread and at the same time got a newspaper. *Salió para comprar pan y de paso compró un periódico.*

at the time — *a la sazón; por la época.*

At the time she was fifty. *A la sazón (Por la época) tenía 50 años.*

at times — *a veces; en ocasiones.*

At times she feels lonesome. *A veces (En ocasiones) se siente sola.*

at times . . . , at (other) times . . . — *ora . . . , ora . . . .*

At times we take wine, at (other) times beer. *Ora tomamos vino, ora cerveza.*

behind the times — *atrasado de noticias.*

As far as political matters are concerned, they are behind the times. *En cuanto a asuntos políticos están atrasados de noticias.*

by that time — *para entonces; para esa época.*

By that time he had retired. *Para entonces (Para esa época) se había jubilado.*

for the time being — *por el momento.*

For the time being, I'm busy. *Por el momento estoy ocupado.*

free time — *horas libres.*

She knits in her free time. *Teje en sus horas libres.*

from time to time — *de vez en cuando; de cuando en cuando.*

We see each other from time to time. *Nos vemos de vez en cuando (de cuando en cuando).*

in due time — *a su tiempo.*

I'll have it in due time. *Lo tendré a su tiempo.*

in no time — *en un abrir y cerrar de ojos.*

He did it in no time. *Lo hizo en un abrir y cerrar de ojos.*

He did it in no time.
Lo hizo en un abrir y cerrar de ojos.

in one's spare time — *a ratos perdidos.*
I read Spanish in my spare time. *Leo el español a ratos perdidos.*

in recent times (years) — *en los últimos tiempos (años).*
In recent times (years) he has gotten fat. *En los últimos tiempos (años) ha engordado.*

It's about time! — *¡A buenas horas! (¡Ya era hora!).*

many is the time — *muchas veces.*
Many is the time that I wanted to go there. *Muchas veces quería ir allí.*

most of the time — *la mayor parte del tiempo.*
It's hot most of the time. *Hace calor la mayor parte del tiempo.*

of that time — *de entonces.*
The kids of that time knew less. *Los chicos de entonces sabían menos.*

on time — *a la hora; a tiempo.*
It started on time. *Empezó a la hora (a tiempo).*

once upon a time there was — *érase una vez.*
Once upon a time there was a wolf. *Erase una vez un lobo.*

several times — *varias veces.*
We worked together several times. *Trabajamos juntos varias veces.*

There is a time for all things. — *Cada cosa a su tiempo.*

253

Time is a great healer. — *El tiempo todo lo cura.*

Time is money. — *El tiempo es oro.*

Time is up. — *Ya es la hora; Ha llegado la hora.*

Time will tell. — *El tiempo lo dirá.*

to be (to arrive) on time — *llegar a tiempo.*
I was (arrived) on time. *Llegué a tiempo.*

to be time to — *ser (la) hora de.*
It's time to go to bed. *Es la hora de acostarse.*

to be time to eat — *ser hora de comer.*
It's about time to eat. *Ya empieza a ser hora de comer.*

to have a good time — *pasarlo bien; divertirse.*
They had a good time. *Lo pasaron bien (Se divirtieron).*

to have a hard time of it — *pasar muchos apuros.*
He had a hard time of it. *Pasó muchos apuros.*

to have a whale of a time — *divertirse como loco.*
We had a whale of a time in Paris. *Nos divertimos como locos en París.*

to have plenty of time — *sobrarle tiempo.*
We have plenty of time. *Nos sobra tiempo.*

to have the time of one's life — *divertirse en grande.*
We went to the party and had the time of our life. *Fuimos a la fiesta y nos divertimos en grande.*

to have time — *darle tiempo.*
I wanted to go but I didn't have time. *Quería ir pero no me dio tiempo.*

to keep good time — *marcar bien la hora; andar bien.*
This watch does not keep good time. *Este reloj no marca bien la hora (no anda bien).*

to keep time — *llevar el compás.*
He keeps time with his foot. *Lleva el compás con el pie.*

to kill time — *matar el (hacer) tiempo; pasar el rato.*
They took a walk to kill time. *Dieron un paseo para matar el (hacer) tiempo (pasar el rato).*

to last a short time — *durar poco tiempo.*
It lasted a short time. *Duró poco tiempo.*

to make good time — *ganar tiempo.*
We made good time on the highway. *Ganamos tiempo por la carretera.*

to make up for lost time — *recuperar el tiempo que se perdió.*
We made up for lost time. *Recuperamos el tiempo que perdimos.*

to pass the time (away) — *pasar el rato (el tiempo).*
They were telling jokes just to pass the time (away). *Contaban chistes para pasar el rato (el tiempo).*

to pass the time of day — *echar un párrafo.*
Every morning she stops by to pass the time of day. *Todas las mañanas pasa para echar un párrafo.*

to spend one's time — *pasar el tiempo.*
He spends his time gambling. *Pasa el tiempo jugando (por dinero).*

to take one's time — *tomar su tiempo.*
He takes his time. *Toma su tiempo.*

to take time — *costar tiempo.*
It takes time. *Cuesta tiempo.*

to take time off — *tomar tiempo libre.*
She took time off. *Tomó tiempo libre.*

to take up someone's time — *quitarle el tiempo.*
She took up our time. *Nos quitó el tiempo.*

to tell time — *decir la hora.*
He doesn't know how to tell time. *No sabe decir la hora.*

to waste time — *perder tiempo.*
He's wasting time. *Está perdiendo tiempo.*

---

tip — *la punta, la propina*
to have at one's finger tips — *saber al dedillo.*
She has it at her finger tips. *Lo sabe al dedillo.*

to have on the tip of one's tongue — *tener en la punta de la lengua.*
I have it on the tip of my tongue. *Lo tengo en la punta de la lengua.*

---

to tip — *dar propina*
to tip over — *volcar.*
The child tipped over the chair. *El niño volcó la silla.*

to tip someone — *darle una propina.*
He tipped her. *Le dio una propina.*

to tip someone off — *informarle bajo cuerda.*
He tipped us off. *Nos informó bajo cuerda.*

---

tiptoe — *la punta del pie*
on tiptoe(s) — *de (en) puntillas.*
She entered on tiptoe(s). *Entró de (en) puntillas.*

---

tit
to give tit for tat — *pagar en la misma moneda.*
He insulted me and I gave him tit for tat. *El me insultó y yo le pagué en la misma moneda.*

---

today — *hoy*
today is the . . . — *estamos a . . . .*
Today's the tenth. *Estamos a diez.*

---

toe — *el dedo del pie*
to be on one's toes — *estar alerta.*
He's always on his toes. *Siempre está alerta.*

to keep on one's toes — *mantener alerto.*
He keeps his students on their toes. *Mantiene alertos a sus alumnos.*

to tread on someone's toes — *ofenderle.*
He changed it without treading on our toes. *Lo cambió sin ofendernos.*

---

together — *juntos*
to be going together — *ser novios.*
They are going together. *Son novios.*

to drink a toast together — *brindar a coro.*
We drank a toast together. *Brindamos a coro.*

to pull oneself together — *calmarse.*
Pull yourself together. *Cálmese.*

token — *la muestra*

  by the same token — *por la misma razón.*

  If we invite Mary, by the same token we must invite Bob. *Si invitamos a María, por la misma razón debemos invitar a Roberto.*

  in token of — *como expresión de; como muestra de.*

  We sent flowers in token of appreciation. *Mandamos flores como expresión (muestra) de gratitud.*

---

tomorrow — *mañana*

  See you tomorrow. — *Hasta mañana.*

---

tone — *el tono*

  in a very sour tone — *hecho un vinagre.*

  He spoke to us in a very sour tone. *Nos habló hecho un vinagre.*

---

tongue — *la lengua*

  native (mother) tongue – *la lengua materna.*

  It's his native (mother) tongue. *Es su lengua materna.*

  to hold one's tongue — *morderse la lengua; callar.*

  He held his tongue. *Se mordió la lengua (Calló).*

  to stick out one's tongue — *sacar la lengua.*

  He sticks out his tongue. *Saca la lengua.*

  to talk with one's tongue in one's cheek — *no hablar en serio.*

  I hope he's talking with his tongue in his cheek. *Ojalá que no hable en serio.*

  tongue twister — *el trabalenguas.*

  It's a tongue twister. *Es un trabalenguas.*

---

tooth — *el diente*

  to fight tooth and nail — *luchar a brazo partido.*

  We fought tooth and nail. *Luchamos a brazo partido.*

  to have a sweet tooth — *ser muy goloso.*

  She has a sweet tooth. *Es muy golosa.*

---

top — *la cumbre*
  at the top of one's voice — *a gritos.*
  I called out at the top of my voice. *Llamé a gritos.*

  from top to bottom — *de arriba abajo.*
  We painted it from top to bottom. *Lo pintamos de arriba abajo.*

  on top of — *encima de.*
  On top of all his troubles, he's ill. *Encima de todas sus penas, está
    enfermo.*

  to be (sitting) on top of the world — *sentirse dueño del mundo.*
  Now that he's won the prize, he's (sitting) on top of the world. *Habiendo
    ganado el premio, se siente dueño del mundo.*

  to be tops — *ser lo mejor.*
  As far as Pepe is concerned, Sylvia's tops. *Para Pepe, Silvia es lo mejor.*

  to blow one's top — *poner el grito en el cielo.*
  I blew my top. *Puse el grito en el cielo.*

---

to top — *coronar*
  to top it off — *rematarlo.*
  We topped it off with a glass of wine. *Lo rematamos con una copa de
    vino.*

  to top someone — *aventajarle.*
  He topped me. *Me aventajó.*

---

torch — *la antorcha*
  to carry the torch for — *estar enamorado de.*
  She is still carrying the torch for him. *Todavía está enamorada de él.*

---

to toss — *arrojar, echar*
  to toss (flip a coin) — *echar a cara o cruz.*
  Let's toss (flip a coin) to see who pays. *Echemos a cara o cruz para ver
    quién paga.*

  to toss about — *dar vueltas.*
  I tossed about all night. *Di vueltas toda la noche.*

---

touch — *el toque*

   to be out of touch — *no comunicarse.*
   We're out of touch. *No nos comunicamos.*

   to get in touch — *ponerse en contacto; comunicarse con.*
   I got in touch with him. *Me puse en contacto (Me comuniqué) con él.*

   to keep in touch — *mantenerse en contacto.*
   He kept in touch with the doctor. *Se mantuvo en contacto con el médico.*

   to lose one's touch — *perder el tiento.*
   She's lost her touch. *Ha perdido el tiento.*

   to put the touch on someone — *darle un sablazo.*
   He put the touch on me. *Me dio un sablazo.*

to touch — *tocar*

   to be touched (in the head) — *estar tocado (de la cabeza).*
   He's a little touched (in the head). *Está un poco tocado (de la cabeza).*

   to touch down — *aterrizar.*
   It touched down at five. *Aterrizó a las cinco.*

   to touch off — *provocar.*
   It touched off World War II. *Provocó la segunda Guerra Mundial.*

   to touch on — *referirse a.*
   He touched on the Peruvian Indians. *Se refirió a los indios peruanos.*

   to touch up — *retocarse.*
   She touched up her face. *Se retocó la cara.*

tow — *el remolque*

   to take in tow — *encargarse de.*
   The father took his son in tow. *El padre se encargó de su hijo.*

   to take in tow — *llevarse a remolque.*
   They took our car in tow. *Se llevaron nuestro coche a remolque.*

towel — *la toalla*

   to throw in the towel — *darse por vencido (abandonar la partida).*
   He finally had to throw in the towel. *Por fin tuvo que darse por vencido
     (abandonar la partida).*

tower — *la torre*
>   **to live in an ivory tower** — *vivir en una torre de marfil.*
>   He lives in an ivory tower. *Vive en una torre de marfil.*

---

town — *el pueblo*
>   **to be the talk of the town** — *dar mucho que hablar (ser la comidilla de la ciudad).*
>   Her divorce is the talk of the town. *Su divorcio da mucho que hablar (es la comidilla de la ciudad).*

>   **to paint the town red** — *ir de juerga (parranda).*
>   They painted the town red. *Fueron de juerga (parranda).*

---

to toy — *jugar*
>   **to toy with the idea** — *acariciar la idea.*
>   He's been toying with the idea all year. *Ha estado acariciando la idea todo el año.*

---

track — *la huella*
>   **off the beaten track** — *fuera del camino trillado.*
>   They travel off the beaten track. *Viajan fuera del camino trillado.*

>   **to be off (the) track** — *andar despistado.*
>   That's not right. You're off (the) track. *No tiene usted razón. Anda usted despistado.*

>   **to be on the right track** — *andar por buen camino.*
>   You're on the right track. *Anda por buen camino.*

>   **to keep track** — *llevar cuenta.*
>   I've kept track of all that I spent. *He llevado cuenta de todo lo que he gastado.*

>   **to keep track** — *preocuparse; estar al corriente.*
>   He keeps track of everything. *Se preocupa (Está al corriente) de todo.*

>   **to lose track of** — *perder de vista.*
>   I've lost track of that family. *He perdido de vista a esa familia.*

>   **to make tracks** — *ir(se) de prisa.*
>   They were really making tracks. *(Se) iban muy de prisa.*

to track — *rastrear*
   to track down — *seguir el rastro.*
   They weren't able to track him down. *No pudieron seguirle el rastro.*

---

trap — *la trampa*
   to fall into the trap — *caer en la trampa (el lazo; la red).*
   I fell into the trap. *Caí en la trampa (el lazo; la red).*

   to lead someone into a trap — *llevarle a la trampa.*
   She led me into a trap. *Me llevó a la trampa.*

---

to tread — *pisar*
   to tread softly — *proceder con prudencia.*
   We trod softly when we first arrived. *Al principio procedimos con prudencia.*

---

treatment — *el tratamiento*
   to give someone the red-carpet treatment — *recibirlo a cuerpo de rey (con todo regalo).*
   They gave him the red-carpet treatment. *Lo recibieron a cuerpo de rey (con todo regalo).*

---

tree — *el árbol*
   to bark up the wrong tree — *ir (andar) descaminado.*
   You're barking up the wrong tree. *Va (Anda) descaminado.*

---

trend — *la dirección*
   It's the trend. — *Es de última hora.*

---

trick — *la maña*
   to be up to one's old trick — *hacer de las suyas.*
   It's evident that he's up to his old tricks. *Se ve que está haciendo de las suyas.*

   to do the trick — *arreglarse.*
   A little soap will do the trick. *Con un poco de jabón se arreglará.*

   to play a dirty trick on someone — *jugarle una mala pasada (mala jugada).*

She played a dirty trick on me. *Me jugó una mala pasada (mala jugada).*

to play a trick on someone — *hacerle una broma.*
She played a trick on me. *Me hizo una broma.*

---

trip — *el viaje*
  to be on a trip — *estar de viaje.*
  They're on a trip. *Están de viaje.*

  to leave (to go) on a trip — *salir de viaje.*
  They're leaving (going) on a trip. *Salen de viaje.*

  to take a trip — *hacer (realizar) un viaje.*
  We took a trip. *Hicimos (Realizamos) un viaje.*

---

trouble — *el apuro*
  That's the trouble. — *Ese es el inconveniente.*

  to be in trouble — *estar en un aprieto.*
  We're in trouble. *Estamos en un aprieto.*

  to cause trouble — *dar guerra.*
  They were always causing trouble. *Siempre daban guerra.*

  to look for trouble — *buscarle tres pies al gato.*
  He goes around looking for trouble. *Le anda buscando tres pies al gato.*

  to put oneself to trouble — *molestarse.*
  Don't put yourself to any trouble. *No se moleste usted.*

to stay out of trouble — *no meterse en líos.*
It's best to stay out of trouble. *Es mejor no meterse en líos.*

to take the trouble to — *tomarse la molestia (el trabajo) de.*
He took the trouble to thank me. *Se tomó la molestia (el trabajo) de darme las gracias.*

What's the trouble? — *¿Qué le pasa?*

---

to trouble — *molestar*
Pardon me for troubling you. — *Perdone la molestia.*

---

true — *verdadero*
It's too good to be true. — *¿Será verdad tanta belleza?*

to be true to one's word — *ser fiel a su palabra.*
He's always true to his word. *Siempre es fiel a su palabra.*

---

truth — *la verdad*
The truth hurts. — *Las verdades amargan.*

to tell the truth — *a decir verdad.*
To tell the truth, I'm not sure. *A decir verdad, no estoy seguro.*

---

to try — *tratar*
to try hard — *hacer todo lo posible.*
He tried hard but couldn't. *Hizo todo lo posible pero no pudo.*

to try on — *probarse.*
He tried on the hat. *Se probó el sombrero.*

to try one's patience — *poner a prueba su paciencia.*
This child tries my patience. *Este chico pone a prueba mi paciencia.*

to try out — *practicar.*
He tried out his Spanish in Mexico. *Practicó su español en México.*

to try out — *probar.*
He's trying out his new bike. *Está probando su nueva bicicleta.*

---

tune — *la melodía*
to be in (out of) tune — *estar (des)afinado.*
The guitar is in (out of) tune. *La guitarra está (des)afinada.*

263

to change one's tune — *cambiar de disco (actitud)*.

He used to talk against the president but now he has changed his tune.
Antes hablaba contra el presidente pero ahora ha cambiado de disco (actitud).

to pay to the tune of — *pagar la friolera de*.

I had to pay to the tune of a hundred dollars. *Tuve que pagar la friolera de cien dólares*.

---

to tune — *afinar*

to tune in — *sintonizar*.

I can't tune in that program. *No puedo sintonizar ese programa*.

---

turn — *la vuelta*

at every turn — *a cada paso*.

At every turn there was a truck. *A cada paso había un camión*.

in turn — *a su vez*.

They all tasted it in turn. *Todos la probaron a su vez*.

One good turn deserves another. — *Bien con bien se paga*.

to be one's turn — *tocarle; corresponderle*.

It's your turn. *Le toca (corresponde) a usted*.

to speak out of turn — *meter su cuchara*.

He spoke out of turn again. *Metió su cuchara otra vez*.

to take a new turn — *tomar nuevo aspecto*.

The news took a new turn. *Las noticias tomaron nuevo aspecto*.

to take a turn for the better (worse) — *mejorarse (empeorarse)*.

He took a turn for the better (worse). *El se mejoró (se empeoró)*.

to take turns (at) — *turnarse*.

We take turns (at) answering the phone. *Nos turnamos para contestar el teléfono*.

---

to turn — *dar vuelta, volverse; doblar*

not to know where to turn (for help) — *no saber a quién dirigirse (por ayuda)*.

He doesn't know where to turn (for help). *No sabe a quién dirigirse (por ayuda)*.

to turn — *dar vueltas a.*
He turned the handle. *Dio vueltas al manubrio.*

to turn around — *dar una vuelta.*
He turned around and saw her. *Dio una vuelta y la vio.*

to turn down — *bajar.*
Turn down the radio. *Baje la radio.*

to turn down — *bajarse.*
Turn down your cuffs. *Bájese los puños.*

to turn down — *rechazar.*
He turned down my request. *Rechazó mi petición.*

to turn half way around — *dar media vuelta.*
He turned half way around. *Dio media vuelta.*

to turn in — *entregar.*
He turned in his equipment. *Entregó su equipo.*

to turn in — *irse a la cama.*
He turned in at ten. *Se fue a la cama a las diez.*

to turn in(to) — *entrar en.*
He turned in(to) our driveway. *Entró en nuestra calzada.*

to turn into — *convertirse en.*
The wine turned into vinegar. *El vino se convirtió en vinagre.*

to turn off — *cerrar.*
Turn off the water. *Cierre la llave del agua.*

to turn off — *doblar.*
He turned off to the left. *Dobló a la izquierda.*

to turn on — *atacar.*
The bear turned on the tourist. *El oso atacó al turista.*

to turn on — *poner.*
Turn on the gas (light). *Ponga el gas (la luz).*

to turn out — *apagar (cerrar).*
They turned out the light. *Apagaron (Cerraron) la luz.*

to turn out — *presentarse.*
All his friends turned out for the wedding. *Todos sus amigos se presentaron para la boda.*

to turn out — *producir.*
The factory turned out ten airplanes in one day. *La fábrica produjo diez aviones en un día.*

to turn out — *resultar.*
It turned out well. *Resultó bien.*

to turn out to be — *salir.*
He turned out to be a Republican. *Salió republicano.*

to turn over (upside down) — *darle vuelta.*
He turned it over (upside down). *Le dio vuelta.*

to turn over — *transferir.*
He turned over his money to his son. *Transfirió su dinero a su hijo.*

to turn over — *volcarse.*
The car turned over. *El coche se volcó.*

to turn over to — *entregar a.*
I turned him over to the principal. *Lo entregué al director.*

to turn pale — *ponerse pálido.*
He turned pale. *Se puso pálido.*

to turn to — *recurrir a.*
He turned to his father for his help. *Recurrió a su padre por su ayuda.*

to turn up — *aparecer.*
They turned up at our house. *Aparecieron en nuestra casa.*

to turn up — *levantarse.*
Turn up your collar. *Levántese el cuello.*

to turn up — *poner más alto.*
Turn up the radio. *Ponga la radio más alto.*

---

twinkling — *el centelleo*
in the twinkling of an eye — *en un abrir y cerrar de ojos; en un santiamén.*
He answered in the twinkling of an eye. *Contestó en un abrir y cerrar de ojos (en un santiamén).*

---

two — *dos*
by twos (two by two) — *de dos en dos; dos a dos.*

They entered by twos (two by two). *Entraron de dos en dos (dos a dos)*.

that makes two of us — *ya somos dos*.

That makes two of us. I arrived late too. *Ya somos dos. Yo también llegué tarde*.

to divide in two (half) — *dividir por la mitad*.

We divided it in two (half). *Lo dividimos por la mitad*.

to put two and two together — *atar cabos*.

By putting two and two together, I understood. *Atando cabos, comprendí*.

U

unaware — *inconsciente*

to be unaware — *ignorar; estar ajeno a*.

I am unaware of the problem. *Ignoro el (Estoy ajeno al) problema*.

to understand — *entender*

to make oneself understood — *hacerse entender*.

She couldn't make herself understood. *No pudo hacerse entender*.

to understand why — *explicarse por qué*.

I can't understand why. *No me explico por qué*.

understanding — *el entendimiento*.

with the understanding that — *con la condición de que*.

We bought the apartment with the understanding that we would share the expenses. *Compramos el apartamento con la condición de que compartiríamos los gastos*.

undertone — *la voz baja*

in an undertone — *por lo bajo*.

He said it in an undertone. *Lo dijo por lo bajo*.

up — *arriba*

Time's up. — *Ya es la hora*.

to be up — *haberse levantado.*
He's not up yet. *Todavía no se ha levantado.*

to be up and about — *haberse restablecido.*
She had the flu last week, but she's up and about now. *Estaba con la gripe la semana pasada, pero ya se ha restablecido.*

to be up and about — *estar levantado.*
At five in the morning, she was already up and about. *A las cinco de la mañana ya estaba levantada.*

to be up on — *conocer bien.*
He's up on physics. *Conoce bien la física.*

to be up on — *estar al corriente de.*
He's up on world news. *Está al corriente de las noticias mundiales.*

to be up to — *sentirse capaz de.*
I'm not up to working today. *No me siento capaz de trabajar hoy.*

to be up to one — *depender de (tocarle a) uno.*
It's up to you. *Depende de (Le toca a) usted.*

to go up — *subir.*
He went up the stairs. *Subió la escalera.*

to keep up — *continuar.*
He couldn't keep up. *No pudo continuar.*

to keep up with — *correr parejas con.*
He couldn't keep up with his class. *No pudo correr parejas con su clase.*

to look up and down — *mirar de arriba abajo.*
We looked up and down. *Miramos de arriba abajo.*

to move upstream (downstream) — *ir aguas arriba (abajo).*
It was moving upstream (downstream). *Iba aguas arriba (abajo).*

up there — *allá arriba.*
It's up there. *Está allá arriba.*

up to now — *hasta ahora; hasta la fecha.*
Up to now, I don't know. *Hasta ahora (la fecha) no sé.*

What are you up to? — *¿Qué está haciendo?*

What's up? — *¿Qué pasa?*

use — *el uso*
  it's no use — *es inútil.*
  It's no use trying to solve it, *Es inútil tratar de resolverlo.*

  to be of no use — *no servir de (para) nada.*
  It's of no use to us. *No nos sirve de (para) nada.*

  to have no use for — *no gustarle.*
  I have no use for that girl. *Esa chica no me gusta.*

  to make use of — *servirse de.*
  He made use of them. *Se sirvió de ellos.*

  what's the use of — *para (a) qué.*
  What's the use of crying? *¿Para (A) qué llorar?*

used — *usado*
  to get used to — *acostumbrarse a.*
  We get used to working hard. *Nos acostumbramos a trabajar mucho.*

usual — *usual*
  as usual — *como de costumbre.*
  She arrived late, as usual. *Llegó tarde, como de costumbre.*

utmost — *el más alto grado*
  to do one's utmost — *desvivirse; hacer todo lo posible.*
  She did her utmost to find us. *Se desvivió (Hizo todo lo posible) por encontrarnos.*

  to the utmost — *hasta más no poder.*
  We must defend our liberty to the utmost. *Tenemos que guardar nuestra libertad hasta más no poder.*

V

vacation — *las vacaciones*
  to be on vacation — *estar de vacaciones.*
  He's on vacation. *Está de vacaciones.*

vain — *vano*
  in vain — *en vano; en balde.*
  They tried in vain. *Se esforzaron en vano (en balde).*

variety — *la variedad*
  Variety is the spice of life. — *En la variedad está el gusto.*

vengeance — *la venganza*
  with a vengeance — *con todas sus fuerzas.*
  He studied with a vengeance. *Estudió con todas sus fuerzas.*

to venture — *aventurarse*
  Nothing ventured, nothing gained. — *El que no se arriesga no pasa la mar.*

verge — *el borde*
  to be on the verge of — *estar a punto (al borde) de.*
  They're on the verge of reaching an agreement. *Están a punto (al borde) de ponerse de acuerdo.*

very — *muy*
  not very — *poco.*
  It was not very interesting. *Fue poco interesante.*

  the very one — *precisamente.*
  He's the very one I'm looking for. *Es precisamente él a quien busco.*

view — *la vista*
  in view of this — *en vista de esto.*
  In view of this, you can't go. *En vista de esto no puede ir.*

  to be on view — *estar en exhibición.*
  The painting is on view. *La pintura está en exhibición.*

  to be on view — *estar expuesto.*
  The body will be on view. *El cadáver estará expuesto.*

  to take a dim view of — *parecerle mal; no entusiasmarse de.*
  He took a dim view of our missing class. *Le pareció mal (No se entusiasmó de) que faltáramos a la clase.*

with a view to — *con miras a; con el propósito de.*
He signed it with a view to earning more money. *Lo firmó con miras a (con el propósito de) ganar más dinero.*

virtue — *la virtud*
  by virtue of — *en virtud de.*
  He presented it by virtue of his authority. *Lo presentó en virtud de su autoridad.*

vision — *la visión*
  to have visions of — *imaginar.*
  I had visions of being late. *Me imaginaba llegando tarde.*

visit — *la visita*
  to pay someone a visit — *hacerle una visita.*
  We paid them a visit. *Les hicimos una visita.*

voice — *la voz*
  at the top of one's voice — *a voz en cuello.*
  He was yelling at the top of his voice. *Gritaba a voz en cuello.*

  in a low (loud) voice — *en voz baja (alta).*
  She spoke in a low (loud) voice. *Habló en voz baja (alta).*

  in a muffled voice — *con voz sorda.*
  She said it in a muffled voice. *Lo dijo con voz sorda.*

  to lower one's voice — *apagar la voz.*
  She lowered her voice. *Apagó la voz.*

  to raise one's voice — *alzar la voz.*
  He raised his voice. *Alzó la voz.*

to vote — *votar*
  to vote in — *elegir por votación.*
  He was voted in. *Fue elegido por votación.*

voyage — *el viaje*
  maiden voyage — *la primera travesía; el viaje inaugural.*

271

It was the ship's maiden voyage. *Fue la primera travesía (el viaje inaugural) del barco.*

W

wait — *espera*

  to have a long wait — *tener que esperar mucho.*
  We had a long wait. *Tuvimos que esperar mucho.*

  to lie in wait — *estar al (en) acecho.*
  He's lying in wait. *Está al (en) acecho.*

---

to wait — *esperar*

  not to be able to wait — *arder en deseos de.*
  I have not seen Mary in five years, and I can't wait until she arrives!
    ¡Hace cinco años que no he visto a María, y ardo en deseos de que llegue!

  to be waiting for — *estar pendiente de.*
  I'm waiting for your orders. *Estoy pendiente de sus órdenes.*

  to wait for — *esperar.*
  He's waiting for us. *Nos espera.*

  to wait on — *servir.*
  She waited on us. *Nos sirvió.*

  to wait up for — *desvelarse esperando a.*
  He waited up for his children. *Se desveló esperando a sus hijos.*

  wait and see — *ya lo veremos.*
  His attitude is "wait and see." *Su actitud es "ya lo veremos."*

---

wake — *la estela*

  in the wake of — *a consecuencia de.*
  They abandoned their home in the wake of the flood. *A consecuencia de la inundación abandonaron su casa.*

---

to wake — *despertar*
  to wake up — *despertarse.*
  She woke up at six. *Se despertó a las seis.*

---

walk — *el paseo*
  all walks of life — *todas las clases sociales.*
  They come from all walks of life. *Son de todas las clases sociales.*

  to take a walk — *dar un paseo (una vuelta).*
  He likes to take a walk. *Le gusta dar un paseo (una vuelta).*

---

to walk — *caminar*
  to walk (to stroll) around — *dar vueltas (pasearse) por.*
  I walked (strolled) around the garden. *Di vueltas (Me paseé) por el jardín.*

  to walk around the block — *dar (la) vuelta a la manzana.*
  He walked around the block. *Dio (la) vuelta a la manzana.*

  to walk back — *volver a pie.*
  We walked back. *Volvimos a pie.*

  to walk off with — *llevarse; robar.*
  He walked off with our typewriter. *Se llevó (Robó) nuestra máquina de escribir.*

  to walk out — *abandonar el trabajo.*
  The employees walked out when the boss insulted them. *Los empleados abandonaron el trabajo cuando el jefe los insultó.*

  to walk up (down) — *subir (bajar) andando (a pie).*
  She walked up (down). *Subió (Bajó) andando (a pie).*

  to walk up and down — *pasearse de arriba abajo.*
  They were walking up and down. *Se paseaban de arriba abajo.*

---

wall — *la pared*
  to have one's back to the wall — *estar entre la espada y la pared.*
  We have our backs to the wall. *Estamos entre la espada y la pared.*

  Walls have ears. — *Las paredes oyen.*

---

to wall — *murar*
  to be walled in — *estar encerrado (con muro).*
  We were walled in. *Estábamos encerrados (con muro).*

---

war — *la guerra*
  to go to war — *ir a la guerra.*
  He went to war. *Fue a la guerra.*

  to wage war — *hacer (la) guerra.*
  He waged war. *Hizo (la) guerra.*

---

warm — *caliente*
  It's warm. — *Hace calor.*

  to be warm — *tener calor.*
  I'm warm. *Tengo calor.*

  to send warm greetings (regards) — *mandar saludos cariñosos.*
  We all send warm greetings (regards). *Todos mandamos saludos cariñosos.*

---

to warm — *calentar*
  to warm up — *calentar.*
  They warmed up the meat. *Calentaron la carne.*

  to warm (oneself) up — *calentarse.*
  Let's warm up near the fire before we leave. *Calentémonos cerca del fuego antes de salir.*

  to warm up — *templar.*
  It (the weather) warmed up. *El tiempo templó.*

  to warm up to — *entrar en confianza con.*
  The lost cat soon warmed up to us. *El gato perdido pronto entró en confianza con nosotros.*

---

waste — *el derroche, el despilfarro*
  to go to waste — *malgastarse; desperdiciarse.*
  It would be a shame for all that money to go to waste. *Sería una lástima que se malgastara (se desperdiciara) todo ese dinero.*

watch — *la guardia, la vigilancia; el reloj*
  to be on the watch for — *estar a la mira de.*
  Be on the watch for my dog. *Esté a la mira de mi perro.*

  to keep (to stand) watch — *hacer la (estar de) guardia.*
  He kept (stood) watch all night. *Hizo la (Estuvo de) guardia toda la noche.*

  to wind up a watch — *dar cuerda a un reloj.*
  I wound up my watch. *Di cuerda a mi reloj.*

to watch — *mirar*
  to watch out for — *tener cuidado con.*
  Watch out for the train. *Tenga cuidado con el tren.*

  to watch over — *guardar.*
  The dog watched over his master. *El perro guardó a su amo.*

water — *el agua*
  not to hold water — *caerse por su base.*
  That explanation doesn't hold water. *Esa explicación se cae por su base.*

  Still waters run deep. — *Del agua mansa me libre Dios, que de la brava me libro yo.*

  That's water under the bridge now. — *Lo hecho hecho está.*

  to be in hot water — *estar en un aprieto.*
  He's in hot water. *Está en un aprieto.*

  to fish in troubled waters — *pescar en agua turbia (revuelta).*
  They are fishing in troubled waters. *Pescan en agua turbia (revuelta).*

  to throw cold water on — *echar una jarra de agua fría a.*
  He threw cold water on our plans. *Echó una jarra de agua fría a nuestros planes.*

  to tread water — *pedalear en el agua.*
  He's treading water. *Está pedaleando en el agua.*

to water — *regar*
  for one's mouth to water — *hacérsele agua la boca.*
  My mouth waters. *Se me hace agua la boca.*

275

to make one's eyes water — *hacerle llorar.*
It made my eyes water. *Me hizo llorar.*

---

way — *la manera, el modo; el camino*

any way one likes — *como quiera.*
I'll make them any way you like. *Los haré como usted quiera.*

by the way — *a propósito (entre paréntesis).*
By the way, do you have it? *A propósito (Entre paréntesis), ¿lo tiene?*

by way of — *a guisa de.*
By way of explanation, he read the letter to us. *A guisa de explicación,
nos leyó la carta.*

by way of — *pasando por.*
We came by way of Chicago. *Vinimos pasando por Chicago.*

either way — *en uno u otro caso.*
Either way, I'll manage. *En uno u otro caso, me las arreglaré.*

halfway through — *a mitad de.*
They got up from the table halfway through the meal. *Se levantaron de la
mesa a mitad de la comida.*

in a big way — *en grande.*
She always celebrates her birthday in a big way. *Siempre celebra su
cumpleaños en grande.*

in a way — *en cierto modo; hasta cierto punto.*
In a way, it will be difficult. *En cierto modo (Hasta cierto punto) será
difícil.*

in one's way — *a su manera.*
In his way he tries to help. *A su manera, trata de ayudar.*

in such a way — *de tal modo.*
She said it in such a way that I didn't understand. *Lo dijo de tal modo que
no comprendí.*

in the same way — *en la misma forma; de la misma manera.*
He does it in the same way. *Lo hace en la misma forma (de la misma
manera).*

in the way of — *en.*
What do you have in the way of a piano? *¿Qué tiene en pianos?*

It's all in the way you say it. — *Todo depende de cómo se dice (diga).*

on the way — *de camino.*
On the way, buy some milk. *De camino, compre leche.*

on the way — *por el camino.*
I saw him on the way. *Lo vi por el camino.*

one way or another — *de algún modo.*
We'll do it one way or another. *Lo haremos de algún modo.*

way of life — *manera (estilo) de vivir.*
He doesn't like our way of life. *No le gusta nuestra manera (nuestro estilo) de vivir.*

the hard way — *el modo más difícil.*
He does it the hard way. *Lo hace del modo más difícil.*

the other way (a)round (just the opposite) — *al revés; al contrario.*
It's the other way (a)round (just the opposite). *Es al revés (al contrario).*

the way in — *la entrada.*
We couldn't find the way in. *No pudimos encontrar la entrada.*

the way out — *la salida.*
Here's the way out. *Aquí está la salida.*

There are no two ways about it. *No hay que darle vueltas.*

this way — *de este modo; de esta manera.*
This way we'll pay less. *De este modo (De esta manera) pagaremos menos.*

this way — *por acá (aquí).*
This way, please. *Por acá (aquí), por favor.*

to be in the way — *estorbar; estar de sobra.*
He's always in the way. *Siempre estorba (está de sobra).*

to be on one's way — *marcharse, irse.*
We ought to be on our way if we want to arrive by ten. *Debemos marcharnos (irnos) si queremos llegar para las diez.*

to block the way — *cerrar el paso.*
It blocked our way. *Nos cerró el paso.*

to find its way to — *ir a parar a.*

Very little food finds its way to the houses of the poor. *Muy poco de la comida va a parar a las casas de los pobres.*

to force (to make) one's way through — *abrir paso.*
They forced (made) their way through. *Abrieron paso.*

to get one's way — *salir(se) con la suya.*
He always gets his way. *Siempre (se) sale con la suya.*

to get out of the way — *quitarse de en medio.*
Get out of the way! *¡Quítese de en medio!*

to get that way — *ponerse así.*
He gets that way often. *Se pone así a menudo.*

to get under way — *ponerse en marcha.*
We got under way late. *Nos pusimos en marcha tarde.*

to give way — *ceder.*
The dam gave way. *La presa cedió.*

to go a long way — *alcanzar para mucho.*
You can go a long way with what you have if you're careful. *Si tiene cuidado, lo que tiene alcanzará para mucho.*

to go a long way — *hacer muchos esfuerzos.*
He goes a long way to help his students. *Hace muchos esfuerzos para ayudar a sus alumnos.*

to go out of one's way — *desvivirse.*
They went out of their way to help us. *Se desvivieron por ayudarnos.*

to have a (nice) way with people — *saber manejar a la gente.*
She has a (nice) way with people. *Sabe manejar a la gente.*

to have come a long way — *haber adelantado mucho.*
Building has come a long way in Mexico City. *La construcción ha adelantado mucho en México.*

to look the other way — *hacer la vista gorda.*
I looked the other way. *Hice la vista gorda.*

to one's way of thinking — *a su modo de ver.*
To my way of thinking, it's a bargain. *A mi modo de ver es una ganga.*

to pave the way for — *abrirle el camino a.*
We paved the way for the new boss. *Le abrimos el camino al nuevo jefe.*

to return to one's old ways — *volver a las andadas.*
He returned to his old ways. *Volvió a las andadas.*

to rub one the wrong way — *irritarle.*
He rubs me the wrong way. *Me irrita.*

to work one's way up — *progresar.*
He has worked his way up until he became manager. *Ha progresado en su
  trabajo hasta hacerse gerente.*

way off — *muy lejos.*
They live way off at the edge of town. *Viven muy lejos, en las afueras de
  la ciudad.*

way off — *muy equivocado.*
His calculations are way off. *Sus cálculos son muy equivocados.*

---

weakness — *la debilidad*
  to have a weakness for — *tener debilidad por.*
  He has a weakness for new ideas. *Tiene debilidad por ideas nuevas.*

---

wear — *el uso*
  wear and tear — *desgaste (por el uso).*
  There was a lot of wear and tear on the car. *Hubo mucho desgaste (por el
    uso) del coche.*

---

to wear — *usar, llevar*
  to be worn out — *estar agotado.*
  I'm worn out. *Estoy agotado.*

  to be worn out — *estar gastado.*
  The motor is worn out. *Este motor está gastado.*

  to wear off — *pasar.*
  Your headache will wear off. *Su dolor de cabeza pasará.*

  to wear one out — *agotarle.*
  Pushing the car wore me out. *Me agotó empujar el coche.*

  to wear well — *durar mucho.*
  This material wears well. *Este género dura mucho.*

---

weather — *el tiempo*
  for the weather to be good (bad) — *hacer buen (mal) tiempo.*
  The weather is good (bad). *Hace buen (mal) tiempo.*

  to be under the weather — *estar indispuesto; no sentirse bien.*
  He's under the weather today. *Está indispuesto (No se siente bien) hoy.*

  weather permitting — *si el tiempo lo permite.*
  Weather permitting, we'll walk. *Si el tiempo lo permite, iremos a pie.*

---

weight — *el peso*
  to lose weight — *rebajar de peso.*
  She's lost weight. *Ha rebajado de peso.*

  to put on weight — *ponerse gordo; engordar.*
  He's putting on weight. *Se está poniendo gordo (Está engordando).*

---

welcome — *la bienvenida*
  to be welcome to — *estar a su disposición.*
  You are welcome to stay at our house. *Nuestra casa está a su disposición.*

  Welcome! — *¡Bienvenido!*

  You are welcome. — *De nada; No hay de qué.*

---

well — *bien*
  as well as — *así como (tanto . . . como . . .).*
  The cat as well as the dog sleeps in the house. *El gato así como el perro (Tanto el gato como el perro) duerme en la casa.*

  to be well off — *ser rico.*
  He's well off. *Es rico.*

  to know only too well — *saber de sobra.*
  I know it only too well. *Lo sé de sobra.*

  to think well of — *tener buena impresión de.*
  He thinks well of them. *Tiene buena impresión de ellos.*

  Well now! — *¡Vaya!*

  well then — *pues bien.*
  Well then! How goes it? *¡Pues bien! ¿Cómo le va?*

---

wet — *mojado*
  to be soaking wet — *estar hecho una sopa.*
  He's soaking wet. *Está hecho una sopa.*

whale — *la ballena*
  to be a whale of a . . . — *ser un as de . . . .*
  He's a whale of a baseball player. *Es un as de béisbol.*

  to be a whale of a . . . — *ser un . . . tremendo.*
  It was a whale of a party. *Fue una fiesta tremenda.*

what — *qué*
  So what? — *¿Qué más da?*

  to know what is what — *saber cuántas son cinco.*
  She knows what is what. *Sabe cuántas son cinco.*

  what a . . . — *qué . . .*
  What a class! *¡Qué clase!*

  what about — *qué hay de.*
  What about that house you were going to build? *¿Qué hay de la casa que iba a construir?*

  what about — *qué le parece si.*
  What about helping me? *¿Qué le parece si me ayuda?*

  What can I do for you? — *¿Qué se le ofrece?*

  What for? — *¿Para qué?*

  What will you have (to drink)? — *¿Qué va a tomar?*

  What's it all about? — *¿De qué se trata?*

  what's it to . . . ? — *¿Qué le importa a . . . ?*
  If I like to live in the country, what's it to you? *Si a mí me gusta vivir en el campo, ¿qué te importa a ti?*

  What's new? — *¿Qué hay de nuevo?*

  What's up? — *¿Qué sucede (ocurre; pasa)?*

whatever — *lo que*
  whatever it may be — *sea lo que sea.*
  Whatever it may be, I can't believe it. *Sea lo que sea, no lo puedo creer.*

wheel — *la rueda*
  to be a big wheel — *ser un pez gordo.*
  He's a big wheel. *Es un pez gordo.*

wherewithal — *con el cual*
  to have the wherewithal — *tener con qué.*
  He has the wherewithal to travel all over. *Tiene con qué viajar por todas
    partes.*

while — *el rato*
  a (little) while ago — *hace un rato.*
  I saw her a (little) while ago. *La vi hace un rato.*

  a while back — *hace un rato.*
  I would have gone a while back, but not now. *Habría ido hace un rato,
    pero ahora no.*

  after a (little) while — *al cabo de un rato.*
  After a (little) while it began. *Al cabo de un rato empezó.*

  every little while — *cada poco; a cada rato.*
  Every little while the sun came out. *Cada poco (A cada rato) salía el sol.*

  in a little while — *dentro de poco.*
  We'll arrive in a little while. *Llegaremos dentro de poco.*

whisper — *el cuchicheo*
  to speak in a whisper — *hablar a media voz.*
  They're speaking in a whisper. *Están hablando a media voz.*

  to speak in whispers — *hablar en susurros.*
  They're speaking in whispers. *Hablan en susurros.*

whistle — *el silbato*
  to wet one's whistle — *echarse un trago.*
  They stopped by the bar to wet their whistle. *Pasaron por el bar para
    echarse un trago.*

to whiz — *moverse rápidamente*
  to whiz by — *pasar como una flecha.*

I saw her whiz by in her convertible. *La vi pasar como una flecha en su convertible.*

They whizzed by.
Pasaron como una flecha.

---

who — *quién; quien*
  Who cares? — *¿Qué más da?*

---

whole — *entero*
  on the whole — *en general.*
  On the whole, he's cooperative. *En general es cooperativo.*

---

why — *por qué*
  that's why — *por eso.*
  That's why she's crying. *Por eso está llorando.*

  why — *pero si.*
  Why, I always greet you! *¡Pero si siempre lo saludo!*

---

wig — *la peluca*
  to be a big wig — *ser un pez gordo.*
  He's a big wig. *Es un pez gordo.*

---

wildfire — *el fuego griego*
  to spread like wildfire — *correr como pólvora en reguera.*
  The news spread like wildfire. *La noticia corrió como pólvora en reguera.*

---

will — *la voluntad*
  against one's will — *a la fuerza; de mala voluntad.*
  He came against his will. *Vino a la fuerza (de mala voluntad).*

at will — *a voluntad.*
They fired at will. *Dispararon a voluntad.*

Where there's a will there's a way. — *Querer es poder.*

***

to win — *ganar*
  to win out over — *poder más que.*
  Love won out over hate. *El amor pudo más que el odio.*

wind — *el viento*
  There's something in the wind. — *Algo está pendiente; Se está tramando algo.*

  to fly into the wind — *volar contra el viento.*
  They flew into the wind. *Volaron contra el viento.*

  to get wind of — *enterarse de.*
  I got wind of their arrival. *Me enteré de su llegada.*

  to take the wind out of one's sails — *desanimarle.*
  It took the wind out of my sails. *Me desanimó.*

***

to wind — *enrollar*
  to wind up — *acabar.*
  He wound up in court. *Acabó en el tribunal.*

  to wind up — *cerrar.*
  We are winding up our school year. *Estamos cerrando nuestro año académico.*

***

windmill — *el molino de viento*
  to tilt at windmills — *luchar con los molinos de viento.*
  He tilts at windmills. *Lucha con los molinos de viento.*

***

window — *la ventana*
  to go window shopping — *mirar los escaparates.*
  She likes to go window shopping. *Le gusta mirar los escaparates.*

***

wing — *el ala (f.)*
  to clip someone's wings — *cortarle las alas.*
  They clipped his wings. *Le cortaron las alas.*

to take under one's wing — *tomar bajo su protección.*
His professor took him under his wing. *Su profesor lo tomó bajo su protección.*

wink — *el guiño*
  as quick as a wink — *en menos que canta un gallo.*
  He grabbed it as quick as a wink. *Lo agarró en menos que canta un gallo.*

  not to sleep a wink — *no pegar (un) ojo.*
  She didn't sleep a wink. *No pegó (un) ojo.*

  to take forty winks — *echar una siesta.*
  He took forty winks before leaving. *Echó una siesta antes de salir.*

to wipe — *secar*
  to wipe out — *destruir.*
  The bombs wiped out the town. *Las bombas destruyeron el pueblo.*

wise — *sabio*
  to be wise to — *conocerle el juego.*
  Be careful. She's wise to you. *Ten cuidado. Te conoce el juego.*

wish — *el deseo*
  Your wish is my command. — *Sus deseos son órdenes para mí.*

to wish — *desear*
  I wish I could. — *ojalá; me gustaría.*

  to wish it off on someone else — *endosárselo.*
  She wished it off on me. *Me lo endosó.*

wit — *el ingenio*
  to be at one's wit's end — *no saber qué hacer.*
  He's at his wit's end. *No sabe qué hacer.*

  to be out of one's wits — *haber perdido el juicio.*
  He's out of his wits. *Ha perdido el juicio.*

  to keep one's wits about one — *conservar su presencia de ánimo.*
  He kept his wits about him. *Conservó su presencia de ánimo.*

  to live by one's wits — *vivir de gorra.*
  He lives by his wits. *Vive de gorra.*

with — *con*
> **to be with it** — *estar al día.*
> He's always with it. *Siempre está al día.*

wolf — *el lobo*
> **to cry wolf** — *dar una falsa alarma.*
> They cried wolf. *Dieron una falsa alarma.*
>
> **to keep the wolf from the door** — *defenderse de la pobreza.*
> They were barely able to keep the wolf from the door. *Apenas pudieron defenderse de la pobreza.*

wonder — *la maravilla*
> **no wonder** — *no es de extrañar; no es extraño.*
> No wonder he's ill. *No es de extrañar (No es extraño) que esté enfermo.*

woods — *el bosque*
> **to be out of the woods** — *estar fuera de peligro.*
> The doctor says that he's out of the woods. *El médico dice que está fuera de peligro.*

wool — *la lana*
> **to pull the wool over one's eyes** — *engañarlo como a un chino.*
> They pulled the wool over his eyes. *Lo engañaron como a un chino.*

word — *la palabra*
> **beyond words** — *indecible.*
> I was grieved beyond words. *Mi pena fue indecible.*
>
> **by word of mouth** — *de palabra.*
> We were informed by word of mouth. *Nos informaron de palabra.*
>
> **for words to fail one** — *quedarse sin palabras.*
> Words fail me. *Me quedo sin palabras.*
>
> **from the word go** — *de pies a cabeza.*
> He's an actor from the word go. *Es un actor de pies a cabeza.*
>
> **in other words** — *en otras palabras.*
> In other words, we need more. *En otras palabras, nos hacen falta más.*
>
> **in so many words** — *sin rodeos.*

He told me in so many words that he considered me an idiot. *Me dijo sin rodeos que me consideraba como un idiota.*

not to utter a word — *no despegar los labios.*
He never utters a word. *Nunca despega los labios*

not to mince words — *hablar sin rodeos (sin morderse la lengua).*
He was the only one who didn't mince words. *Fue el único que habló sin rodeos (sin morderse la lengua).*

to eat one's words — *tragarse las palabras.*
We made him eat his words. *Lo hicimos tragarse las palabras.*

to get a word in edgewise — *meter baza.*
They don't let him get a word in edgewise. *No lo dejan meter baza.*

to have a word with — *hablar dos palabras con.*
He'd like to have a word with us. *Quisiera hablar dos palabras con nosotros.*

to keep one's word — *cumplir con su palabra.*
He keeps his word. *Cumple con su palabra.*

to leave word — *dejar recado (dicho).*
He left word that he couldn't come. *Dejó recado (dicho) que no podía venir.*

to mark someone's words — *advertir lo que se le dice.*
Mark my words. *Advierta lo que le digo.*

to put in a good word for — *interceder por.*
I put in a good word for her. *Yo intercedí por ella.*

to put into words — *encontrar palabras.*
I can't put into words my gratitude. *No puedo encontrar palabras para expresar mi gratitud.*

to put words in someone's mouth — *atribuirle algo que no dijo.*
You're putting words in my mouth. *Me está atribuyendo algo que no he dicho.*

to say (give) the word — *avisar, dar permiso.*
We were waiting for him to give the word. *Esperábamos a que nos avisara (diera permiso).*

to send word — *mandar recado.*
He sent word that I was to come. *Mandó recado que debía venir.*

287

to take someone at his word — *tomar en serio lo que dice.*
She took me at my word. *Tomó en serio lo que dije.*

to take someone's word for it — *creerle.*
He wouldn't take my word for it. *No quiso creerme.*

to take the words right out of one's mouth — *quitarle las palabras de la boca.*
He took the words right out of my mouth. *Me quitó las palabras de la boca.*

word for word — *palabra por palabra.*
He recited it to me word for word. *Me lo recitó palabra por palabra.*

---

to work — *trabajar*

to get all worked up — *excitarle.*
We got all worked up over the idea. *La idea nos excitó.*

to work one's way — *abrirse paso.*
We worked our way into the house. *Nos abrimos paso hasta la casa.*

to work one's way through college — *trabajar para costear sus estudios universitarios.*
He's working his way through college. *Está trabajando para costear sus estudios universitarios.*

to work out — *preparar; planear.*
We worked out the details. *Preparamos (Planeamos) los detalles.*

to work out — *resolver.*
We worked out the problem. *Resolvimos el problema.*

to work out — *ejercitarse (entrenarse).*
She works out in the gym every day. *Se ejercita (Se entrena) en el gimnasio todos los días.*

to work out well — *salir (resultar) bien.*
It worked out well. *Salió (Resultó) bien.*

to work up — *preparar.*
He's working up a lecture for tomorrow. *Está preparando una conferencia para mañana.*

---

world — *el mundo*

   to set the world on fire — *hacerse famoso.*
   He'll never set the world on fire. *Nunca se hará famoso.*

   not for (anything in) the world — *por nada del mundo.*
   I wouldn't accept it for (anything in) the world. *No lo aceptaría por nada del mundo.*

   to be a man of the world — *ser un hombre de mundo.*
   He's a man of the world. *Es un hombre de mundo.*

   to be out of this world — *ser algo de sueño.*
   Her cooking is out of this world. *Su cocina es algo de sueño.*

   to come down in the world — *venir a menos.*
   The family came down in the world. *La familia vino a menos.*

to worry — *preocupar*

   to worry about — *preocuparse por.*
   Don't worry about me. *No te preocupes por mí.*

worse — *peor*

   to get worse and worse — *ir de mal en peor.*
   He's getting worse and worse. *Va de mal en peor.*

worst — *el peor*

   if worst comes to worst — *en el peor de los casos.*
   If worst comes to worst, we'll buy another one. *En el peor de los casos, compraremos otro.*

worth — *el valor*

   for all one is worth — *a (hasta) más no poder; con todas sus fuerzas.*
   They're playing for all they're worth. *Están jugando a (hasta) más no poder (con todas sus fuerzas).*

   Take it for what it is worth. — *Lléveselo por el valor que pueda tener.*

   to be worthwhile — *valer (merecer) la pena.*
   It's worthwhile. *Vale (Merece) la pena.*

   to get one's money worth — *sacar el valor de lo que pagó.*

We didn't get our money's worth. *No sacamos el valor de lo que pagamos.*

---

wreck — *la ruina*

  to be a nervous wreck — *ser un manojo (saco) de nervios.*
  She's a nervous wreck. *Es un manojo (saco) de nervios.*

writing — *la escritura*

  in writing — *por escrito.*
  He complained in writing. *Se quejó por escrito.*

  to commit to writing — *poner por escrito.*
  He committed it to writing. *Lo puso por escrito.*

---

wrong — *equivocado*

  to be in the wrong — *ser (el) culpable.*
  He was in the wrong. *Era (el) culpable.*

  to go wrong — *salir mal.*
  Things went wrong. *Las cosas salieron mal.*

  to take the wrong . . . — *equivocarse de. . . .*
  I took the wrong street. *Me equivoqué de calle.*

---

year — *el año*

  all year round — *todo el año.*
  They live here all year round. *Viven aquí todo el año.*

  in recent years — *en estos últimos años.*
  In recent years it has rained a lot. *En estos últimos años ha llovido mucho.*

  to be well along in years — *estar muy entrado (metido) en años.*
  He's well along in years. *Está muy entrado (metido) en años.*

Guía de Pronunciación del Inglés

Letra o Combinación de Letras	Pronunciación Aproximada	Ejemplo en Inglés	Equivalente en Español
a	a	bat	papa
a	e	any	pero
a	ei	may	seis
au	o	nautical	nombrar
aw	o	saw	no
e	e	get	mete
ea	i	seal	risa
ee	i	feet	sin
i	i	hit	niño
i	ai	site	hay
o	o	sonic	sonido
o	a	come	cama
o	ou	bone	bondad
oa	ou	boat	botar
oo	u	boot	común
ou	u	youth	yuca
ow	ou	know	(inexistente)
u	u	rule	mula
u	uh	but	(inexistente)
u	yu	cute	yunque
ur	er	curtain	mercurio
uy	ai	buy	naipe
b	b	bold	baño
c	k	car	casa
c	c	city	cinta
ch	ch	change	chino
d	d	doll	dato
f	f	fine	fino
g	g	goat	gordo
g	j	germ	gime
h	j	hard	jardín
h	(muda)	hour	hora
j	j	jam	como la "y" de reyes
k	k	keep	kilo
l	l	lost	lino
m	m	mix	mala
n	n	no	no
ny	ñ	canyon	cañón

Letra o Combinación de Letras	Pronunciación Aproximada	Ejemplo en Inglés	Equivalente en Español
p	p	pit	pala
q	ku	quick	quántum
r	r	rest	marca
s	s	sea	sol
sh	ch	show	(inexistente)
t	t	mat	tiene
th	s	third	como la "d" de to*d*o
v	v	volt	aviso
w	u + vocal	West	(inexistente)
x	x	ax	experto
y	y	yes	yeso
z	z	zebra	zapato

Spanish Pronunciation Guide

Letter	Approximate Pronunciation	English Equivalent
VOWELS		
a	*ah*	father
e	*eh*	net
i (and **y** meaning "and")	*ee*	machine
o	*oh*	note
u	*oo*	flute
DIPHTHONGS		
ai, ay	*I*	by
au	*ow*	cow
ei, ey	*ay*	day
eu	*eh-oo*	net
i (followed by another vowel)	*y*	yet
oi, oy	*oy*	boy
CONSONANTS		
b, f, k, l, m, n, p, s, t, v, x, y	same as English	
ce, ci	*seh, see*	cent (Hispanic America)
	th	thin (Spain)
ca, co, cu	*kah, koh, koo*	cat
ch	*ch*	chin
d	*th*	them
ge, gi	*heh, hee*	heat
gue, gui	*u* is silent	
güe, güi	*gweh, gwee*	Gwen
h	always silent	
j	*h*	hat
ll	*y*	yet
ñ (a separate letter of the alphabet in Spanish)	*ny*	canyon
que, qui	*k* (*u* is silent)	kite
r	*r* (rolled or trilled)	roll
z	*s*	say (Hispanic America)
	th	thin (Spain)

293

Abreviaturas — Inglés-Español

Abreviatura	Significado	Equivalente en Español	Abreviatura en Español

A

A.B.	Bachelor of Arts	Bachiller en Artes	
a.c.	alternating current	corriente alterna	c.a.
A.D.	Anno Domini	Después de Cristo	D. de C.
ADC	aide-de-camp	ayudante de campo; edecán	
ad lib	at will; without restraint	a libertad	ad lib.
Ala., AL	Alabama	Alabama	
Alas., AK	Alaska	Alaska	
A.M., a.m.	ante meridiem; before noon	de la mañana	a.m.
anon.	anonymous	anónimo	X.
Apr.	April	abril	ab.
apt.	apartment	apartamento	
Ariz., AZ	Arizona	Arizona	
Ark., AR	Arkansas	Arkansas	
assn.	association	asociación	
asst.	assistant	asistente; ayudante	
att(n).	(to the) attention (of)	atención	
atty.	attorney	abogado	
at. wt.	atomic weight	peso atómico	p.a.
Aug.	August	agosto	agto.
Av., Ave.	Avenue	avenida	Av., avda.
AWOL	absent without official leave	ausente sin licencia	

B

b.	born	nacido	n.
B.A.	Bachelor of Arts	Bachiller en Artes	
B.C.	Before Christ	antes de Jesucristo	A. de C.
B.D.	Bachelor of Divinity	Bachiller en divinidad	
bldg.	building	edificio	
Blvd.	Boulevard	bulevar	
Br.	British	Británico	
B.S.	Bachelor of Science	Bachiller en Ciencias	

C

C.A.	Central America	Centro América	C.A.
Calif., Cal., CA	California	California	
Can.	Canada	Canadá	

Abreviatura	Significado	Equivalente en Español	Abreviatura en Español
Capt.	Captain	Capitán	Cap., Capn.
cf.	compare	compárese	comp.
ch., chap.	chapter	capítulo	capo., cap.
cm.	centimeter	centímetro	cm.
c/o	in care of	casa de	a/c, c/de
Co.	Company	compañía	Cía., C.
C.O.D.	Collect (or Cash) on Delivery	cóbrese al entregar	C.A.E
Col.	Colonel	Coronel	Cnel.
Colo., CO	Colorado	Colorado	
Comdr.	Commander	Comandante	Cdte.
Conn., Ct., CT	Connecticut	Connecticut	
Corp.	Corporation	Sociedad Anónima	S.A.
C.P.A.	Certified Public Accountant	Contador Público Títulado	C.P.T.
cr.	credit	crédito	
cu.	cubic	cúbico	cú.
C.Z.	Canal Zone	Zona del Canal	

D

D.A.	District Attorney	Fiscal de Distrito	
d.c.	direct current	corriente directa	c.d.
D.D.	Doctor of Divinity	Doctor en Divinidad	D.D.
dec.	deceased	difunto	
Dec.	December	diciembre	dic.
Del., DE	Delaware	Delaware	
dept.	department	departamento	dpto.
dist.	district	distrito	d.
do.	ditto	lo mismo	do.
doz.	dozen	docena	dna., doc.
Dr.	Doctor	doctor	Dr.

E

ea.	each	cada uno	c/u.
ed.	editor	redactor	red.
ed(s).	edition(s)	edición(es)	ed(s).
e.g.	for example	por ejemplo	p. ej.
enc.	enclosure	incluso	incl.
Eng.	England; English	Inglaterra; inglés	
Esq.	Esquire	Señor	Sr.
et al.	and others	y otros	et al.
etc.	and so forth; etcetera	etcétera	etc.
ext.	extension	extensión	ext.

Abreviatura	Significado	Equivalente en Español	Abreviatura en Español

F

Abreviatura	Significado	Equivalente en Español	Abreviatura en Español
F°	Fahrenheit	Fahrenheit	F°
F.B.I.	Federal Bureau of Investigation	Oficina Federal de Investigaciones	
Feb.	February	febrero	feb.
fed.	federal	federal	
fem.	feminine	femenino	fem.
fig.	figurative; figure	figurativa; figura	fig.
fl.	fluid	fluido	
Fla., FL	Florida	Florida	
F.M.	Frequency Modulation	modulación de frecuencia	m.f.
f.o.b.	free on board	franco a bordo	f.a.b.
for.	foreign	extranjero	
Fri.	Friday	viernes	vier.
ft.	foot; feet	pie(s)	

G

Abreviatura	Significado	Equivalente en Español	Abreviatura en Español
Ga., GA	Georgia	Georgia	
gen.	gender	género	gen.
Gen.	General	General	Genl., Gral.
Ger.	Germany; German	Alemania; Alemán	
govt.	government	gobierno	gob.
gr.	gram	gramo	g.; gr.
GB	Great Britain	Gran Bretaña	
gro. wt.	gross weight	peso bruto	p.b.

H

Abreviatura	Significado	Equivalente en Español	Abreviatura en Español
hdqrs., HQ	headquarters	dirección general	D.G.
H.I., HI	Hawaiian Islands	Islas Hawaianas	
H.M.	Her (His) Majesty	Su Majestad	
H.M.S.	Her (His) Majesty's Ship		
Hon.	(The) Honorable	honorable	
HP	horsepower	caballo de fuerza	HP, c.f., c. de f.
hr.	hour	hora	h.

I

Abreviatura	Significado	Equivalente en Español	Abreviatura en Español
Ia., IA	Iowa	Iowa	
id.	the same	lo mismo	id.
Ida., ID	Idaho	Idaho	

Abreviatura	Significado	Equivalente en Español	Abreviatura en Español
i.e.	that is	esto es	i.e.
Ill., IL	Illinois	Illinois	
in(s).	inch(es)	pulgada(s)	pulg(s).
Inc.	incorporated	sociedad anónima	S.A.
Ind., IN	Indiana	Indiana	
Inst.	Institute	instituto	
I.O.U.	I owe you	vale	
I.Q.	intelligence quotient	cociente intelectual	c.i.
It.; Ital.	Italy; Italian	Italia; italiano	ital.
ital.	italics	itálica; bastardilla	

J

Jan.	January	enero	en.
Jap.	Japan	Japón	
J.C.	Jesus Christ	Jesucristo	J.C.
J.P.	Justice of the Peace	juez de paz	
Jr.	Junior	menor; hijo	h.
Jul.	July	julio	jul.
Jun.	June	junio	jun.

K

Kan(s)., KS	Kansas	Kansas	
kg.	kilogram	kilogramo	Kg.
km.	kilometer	kilómetro	Km.
kw.	kilowatt	kilovatio	Kv., Kw.
Ky., KY	Kentucky	Kentucky	

L

La., LA	Louisiana	Louisiana	
lab.	laboratory	laboratorio	
lat.	latitude	latitud	lat.
Lat.	Latin	latín	
lb(s).	pound(s)	libra(s)	lib(s).
l.c.	lower case	caja baja	c.b.
L.C.	Library of Congress	Biblioteca del Congreso	
Lieut., Lt.	Lieutenant	Teniente	Tte., Tente.
Lit. D.	Doctor of Letters	Doctor en Letras	Dr. en Let.
LL.D.	Doctor of Laws	Doctor en Leyes	Dr. en L.
loc. cit.	in the place cited	loco citado	loc. cit.
long.	longitude	longitud	long.
Ltd.	Limited	Limitada	Ltda.

Abreviatura	Significado	Equivalente en Español	Abreviatura en Español

M

Abreviatura	Significado	Equivalente en Español	Abreviatura en Español
M.A.	Master of Arts	Maestro en Artes	A.M.
Maj.	Major	Comandante	
Mar.	March	marzo	mrz., mro.
masc.	masculine	masculino	m.
Mass., MA	Massachusetts	Massachusetts	
M.C.	Master of Ceremonies	Maestro de Ceremonias	
Md., MD	Maryland	Maryland	
M.D.	Doctor of Medicine	Doctor en Medicina	
Me., ME	Maine	Maine	
Messrs.	plural of Mr.	Señores	Sres.
Mex.	Mexico; Mexican	México; mexicano	Méx.; mex.
mfg.	manufacturing	fabricación	
mfr.	manufacturer	fabricante	
mg.	milligram	miligramo	mg.
Mgr.	Monsignor	monseñor	Mons.
Mich., MI	Michigan	Michigan	
min.	minute	minuto	m.
Minn., MS	Minnesota	Minnesota	
misc.	miscellaneous	misceláneo	
Miss.	Mississippi	Mississippi	
mm.	millimeter	milímetro	mm.
mo(s).	month(s)	mes(es)	m(s).
Mo., MO	Missouri	Missouri	
Mon.	Monday	lunes	lun.
Mont., MT	Montana	Montana	
M.P.	Military Police	Policía Militar	P.M.
m.p.h.	miles per (or an) hour	millas por hora	m.p.h.
Mr.	Mister	Señor	Sr.
Mrs.	Mistress, Mrs.	Señora	Sra.
Ms.	Miss or Mrs.	no Spanish equivalent	
ms.	manuscript	manuscrito	ms.
M.S.	Master of Science	Maestro en Ciencias	
Mt.	Mount; mountain	monte; montaña	

N

Abreviatura	Significado	Equivalente en Español	Abreviatura en Español
n.	number; noun	número; sustantivo	n.
N.A.	North America	Norteamérica	
nat., nat'l.	national	nacional	nac.
N.C., NC	North Carolina	Carolina del Norte	
N.D., ND	North Dakota	Dakota del Norte	
N.E.	New England	New England	

Abreviatura	Significado	Equivalente en Español	Abreviatura en Español
Neb., NE	Nebraska	Nebraska	
neut.	neuter	neutro	neut.
Nev., NV	Nevada	Nevada	
N.H., NH	New Hampshire	New Hampshire	
N.J., NJ	New Jersey	New Jersey	
N. Mex., N.M., NM	New Mexico	New Mexico	
No.	number	número	n°.; núm.
Nov.	November	noviembre	nov.
nt. wt.	net weight	peso neto	no. n°.
N.Y., NY	New York	Nueva York	

O

Oct.	October	octubre	oct.
O.K.	all right	visto bueno	V°.B°.
Okla., OK	Oklahoma	Oklahoma	
Ore., OR	Oregon	Oregon	
Oxf.	Oxford	Oxford	
oz(s).	ounce(s)	onza(s)	on(s). onz.

P

p.	page	página	pág.
Pa., PA	Pennsylvania	Pennsylvania	
Pac.	Pacific	Pacífico	
Pan.	Panama	Panamá	
par.	paragraph	párrafo	
p.c.	per cent	por ciento	p.c.
pd.	paid	pagado	
Pfc.	Private first-class	soldado de primera	
Ph.D.	Doctor of Philosophy	Doctor en Filosofía	
Phila.	Philadelphia	Philadelphia	
P.I.	Philippine Islands	Islas Filipinas	
pl., plu.	plural	plural	pl.
P.M., p.m.	post meridiem; in the afternoon	de la tarde	p.m.
P.M.	Postmaster	Administrador de Correos	
P.O.	post office	oficina de correos	
P.O. Box	Post Office Box	apartado	apdo.
pp.	pages	páginas	págs.
ppd.	prepaid	prepagado	p.p.
p.p.	parcel post	paquetes postales	

Abreviatura	Significado	Equivalente en Español	Abreviatura en Español
pr.	pair	par	
P.R.	Puerto Rico	Puerto Rico	P.R.
pres.	present	presente	pres.
Prof.	Professor	profesor	prof.
pron.	pronoun	pronombre	pron.
P.S.	Postscript	posdata	P.D., P.S.
pt.	pint	pinta	
pvt.	private	soldado raso	
POW	Prisoner of War	prisionero de guerra	
pub., publ.	publisher	publicador	publ.

Q

qt(s).	quarts	cuarto(s) de galón	
Que.	Quebec	Quebec	

R

R.A.F.	Royal Air Force	Real Fuerza Aérea	
R.C.	Roman Catholic	católico romano	
Rd.	road	camino	
ref.	reference	referencia	ref.
reg.	registered	registrado	reg.
regt.	regiment	regimento	
Rep.	Representative	representante	
Rep.	Republic	república	rep.
Rev.	Reverend	reverendo	R.; Rdo.
Rev.	Revolution	revolución	
R.I., RI	Rhode Island	Rhode Island	
riv.	river	río	
R.N.	Registered Nurse	Enfermera Titulada	
r.p.m.	revolutions per minute	revoluciones por minuto	r.p.m.
R.R.	Railroad	ferrocarril	f.c.
Ry.	Railway	ferrocarril	f.c.
R.S.V.P.	Please answer	Sírvase responder	R.S.V.P.

S

S.A.	South America	América del Sur	
Sat.	Saturday	sábado	sáb.
S.C., SC	South Carolina	South Carolina	
Scot.	Scotland	Escocia	
S.D., SD	South Dakota	Dakota del Sur	
sec.	second; section	segundo; sección	

Abreviatura	Significado	Equivalente en Español	Abreviatura en Español
secy.	secretary	secretario	secret^o.; srio.
Sen.	Senator	Senador	Sen.
Sept.	September	septiembre	sept^e.; set^e.; se^{bre}.
Sgt.	Sergeant	sargento	sgto.
sing.	singular	singular	
So.	South	sur	
Soc.	Society	sociedad	soc.
Sp.	Spain; Spanish	España; español	
sq.	square	cuadrado	cuad.
Sr.	Sister	hermana	
S.S.	steamship	vapor	
St.	Saint	San; Santo (-a)	S.; Sto.; Sta.
St.	Street	calle	
subj.	subject	sujeto	
Sun.	Sunday	domingo	dom^o.
supp.	supplement	suplemento	
Supt.	Superintendent	superintendente	supert^{te}.

T

tbs.	tablespoon	cuchara grande	
tel.	telephone; telegram	teléfono; telegrama	tel.; TLF
Tenn., TN	Tennessee	Tennessee	
Test.	Testament	Testamento	Test^{mto}.
Tex., TX	Texas	Texas	
Thur(s).	Thursday	jueves	juev.
TNT	trinitrotoluene	trinitrotuoleno	TNT
trans.	transitive; transportation	transitivo; transporte	
tsp.	teaspoon	cucharita	
Tue(s).	Tuesday	martes	mart.
TV	Television	televisión	T.V.

U

U., Univ.	University	universidad	
u.c.	upper case	caja alta	
U.K.	United Kingdom	Reino Unido	R.U.
U.N.	United Nations	Naciones Unidas	O.N.U.
U.S.A.	United States of America	Estados Unidos de América	E.U.A.

Abreviatura	Significado	Equivalente en Español	Abreviatura en Español
U.S.A.	United States Army	Ejército de los Estados Unidos	
U.S.A.F.	United States Air Force	Fuerzas Aéreas de los Estados Unidos	
U.S.N.	United States Navy	Marina de Guerra de los Estados Unidos	
U.S.S.R.	Union of Soviet Socialist Republics	Unión de Repúblicas Socialistas Soviéticas.	U.R.S.S.
Ut., UT	Utah	Utah	

V

v.	verb; volt	verbo; voltio	v.
Va., VA	Virginia	Virginia	
V.D.	venereal disease	enfermedad venérea	
Ven.	Venerable	venerable	
Visc.	Viscount	vizconde	
viz.	namely	a saber	v.g., v.gr.
vol.	volume	tomo; volumen	t.; vol.
V.P.	Vice President	vice presidente	
vs.	versus; against	contra	
Vt., VT	Vermont	Vermont	

W

w.	watt	vatio, watio	v., w.
Wash., WA	Washington	Washington	
W.C.	water closet	servicio higiénico	serv.
Wed.	Wednesday	miércoles	miérc.
Wisc., WI	Wisconsin	Wisconsin	
wk(s).	week(s)	semana(s)	
wt.	weight	peso	p°.
W. Va., WV	West Virginia	West Virginia	
Wyo., WY	Wyoming	Wyoming	

Y

yd(s).	yard(s)	yarda(s)	yd(a).
yr(s)	year(s)	año(s)	

Z

Z.	Zone	zona	

Abbreviations — Spanish-English

Abbreviation	Meaning	English Equivalent	English Abbreviation

A

ab.	abril	April	Apr., Apl.
A. de C.	antes de Jesucristo	Before Christ	B.C.
admor.	administrador	administrator	adm., admin.
afmo.	afectísimo	yours truly	yrs. trly.
agr.	agricultura	agriculture	agric.
agto.	agosto	August	Aug.
a.m.	de la mañana	in the morning	A.M., a.m.
art.	artículo	article	art.
Arzbpo.	Arzobispo	Archbishop	Arch.
apdo.	apartado	post office box	P.O. Box
atto.	atento	yours truly	yrs. trly.
av.	avenida	avenue	Av., Ave.

B

Br.	Bachiller	Bachelor (academic)	B., b.

C

c.	centígrado	centigrade	c., cent.
c.a.	corriente alterna	alternating current	a.c.
cap.	capítulo	chapter	ch., chap.
Cap., capn.	Capitán	Captain	Capt.
c.d.	corriente directa	direct current	d.c.
c.f., c. de f.	caballo de fuerza	horsepower	hp., h.p.
cg.	centigramo	centigram	cent.
Cía.	Compañía	Company	Co.
cm.	centímetro	centimeter	cm.
Cnel.	Coronel	Colonel	Col.
C.P.T.	Contador Público Titulado	Certified Public Accountant	C.P.A.
c/u	cada uno	each	ea.

D

D.; Da.	Don; Doña	(titles of respect; no English equiv.)	
D. de C.	Después de Cristo	Anno Domini	A.D.
der., dra(-o).	derecha(-o)	right	r., rt.
D.F.	Distrito Federal	Federal District	F.D.

Abbreviation	Meaning	English Equivalent	English Abbreviation
dic.	diciembre	December	Dec.
dls.	dólares	dollars	dls.
dom.	domingo	Sunday	Sun.
Dr.	Doctor	Doctor	Dr.

E

EE.UU.	Estados Unidos	United States	U.S.(A.)
en.	enero	January	Jan.
etc.	etcétera	and so on	etc.
E.U.(A.)	Estados Unidos (de América)	United States (of America)	U.S.(A.)
Exca.	Excelencia	(Your) Excellency	Exc.

F

F°	Fahrenheit	Fahrenheit	F°
f.a.b.	franco a bordo	free on board	f.o.b.
facta., fra.	factura	invoice	inv.
F.C.	ferrocarril	railway; railroad	ry.; rr., R.R.
feb.	febrero	February	Feb.

G

g(r).	gramo	gram	gr.
gnte., gte.	gerente	manager	mgr.
gob.	gobierno; gobernador	government; governor	govt.; gov.
Gral.	General	General	Gen.

H

h.	hijo; hora	son; Junior; hour	Jr., h.
hect.	hectárea	hectare	ha.
Hnos.	Hermanos	Brothers	Bros.
hosp.	hospital	hospital	hosp.

I

ib.	ibídem	in the same place	Ibid.
id.	ídem	the same	id.
Ilmo(-a)	Ilustrísimo(-a)	Most Illustrious	Mt. Illus.
impr.	imprenta	publishing house	pub., publ.
Ing.	Ingeniero	engineer	engr.
ingl.	inglés	English	Eng., Engl.
izq.	izquierda	left	l.

Abbreviation	Meaning	English Equivalent	English Abbreviation

J

J.C.	Jesucristo	Jesus Christ	J.C.
jue.	jueves	Thursday	Thur., Thurs.

K

kg.	kilogramo	kilogram	kilo.
km.	kilómetro	kilometer	km., kilom.
kv.	kilovatio	kilowatt	kw.
k.p.h.	kilómetros por hora	kilometers per hour	k.p.h.

L

l.	litro	liter	lit.
L.A.B.	libre a bordo	free on board	f.o.b.
lb(s).	libra(s)	pound(s)	lb(s).
Lic.	Licenciado	Licentiate	Lic., L.
lun.	lunes	Monday	Mon.

M

mar.	martes	Tuesday	Tu., Tue., Tues.
med.	medicina	medicine	med.
mg.	miligramo	milligram	mg.
miérc.	miércoles	Wednesday	Wed.
mm.	milímetro	millimeter	mm.
m/n	moneda nacional	national currency	
Mons.	Monseñor	Monsignor	Msgr., Monsig.
mrz., mzo.	marzo	March	Mar.
m.p.h.	millas por hora	miles per hour	m.p.h.

N

n.	nacido	born	b.
nac.	nacional	national	nat., natl.
No., núm.	número	number	no.
nov.	noviembre	November	Nov.
N.S.	Nuestro Señor	Our Lord	

O

oct.	octubre	October	Oct.
(O)NU	(Organización de) Naciones Unidas	(Organization of) United Nations	U.N.
onz., on(s).	onza(s)	ounce(s)	oz(s).

Abbreviation	Meaning	English Equivalent	English Abbreviation

P

pág(s).	página(s)	page(s)	p., pp.
P.D., P.S.	Posdata	postscript	P.S.
p.ej.	por ejemplo	for example	e.g.
pl.	plural	plural	pl., plu.
p.p.	porte pagado	postage paid	p.p., P.P.
ppdo.	próximo pasado	last	
P.R.	Puerto Rico	Puerto Rico	P.R.
pral.	principal	principal	pral.
prof.	profesor	professor	prof.
pta(s).	peseta(s)	peseta(s)	

Q

Q.E.D.P.	que en paz descanse	(May he) Rest in Peace	R.I.P.

R

Rep.	República	Republic	Repub.
r.p.m.	revoluciones por minuto	revolutions per minute	r.p.m.

S

S.	San(to); Santa	Saint	St.
S.A.	Sociedad Anónima	Corporation	Corp., Inc.
sáb.	sábado	Saturday	Sat.
S.A. de C.V.	Sociedad Anónima de Capital Variable	Corporation with variable capital	
sept.	septiembre	September	Sep., Sept.
S.M.	Su Majestad	His (Her) Majesty	H.M.
Sr(es)	Señor(es)	Sir, Mister; Sirs, Gentlemen	Mr.; Messrs.
Sra(s).	Señora(s)	Madam, Mrs.; Mesdames, Ladies	Mrs., Ms.
Srta(s).	Señorita(s)	Miss(es)	Miss, Ms.
sria.	secretaria	secretary	sec., secy.
sría.	secretaría	Office of the Secretary	
S.S.	seguro servidor	Yours truly	yrs. trly.
S.S.S.	su seguro servidor	Yours truly	yrs. trly.

Abbreviation	Meaning	English Equivalent	English Abbreviation

T

t(on).	tonelada	ton	t.
TNT	trinitrotolueno	trinitrotoluene	TNT
Tte., Tente.	Teniente	Lieutenant	Lt., Lieut.

U

U., Ud.	usted	you (polite sing. or pl.)	
U.R.S.S.	Unión de Repúblicas Socialistas Soviéticas	Union of Soviet Socialist Republics	U.S.S.R.

V

V., Vd.; Vds.	usted; ustedes	you (polite sing.); you (pl.)	
v.	verbo	verb	v., vb.
v.gr.	verbigracia	for example	e.g.
vier.	viernes	Friday	Fri.
V.M.	Vuestra Majestad	Your Majesty	
vol.	volumen	volume	vol.

Y

yd(a).; yd(as).	yarda(s)	yard(s)	yd(s).

Pesos y Medidas

WEIGHTS
(Pesos)

Onza (avoirdupois)	28.35 gms.	Ounce (avoirdupois)	28.35 grams.
Libra	0.4536 kgs.	Pound	0.4536 kgs.
Tonelada larga	1.0161 ton. met.	Long ton	1.0161 met. tons.
Tonelada corta	0.9072 ton. met.	Short ton	0.9072 met. tons.
Grano	0.0648 gms.	Grain	0.0648 grams.

LINEAR
(Lineales)

Milla	1.6093 kms.	Mile	1.6093 kms.
Milla marina	1.853 kms.	Naut. mile	1.853 kms.
Yarda	0.9144 ms.	Yard	0.9144 ms.
Pie	0.3048 ms.	Foot	0.3048 ms.
Pulgada	2.54 cms.	Inch	2.54 cms.

CAPACITY
(Capacidad)

Cuarto del gal. (líq.)	0.9463 litros	Liquid quart	0.9463 liters
Cuarto de gal. (áridos)	1.101 litros	Dry quart	1.101 liters
Galón	3.785 litros	Gallon	3.785 liters
Bushel	35.24 litros	Bushel	35.24 liters

CUBIC
(Volumen)

Pulgada cúbica	16.387 cm.^{3}	Cubic inch	16.387 cu. cm.
Pie cúbico	0.0283 m.^{3}	Cubic foot	0.0283 cu. ms.
Yarda cúbica	0.7646 m.^{3}	Cubic yard	0.7646 cu. ms.

SURFACE
(Superficie)

Acre	0.4453 hectáreas	Acre	0.4453 hectares
Milla cuadrada	259 hectáreas	Square mile	259 hectares
Yarda cuadrada	0.8361 m.^{2}	Square yard	0.8351 sq. meters
Pie cuadrado	929.03 cms.^{2}	Square foot	929.03 sq. cms.
Pulgada cuadrada	6.456 cms.^{2}	Square inch	6.4516 sq. cms.

Weights and Measures

Medidas Métricas   (Metric Measures)

PESOS
(Weights)

Tonelada	2204.6 lb.	Ton	2204.6 lbs.
Kilogramo	2.2046 lb.	Kilogram	2.2046 lbs.
Gramo	15.432 granos	Gram	15.432 grains
Centigramo	0.1543 granos	Centigram	0.1543 grains

LINEALES
(Linear)

Kilómetro	0.62137 millas	Kilometer	0.62137 miles
Metro	39.37 pulgadas	Meter	39.37 inches
Decímetro	3.937 pulgadas	Decimeter	3.937 inches
Centímetro	0.3937 pulgadas	Centimeter	0.3937 inches
Milímetro	0.03937 pulgadas	Millimeter	0.03937 inches

CAPACIDAD
(Capacity)

Hectolitro		2.838 bushels	Hectoliter		2.838 bushels
	o	26.418 galones		or	26.418 gallons
Litro		0.9081 cuarto de galón (áridos)	Liter		0.9081 dry qt.
	o	1.0567 cuarto de galón (líq.)		or	1.0567 liq. qts.

VOLUMEN
(Cubic)

Metro cúbico	1.308 yardas^3	Cubic meter	1.308 cu. yards
Decímetro cúbico	61.023 pulgadas^3	Cubic decimeter	61.023 cu. inches
Centímetro cúbico	0.0610 pulgadas^3	Cubic centimeter	0.0610 cu. inches

SUPERFICIE
(Surface)

Kilómetro cuadrado	247.104 acres	Sq. kilometer	247.104 acres
Hectárea	2.471 acres	Hectare	2.471 acres
Metro cuadrado	1550 pulgadas^2	Square meter	1550 sq. inches
Decímetro cuadrado	15.50 pulgadas^2	Square decimeter	15.50 sq. inches
Centímetro	0.155 pulgadas^2	Square centimeter	0.155 sq. inches

Modismos Españoles Corrientes

Las palabras inglesas entre paréntesis representan a la palabra clave que ha de buscarse para encontrar el modismo español deseado. Los números revelan la página en que se halla dicha palabra.

A

a cada paso 264 (*turn*)
a cada rato 282 (*while*)
a cámara lenta 154 (*motion*)
a cambio de 73 (*exchange*)
a causa de 17 (*because*)
a ciencia cierta 39 (*certain*)
¡A comer! 44 (*to come*)
¿A cómo se vende? 156 (*much*)
a consecuencia de 272 (*wake*)
a costa de 74 (*expense*)
a crédito 51 (*credit*)
a cuestas 13 (*back*)
a decir verdad 263 (*truth*)
a diestra y siniestra 195 (*right*)
a duras penas 60 (*difficulty*)
a escondidas 219 (*sly*)
a eso de la(s) 11 (*at*)
a estas alturas 181 (*point*)
a este paso 189 (*rate*)
a expensas de 74 (*expense*)
a fines de 70 (*end*)
a fuerza de 60 (*dint*)
a gritos 258 (*top*)
a guisa de 276 (*way*)
a hora fija 251 (*time*)
a instancia de 193 (*request*)
a justo título 196 (*rightly*)
a juzgar por 123 (*to judge*)
a la carrera 199 (*run*)
a la fuerza 283 (*will*)
a la hora 253 (*time*)
a la hora de la verdad 63 (*down*)
a la larga 199 (*run*)
a la merced de. . . 149 (*mercy*)
a la sazón 252 (*time*)

a la vez 109 (*once*)
a la(s) . . . en punto 210 (*sharp*)
A lo hecho, pecho. 61 (*to do*)
a lo lejos 61 (*distance*)
a lo mejor 136 (*likely*)
a mano 102 (*hand*)
a manos llenas 105 (*handful*)
a más no poder 289 (*worth*)
a más tardar 128 (*latest*)
a mediados 150 (*middle*)
a medio cerrar 102 (*half*)
a mitad de 276 (*way*)
A otro perro con ese hueso. 146 (*marine*)
a pasos agigantados 130 (*leap*)
a pesar de 225 (*spite*)
a petición de 193 (*request*)
a pie 87 (*foot*)
a poco de 212 (*shortly*)
a primera hora de 67 (*early*)
a primera vista 95 (*glance*)
a propósito 276 (*way*)
a punto fijo 237 (*sure*)
a quemarropa 181 (*point*)
A quien le corresponda. 47 (*to concern*)
a ratos perdidos 253 (*time*)
a razón de 189 (*rate*)
a solas 8 (*alone*)
a su manera 276 (*way*)
a su modo 80 (*fashion*)
a su modo de ver 206 (*to see*)
a su parecer 170 (*opinion*)
a su vez 264 (*turn*)
a tal punto 74 (*extent*)
a tiempo 253 (*time*)

a toda carrera 224 (*speed*)
a toda costa 49 (*cost*)
a toda hora 115 (*hour*)
a toda prisa 105 (*haste*)
a todo trance 49 (*cost*)
a última hora 151 (*minute*)
a última hora de la mañana 128 (*late*)
a ver 206 (*to see*)
a viva fuerza 89 (*force*)
a voz en cuello 271 (*voice*)
a vuelo de pájaro 51 (*crow*)
abierto de par en par 170 (*open*)
abrirle el apetito 9 (*appetite*)
aburrirse como una ostra 26 (*boredom*)
acabar por 71 (*to end*)
aceptarlo con los brazos cruzados 133 (*to lie*)
acostarse con las gallinas 18 (*bed*)
acto seguido 4 (*afterwards*)
aficionarse a 243 (*taste*)
ahí será el diablo 59 (*devil*)
ahogar las penas 223 (*sorrow*)
ahora bien 164 (*now*)
ahora mismo 195 (*right*)
al aire libre 5 (*air*)
al alcance de la voz 35 (*call*)
al amanecer 55 (*dawn*)
al anochecer 160 (*night*)
al atardecer 66 (*dusk*)
al azar 188 (*random*)
al contrario 48 (*contrary*)
al cuidado de 36 (*care*)
al descubierto 170 (*open*)
al fiado 51 (*credit*)
al fin y al cabo 203 (*to say*)
Al freír será el reír. 184 (*pudding*)
al menos 130 (*least*)
al mismo tiempo 169 (*once*)
al oído 67 (*ear*)
al principio 84 (*first*)

Al que madruga. Dios le ayuda. 22 (*bird*)
al rayar el alba 55 (*dawn*)
al revés 277 (*way*)
al rojo (vivo) 191 (*red-hot*)
al romper el alba 50 (*crack*)
alcanzar para mucho 278 (*way*)
algo por el estilo 223 (*sort*)
alzar el vuelo 86 (*flight*)
alzarse en armas 10 (*arm*)
Allá él (ella, etc.) 33 (*business*)
Allá usted. 183 (*problem*)
¡Allá voy! 44 (*to come*)
andar a la greña con 167 (*odds*)
andar con rodeos 33 (*bush*)
andar de capa caída 131 (*leg*)
andar de prisa 116 (*hurry*)
andar en andrajos 187 (*rag*)
andar en quisquillas 102 (*hair*)
andar escaso de 212 (*short*)
andar por buen camino 260 (*track*)
andar por las ramas 33 (*bush*)
ante todo 6 (*all*)
aparte de 11 (*aside*)
aprender de memoria 109 (*heart*)
aquí dentro 111 (*here*)
aquí mismo 111 (*here*)
armar un alboroto 34 (*Cain*)
armar un escándalo 204 (*scene*)
armarse un bochinche 198 (*row*)
arrimar el hombro 213 (*shoulder*)
así así 221 (*so*)
así como 280 (*well*)
así de 248 (*this*)
así y todo 72 (*even*)
asomarse a 9 (*to appear*)
Asunto terminado. 36 (*care*)
atar cabos 267 (*two*)
Aunque la mona se vista de seda, mona se queda. 185 (*purse*)
anque parezca mentira 19 (*to believe*)

B

bailarle el agua a 180 (*to play*)
bajarle los humos 162 (*notch*)
bajo ningún pretexto 1 (*account*)
boca abajo 75 (*face*)
boca arriba 76 (*face*)
brillar por su ausencia 47
  (*conspicuous*)
burlarse de 90 (*fun*)
buscarle tres pies al gato 262
  (*trouble*)

C

cada cuánto (tiempo) 167 (*often*)
cada poco 282 (*while*)
cada vez más 153 (*more*)
caer de bruces 76 (*face*)
caer de plano 86 (*flat*)
caer de redondo 86 (*flat*)
caer en la cuenta 135 (*light*)
caerle bien 135 (*to like*)
caerse por su base 275 (*water*)
caérsele las alas 60 (*discouraged*)
cambiar opiniones 163 (*note*)
casarse con 146 (*to marry*)
cerrar el paso 277 (*way*)
cerrarle la puerta en las narices
  63 (*door*)
citarse con 9 (*appointment*)
cocer en su propia salsa 123
  (*juice*)
comerse las uñas 157 (*nail*)
como alma que lleva el diablo
  16 (*bat*)
como caído de las nubes 24 (*blue*)
como de costumbre 269 (*usual*)
cómo no 50 (*course*)
como si esto fuera poco 120
  (*insult*)
comprar a ciegas 178 (*pig*)
comprar regalado 222 (*song*)

con arreglo a 1 (*according*)
con el propósito de 271 (*view*)
con el transcurso del tiempo 50
  (*course*)
con la mayor brevedad 222 (*soon*)
con las manos en la masa 3 (*act*)
con miras a 271 (*view*)
con motivo de 166 (*occasion*)
con mucho 79 (*far*)
con pulso firme 104 (*hand*)
con todo 72 (*even*)
concertar un acuerdo 245 (*term*)
conciliar el sueño 11 (*asleep*)
conformarse con 209 (*to settle*)
confundir con 152 (*mistake*)
conocer a fondo 26 (*book*)
conocerle el juego 17 (*to be*)
consultarlo con la almohada 218
  (*to sleep*)
contar con 49 (*to count*)
contra viento y marea 110 (*hell*)
cortar de raíz 32 (*bud*)
cortarle las alas 284 (*wing*)
costar trabajo 105 (*hard*)
costarle un dineral 176 (*penny*)
costarle un ojo de la cara 162
  (*nose*)
crisparle los nervios 159 (*nerve*)
Cuando el río suena, agua lleva.
  220 (*smoke*)
cuando más 154 (*most*)
cuando menos 130 (*least*)
cuando menos se piense 74
  (*expected*)
cuanto antes 182 (*possible*)
cuanto más . . . (tanto) más . . .
  154 (*more*)
cuánto tiempo 138 (*long*)
cueste lo que cueste 49 (*cost*)
cuidado con . . . 36 (*careful*)
cuidar a cuerpo de rey 104
  (*hand*)

D

dadas las circunstancias 41 (*circumstance*)
dar a 76 (*to face*)
dar a conocer 126 (*to know*)
dar a entender 94 (*to give*)
dar alcance 38 (*to catch*)
dar cabezadas 161 (*to nod*)
dar cuenta de 192 (*to report*)
dar cuerda al reloj 42 (*clock*)
dar el pésame 238 (*sympathy*)
dar en el clavo 157 (*nail*)
dar fin a 70 (*end*)
dar guerra 262 (*trouble*)
dar la mano a 104 (*hand*)
dar la razón a 2 (*to acknowledge*)
dar lugar a 196 (*rise*)
dar media vuelta 265 (*to turn*)
dar origen a 196 (*rise*)
dar palmadas 103 (*hand*)
dar principio con 170 (*to open*)
dar que pensar 87 (*food*)
dar rienda suelta a 192 (*rein*)
dar un paseo 273 (*walk*)
dar un paseo (en coche) 194 (*ride*)
dar un paso 230 (*step*)
dar un portazo 63 (*door*)
dar un vistazo 169 (*once-over*)
dar una vuelta 265 (*to turn*)
dar vueltas 258 (*to toss*)
darle con la puerta en las narices 63 (*door*)
darle escalofríos 51 (*creeps*)
darle lo suyo 58 (*desert*)
darle por 241 (*to take*)
darle rabia 143 (*mad*)
darle tiempo 254 (*time*)
darse buena vida 138 (*to live*)
darse por aludido 111 (*hint*)
darse por vencido 94 (*to give*)
darse tono 6 (*air*)
de . . . en . . . 90 (*from*)

de acuerdo con 1 (*according*)
de algún modo 277 (*way*)
de aquí en adelante 164 (*now*)
de arriba abajo 258 (*top*)
de balde 89 (*free*)
de beuna fe 77 (*faith*)
de cabeza 107 (*head*)
de cerca 188 (*range*)
de cuando en cuando 252 (*time*)
de día 65 (*during*)
de dos en dos 266 (*two*)
de golpe 236 (*sudden*)
De la mano a la boca se pierde la sopa. 219 (*slip*)
de la noche a la mañana 160 (*night*)
de mala fe 77 (*faith*)
De noche todos los gatos son pardos. 38 (*cat*)
de momento 152 (*moment*)
De nada 280 (*welcome*)
de ningún modo 40 (*circumstance*)
de ninguna manera 148 (*means*)
de noche 160 (*night*)
de oído 67 (*ear*)
de palabra 286 (*word*)
de pies a cabeza 249 (*through*)
de pronto 6 (*all*)
de punta en blanco 192 (*regalia*)
de puntillas 256 (*tiptoe*)
de repente 236 (*sudden*)
de sobra 171 (*over*)
De tal palo, tal astilla. 40 (*chip*)
de todas formas 37 (*case*)
de todas maneras 72 (*event*)
de todos modos 189 (*rate*)
de un momento a otro 250 (*time*)
de un salto 85 (*flash*)
de una vez 61 (*to do*)
de una vez por todas 169 (*once*)
de uno en uno 169 (*one*)

314

de vez en cuando 252 (*time*)

decir mil bienes de 224 (*to speak*)

decirle cuántas son cinco 178 (*piece*)

decirle que se vaya a freír espárragos 141 (*to lose*)

defenderse bien 92 (*to get*)

dejar cesante 129 (*to lay*)

dejar colgado 44 (*cold*)

dejar con la carga en las costillas 14 (*bag*)

dejar en paz 132 (*to let*)

dejar en paz 8 (*alone*)

dejar huella 118 (*impression*)

dejar recado 287 (*word*)

dejarle boquiabierto 30 (*breath*)

Del agua mansa me libre Dios, que de la brava me libro yo. 275 (*water*)

delante de las narices 162 (*nose*)

depender de 58 (*to depend*)

desde luego 50 (*course*)

desde un principio 8 (*along*)

desempeñar el papel 187 (*role*)

deshacerse de 194 (*to rid*)

deshacerse en lágrimas 29 (*to break*)

desnudar a un santo para vestir a otro 177 (*Peter*)

despedirse de 130 (*leave*)

Dicho y hecho. 223 (*sooner*)

Díos los cría y ellos se juntan. (*bird*)

¡Dios me libre! 79 (*far*)

distar mucho de ser 52 (*cry*)

doblar la cabeza 94 (*to give*)

dolerle la cabeza 108 (*headache*)

Donde comen seis comen siete. 197 (*room*)

Donde fueres, haz lo que vieres. 197 (*Rome*)

dorar la píldora 178 (*pill*)

dormir a pierna suelta 138 (*log*)

dormir la mona 218 (*to sleep*)

dormir la siesta 158 (*nap*)

dormirse en las pajas 99 (*grass*)

dormirse sobre sus laureles 129 (*laurel*)

dos a dos 266 (*two*)

E

echar a perder 199 (*to ruin*)

echar aceite al fuego 90 (*fuel*)

echar chispas 114 (*to hop*)

echar de menos 152 (*to miss*)

echar la casa por la ventana 96 (*to go*)

echar la vista encima 75 (*eye*)

echar leña al fuego 168 (*oil*)

echar margaritas a los cerdos 176 (*pearl*)

echar raíces 198 (*root*)

echar tierra al escándalo 116 (*to hush*)

echar una carta 143 (*to mail*)

echar una mano 104 (*hand*)

echar una ojeada a 190 (*to read*)

echar una siesta 158 (*nap*)

echarle la culpa a 23 (*blame*)

echarse encima 241 (*to take*)

echárselas de 25 (*to boast*)

echárselo en la cara 249 (*to throw*)

el alma de la fiesta 133 (*life*)

el día menos pensado 74 (*expected*)

el mes (año, semana, etc.) que viene 160 (*next*)

el séptimo cielo 43 (*cloud*)

ello es 77 (*fact*)

empeñarse en 20 (*bent*)

empezar la casa por el tejado 37 (*cart*)

en absoluto 7 (*all*)

en algún tiempo 251 (*time*)
en alta mar 205 (*sea*)
en balde 270 (*vain*)
En boca cerrada no entran moscas. 216 (*silence*)
en broma 122 (*joke*)
en cambio 103 (*hand*)
en caso contrario 162 (*not*)
en cierto modo 276 (*way*)
en confianza 190 (*record*)
en contra de 170 (*opposition*)
en cuanto a 10 (*as*)
en cuanto sea posible 182 (*possible*)
en demasía 73 (*excess*)
en efecto 147 (*matter*)
en el acto 225 (*spot*)
en el mejor de los casos 20 (*best*)
en el momento actual 183 (*present*)
en el peor de los casos 289 (*worst*)
en el quinto infierno 70 (*end*)
en especial 174 (*particular*)
en fecha próxima 54 (*date*)
en fila india 83 (*file*)
en flagrante 3 (*act*)
en gran parte 74 (*extent*)
en grande 203 (*scale*)
en la actualidad 251 (*time*)
en la cara 76 (*face*)
en la flor de la vida (de edad) 183 (*prime*)
en lo más mínimo 130 (*least*)
en lo posible 182 (*possible*)
en lo que va de 79 (*far*)
en lo sucesivo 91 (*future*)
en mangas de camisa 218 (*sleeve*)
en masa 89 (*force*)
en medio de 150 (*middle*)
en menos que canta un gallo 285 (*wink*)

en nombre de 19 (*behalf*)
en números redondos 165 (*number*)
en obras 47 (*construction*)
en pie 69 (*effect*)
en pleno día 56 (*daylight*)
en primer lugar 179 (*place*)
en puntillas 256 (*tiptoe*)
en punto 63 (*dot*)
en regla 170 (*order*)
en resumidas cuentas 233 (*story*)
en seguida 169 (*once*)
en su vida 133 (*life*)
en todas partes 7 (*all*)
en todo caso 72 (*event*)
en total 7 (*all*)
en último caso 193 (*resort*)
en un abrir y cerrar de ojos 252 (*time*)
en un dos por tres 121 (*jiffy*)
en un futuro próximo 91 (*future*)
en un principio 84 (*first*)
en un santiamén 266 (*twinkling*)
en uno u otro caso 276 (*way*)
en vigor 69 (*effect*)
en virtud de 271 (*virtue*)
en voz baja 271 (*voice*)
enamorarse de 78 (*to fall*)
encargarse de 206 (*to see*)
encogerse de hombros 213 (*shoulder*)
encontrarse entre la espada y la pared 13 (*back*)
entenderse bien 111 (*to hit*)
enterarse de 83 (*to find*)
entrar en razón 207 (*sense*)
entrar en vigor 69 (*effect*)
entre bastidores 204 (*scene*)
entre la espada y la pared 59 (*devil*)
entregar el alma 94 (*ghost*)
érase una vez 253 (*time*)

Es como buscar una aguja en un pajar. 159 (*needle*)
es decir 203 (*to say*)
¡Es el colmo! 234 (*straw*)
Es igual. 60 (*difference*)
Eso es cosa suya. 183 (*problem*)
Eso es harina de otro costal. 114 (*horse*)
Eso es lo de menos. 130 (*least*)
Eso es. 195 (*right*)
¡Eso ni pensarlo! 186 (*question*)
Eso sí que no. 119 (*indeed*)
Eso sí. 119 (*indeed*)
estar a cargo 39 (*charge*)
estar a dieta 59 (*diet*)
estar a la altura de 71 (*equal*)
estar a la mira 140 (*lookout*)
estar a la mira de 275 (*watch*)
estar a punto de 1 (*about*)
estar a régimen 59 (*diet*)
estar a salvo 201 (*safe*)
estar a su alcance 189 (*reach*)
estar a sus anchas 46 (*comfortable*)
estar a tiro 188 (*range*)
estar a un paso de 230 (*step*)
estar agotado 183 (*print*)
estar agotado 206 (*to sell*)
estar agotado 279 (*to wear*)
estar al acecho 272 (*wait*)
estar al borde de 270 (*verge*)
estar al corriente 54 (*date*)
estar al corriente de 119 (*informed*)
estar al día 54 (*date*)
estar al frente 39 (*charge*)
estar al sol 237 (*sun*)
estar al tanto 54 (*date*)
estar al tanto de 12 (*aware*)
estar conforme 5 (*agreement*)
estar de acuerdo 5 (*agreement*)
estar de buen humor 153 (*mood*)

estar de cuidado 117 (*ill*)
estar de luto 155 (*mourning*)
estar de mal humor 153 (*mood*)
estar de moda 118 (*in*)
estar de servicio 66 (*duty*)
estar de turno 66 (*duty*)
estar de vuelta 13 (*back*)
estar en ascuas 178 (*pin*)
estar en blanco 23 (*blank*)
estar en buenas relaciones 245 (*term*)
estar en desorden 149 (*mess*)
estar en el caso de 166 (*obligated*)
estar en juego 226 (*stake*)
estar en las últimas 131 (*leg*)
estar en lo firme 100 (*ground*)
estar en los huesos 217 (*skin*)
estar en marcha 155 (*move*)
estar en perspectiva 167 (*offing*)
estar en plena actividad 238 (*swing*)
estar en su juicio 150 (*mind*)
estar en su pellejo 211 (*shoe*)
estar en sus cabales 150 (*mind*)
estar en vena (para) 153 (*mood*)
estar en vigor 89 (*force*)
estar en vísperas de 72 (*eve*)
estar fuera de sí 20 (*beside*)
estar fuera de su alcance 189 (*reach*)
estar hasta la coronilla de 81 (*fed*)
estar hecho a la medida 171 (*order*)
estar hecho una sopa 281 (*wet*)
estar libre de palabra 174 (*parole*)
estar mojado hasta los huesos 217 (*skin*)
estar muy a gusto 46 (*comfortable*)
estar muy de moda 8 (*all*)
estar muy entrado en años 290 (*year*)

317

estar muy pagado de sí mismo 248 (*to think*)

estar para 1 (*about*)

estar pendiente de 272 (*to wait*)

estar que arde 108 (*head*)

estar rendido 7 (*all*)

estar sin aliento 30 (*breath*)

estar sin blanca 28 (*to break*)

estar sobre aviso 100 (*guard*)

estarle bien empleado 195 (*right*)

estrechar la mano a 104 (*hand*)

F

faltar a 77 (*to fail*)

faltar a clase 53 (*to cut*)

felicitarle el cumpleaños 194 (*returns*)

formar parte de 174 (*part*)

forrarse el riñón 160 (*nest*)

freír en su aceite 123 (*juice*)

frente a 2 (*across*)

frente a frente 76 (*face*)

frisar en los . . . años 43 (*close*)

fruncir el ceño 31 (*brow*)

G

ganarle la acción 123 (*jump*)

ganarse la vida 138 (*living*)

Genio y figura hasta la sepultura. 132 (*leopard*)

guardar cama 18 (*bed*)

guardar rencor 100 (*grudge*)

guardar silencio 216 (*silent*)

gustarle más 136 (*to like*)

H

haber perdido el juicio 285 (*wit*)

hablar hasta por los codos 67 (*ear*)

hacer calor 114 (*hot*)

hacer frío 44 (*cold*)

hace poco 251 (*time*)

hacer acto de presencia 9 (*appearance*)

hacer alarde de 213 (*show*)

hacer añicos 178 (*piece*)

hacer buen tiempo 280 (*weather*)

hacer caso 110 (*heed*)

hacer cola 137 (*line*)

hacer el papel 197 (*role*)

hacer el ridículo 87 (*fool*)

hacer el tonto 87 (*fool*)

hacer escala 233 (*to stop*)

hacer furor 188 (*rage*)

hacer honor a su fama 192 (*reputation*)

hacer juego con 97 (*to go*)

hacer la vista gorda 75 (*eye*)

hacer las maletas 173 (*to pack*)

hacer las paces 176 (*peace*)

hacer las paces con 144 (*to make*)

hacer las veces de 3 (*to act*)

hacer lo posible 20 (*best*)

hacer mal tiempo 280 (*weather*)

hacer su agosto 125 (*killing*)

hacer una mueca 76 (*face*)

hacer una pregunta 186 (*question*)

hacerle compañía 46 (*company*)

hacerle daño 116 (*to hurt*)

hacerle falta 159 (*to need*)

hacerle tragar saliva 52 (*crow*)

hacerse el muerto 56 (*dead*)

hacerse el santo 202 (*saintly*)

hacerse el sordo 67 (*ear*)

hacerse el tonto 180 (*to play*)

hacerse entender 267 (*to understand*)

hacérsele agua la boca 155 (*mouth*)

hacérsele tarde 128 (*late*)

hacia atrás 14 (*backward*)

lo mismo. . . que . . . 27 (*both*)
Lo mismo da. 7 (*all*)
lo mismo que 123 (*just*)
lo que es 10 (*as*)

LL

llamar a filas 44 (*color*)
llamar al pan, pan y al vino, vino 224 (*spade*)
llamar la atención 47 (*conspicuous*)
llamarle la atención (sobre) 12 (*attention*)
llegar a las manos 24 (*blow*)
llegar a su punto cumbre 176 (*peak*)
llegar a un acuerdo 5 (*agreement*)
llegar a una inteligencia 190 (*to reach*)
llegar tarde 128 (*late*)
llevar a cabo 36 (*to carry*)
llevar adelante 5 (*ahead*)
llevar de paseo (en coche) 194 (*ride*)
llevar el compás 254 (*time*)
llevar el nombre de 158 (*to name*)
llevar encima 169 (*on*)
llevar una ventaja 4 (*advantage*)
llevar una vida. . . 134 (*life*)
llevarle la ventaja 68 (*edge*)
llevarse a rastras 64 (*to drag*)
llevarse bien con 92 (*to get*)
llorar a mares 75 (*eye*)
llorar lágrimas de cocodrilo 244 (*tear*)
llover a cántaros 38 (*cat*)

M

mandar contra reembolso 37 (*cash*)
¡Manos arriba! 231 (*to stick*)

mantenerse en contacto 259 (*touch*)
más allá 79 (*farther*)
más allá de 214 (*side*)
Más vale tarde que nunca. 21 (*better*)
matar a palos 57 (*death*)
matar dos pájaros de un tiro 22 (*bird*)
mejor que mejor 7 (*all*)
merecer la pena 289 (*worth*)
meter la pata 88 (*foot*)
meter su cuchara 165 (*oar*)
meterse en gastos 74 (*expense*)
meterse en un lío 149 (*mess*)
metérsele en la cabeza 108 (*head*)
mientras más . . . más . . . 154 (*more*)
mirar de hito en hito 229 (*to stare*)
mirar de reojo 49 (*corner*)
morder el polvo 66 (*dust*)
morderse la lengua 257 (*tongue*)
morir al pie del cañón 26 (*boot*)
morir en la hoguera 226 (*stake*)
morir vestido 26 (*boot*)
mostrarse a la altura de las circunstancias 166 (*occasion*)
Mucho ruido y pocas nueces. 4 (*ado*)
mucho tiempo 251 (*time*)
muy de tarde en tarde 153 (*moon*)
muy entrada la mañana 128 (*late*)

N

nada de eso 125 (*kind*)
nadar en la abundancia 80 (*fat*)
ni a tiros 142 (*love*)
¡Ni con mucho! 79 (*far*)
¡Ni hablar! 149 (*to mention*)
¡Ni mucho menos! 79 (*far*)
ni pizca 22 (*bit*)

321

pasar de moda 80 (*fashion*)
pasar el tiempo 255 (*time*)
pasar las mocedades 166 (*oats*)
pasar por 175 (*to pass*)
pasar sin 61 (*to do*)
pasarlas muy duras 198 (*rough*)
pasarlo bien 71 (*to enjoy*)
pasarlo en grande 15 (*ball*)
pasarse sin 92 (*to get*)
paso a paso 230 (*step*)
pedir cuentas 74 (*explanation*)
pedir la palabra 86 (*floor*)
pegar fuego a 84 (*fire*)
pensándolo bien 248 (*thought*)
pensión completa 197 (*room*)
peor que peor 7 (*all*)
perder el juicio 130 (*leave*)
perder el seso 151 (*mind*)
perder la ocasión 39 (*chance*)
perder la razón 119 (*insane*)
perder los estribos 108 (*head*)
perder tiempo 255 (*time*)
Perro ladrador, poco mordedor.
    15 (*bark*)
pisarle los tacones 110 (*heel*)
poco a poco 137 (*little*)
poner a prueba 245 (*test*)
poner a un lado 208 (*to set*)
poner al corriente de 54 (*date*)
poner atención 12 (*attention*)
poner el dedo en la llaga 226
    (*spot*)
poner el grito en el cielo 38
    (*ceiling*)
poner en claro 42 (*to clear*)
poner en duda 63 (*doubt*)
poner en libertad 89 (*free*)
poner en ridículo 195 (*ridiculous*)
poner en su punto 208 (*to set*)
poner la mano encima 83
    (*finger*)
poner la mesa 239 (*table*)

poner las cartas boca arriba 36
    (*card*)
poner las cartas sobre la mesa 36
    (*card*)
poner los pies en 88 (*foot*)
poner manos a la obra 60 (*to dig*)
poner pies en polvorosa 110 (*heel*)
poner sobre las nubes 217 (*sky*)
poner un huevo 69 (*egg*)
ponerle en ridículo 87 (*fool*)
ponerle los pelos de punta 101
    (*hair*)
ponerse a dieta 60 (*diet*)
ponerse a régimen 60 (*diet*)
ponerse de acuerdo 5 (*agreement*)
ponerse de moda 80 (*fashionable*)
ponerse de pie 228 (*to stand*)
ponerse en camino 208 (*to set*)
ponerse en contacto 259 (*touch*)
ponerse en fila 137 (*to line*)
ponerse en marcha 93 (*to get*)
ponerse las botas 182 (*pot*)
ponerse por las nubes 217
    (*sky*)
por algo 163 (*nothing*)
por allá 172 (*over*)
por casualidad 39 (*chance*)
por consideración a 47
    (*consideration*)
por decirlo así 224 (*to speak*)
por escrito 290 (*writing*)
por eso 283 (*why*)
por fas o por nefas 113 (*hook*)
por fin 127 (*last*)
por ganas de 202 (*sake*)
por gusto 90 (*fun*)
por las buenas y las malas 246
    (*thick*)
por lo general 91 (*general*)
por lo menos 130 (*least*)
por lo que a mí me toca 46 (*to
    concern*)

por los pelos 217 (*skin*)
por más. . . que 147 (*matter*)
por motivo de 1 (*account*)
por nada del mundo 289
    (*world*)
por poder 184 (*proxy*)
por regla general 199 (*rule*)
por resultas de 193 (*result*)
por si acaso 37 (*case*)
por si las moscas 37 (*case*)
por supuesto 50 (*course*)
por término medio 12 (*average*)
por todas partes 171 (*over*)
por vuelta de correo 143
    (*mail*)
preguntar por 119 (*to inquire*)
prender fuego a 84 (*fire*)
prestar atención 12 (*attention*)
probar fortuna 142 (*luck*)
Puede que sí (no). 147 (*maybe*)

Q

qué ha sido de 18 (*to become*)
qué le parece. . . 135 (*to like*)
¿Qué más da? 283 (*who*)
¿Qué mosca le ha picado? 93 (*to
    get*)
qué se ha hecho 18 (*to become*)
¡Qué va! 161 (*nonsense*)
quedar en 5 (*to agree*)
quedarse con el día y la noche
    176 (*penniless*)
quedarse con la carga en las
    costillas 201 (*sack*)
quemarse las cejas 168 (*oil*)
querer decir 65 (*to drive*)
Querer es poder. 284 (*will*)
Quien calla otorga. 216 (*silence*)
quitarle un peso de encima 138
    (*load*)
quitarse de en medio 278 (*way*)

R

recibirlo a cuerpo de rey 261
    (*treatment*)
reírse de 128 (*to laugh*)
representar su papel 197 (*role*)
respecto a 193 (*respect*)
romper a reír (llorar) 33 (*to burst*)
romper el hielo 117 (*ice*)

S

saber a 244 (*to taste*)
saber a qué atenerse 227 (*to
    stand*)
saber al dedillo 255 (*tip*)
saber cuántas son cinco 281
    (*what*)
saber de memoria 109 (*heart*)
saber de qué pie cojea 165
    (*number*)
saber de sobra 280 (*well*)
sacar a relucir 31 (*to bring*)
sacar el (premio) gordo 183
    (*prize*)
sacar el pecho 40 (*chest*)
sacar en claro 42 (*clear*)
sacar la lengua 231 (*to stick*)
sacar provecho de 184 (*to profit*)
sacar punta a un lápiz 176
    (*pencil*)
sacar una foto 178 (*picture*)
sacarle de sus casillas 65 (*to
    drive*)
sacarle las castañas del fuego 41
    (*chestnut*)
salir de viaje 262 (*trip*)
salir ganando 45 (*to come*)
salirse con la suya 278 (*way*)
salvar las apariencias 76 (*face*)
salvarse por los pelos 35 (*call*)
sano y salvo 201 (*safe*)
sea como sea 147 (*matter*)
sea lo que sea 281 (*whatever*)

seguir adelante 96 (*to go*)

Según y conforme. 58 (*to depend*)

sentar la cabeza 209 (*to settle*)

ser aficionado a 78 (*fan*)

ser cosa de coser y cantar 63 (*downhill*)

ser de encargo 171 (*order*)

ser de la pasta de 240 (*to take*)

ser de su agrado 136 (*liking*)

ser de su puño y letra 105 (*handwriting*)

ser el hombre indicado 145 (*man*)

ser el ojo derecho de. . . 54 (*darling*)

ser fuerte como un roble 172 (*ox*)

ser hora de 254 (*time*)

ser más bueno que el pan 98 (*gold*)

ser mayor de edad 4 (*age*)

ser muy de adentro 78 (*family*)

ser muy ligero de palabra 243 (*talker*)

ser para tanto 246 (*that*)

ser sólo un decir 145 (*manner*)

ser tal para cual 125 (*kind*)

ser un buen partido 38 (*catch*)

ser un caso de fuerza mayor 3 (*act*)

ser un cero a la izquierda 161 (*no*)

ser un hombre hecho y derecho 118 (*inch*)

ser un pez gordo 212 (*shot*)

ser una desgracia para 114 (*hopeless*)

ser una perla 121 (*jewel*)

ser uña y carne 103 (*hand*)

¿Será verdad tanta belleza? 263 (*true*)

si mal no recuerdo 149 (*memory*)

Siempre llueve sobre mojado. 188 (*to rain*)

sin duda 63 (*doubt*)

sin efecto 165 (*null*)

sin más ni más 4 (*ado*)

sin más vueltas 187 (*question*)

sin pestañear 75 (*eye*)

sin rodeos 286 (*word*)

sin ton ni son 194 (*rhyme*)

sin tregua 133 (*to let*)

Sobre gustos no hay nada escrito. 148 (*meat*)

sobre todo 6 (*all*)

sonarle (a algo conocido) 19 (*bell*)

soñar con 64 (*to dream*)

su media naranja 21 (*better*)

subírsele a la cabeza 108 (*head*)

T

tan claro como el agua 55 (*day*)

tanto. . . como. . . 27 (*both*)

tanto es así 221 (*so*)

tanto mejor 7 (*all*)

tanto peor 7 (*all*)

tarde o temprano 223 (*sooner*)

tener celos 121 (*jealous*)

tener. . . años 168 (*old*)

tener a bien 85 (*fit*)

tener a menos 19 (*beneath*)

tener a raya 16 (*bay*)

tener al corriente 182 (*posted*)

tener algo de 222 (*something*)

tener algo de . . . 222 (*something*)

tener algo tramado 218 (*sleeve*)

tener buen aspecto 140 (*to look*)

tener buen ver 108 (*healthy*)

tener buena cara 140 (*to look*)

tener calor 274 (*warm*)

tener cara de enfado 143 (*mad*)

tener carta blanca 103 (*hand*)

tener corazón de piedra 105 (*hard-hearted*)

tener cuidado con 275 (*to watch*)

tener derecho a 195 (*right*)

tener el corazón en la mano 109 (*heart*)

tener el corazón en un puño 109 (*heart*)

tener el papel principal 129 (*lead*)

tener en cuenta 2 (*account*)

tener en existencia 232 (*stock*)

tener en la punta de la lengua 255 (*tip*)

tener en su poder 104 (*hand*)

tener entre algodones 95 (*glove*)

tener éxito 144 (*to make*)

tener fama de 192 (*reputation*)

tener frío 44 (*cold*)

tener ganas de 81 (*to feel*)

tener gracia 90 (*funny*)

tener hambre 116 (*hunger*)

tener inconveniente 151 (*to mind*)

tener la bondad de 98 (*good*)

tener la costumbre de 2 (*accustomed*)

tener la culpa 23 (*blame*)

tener la forma de 209 (*shape*)

tener la mira puesta en 5 (*to aim*)

tener los días contados 55 (*day*)

tener lugar 180 (*place*)

tener madera para 143 (*to make*)

tener mal aspecto 140 (*to look*)

tener mala cara 140 (*to look*)

tener por qué 190 (*reason*)

tener presente 151 (*mind*)

tener prisa 116 (*hurry*)

tener puesto 106 (*to have*)

tener que 106 (*to have*)

tener que ver con 106 (*to have*)

tener razón 195 (*right*)

tener salud de piedra 172 (*ox*)

tener sed 248 (*thirst*)

tener sentido 207 (*sense*)

tener sueño 218 (*sleepy*)

tener suerte 142 (*lucky*)

tener un alto concepto de 248 (*to think*)

tener un nudo en la garganta 142 (*lump*)

tener vergüenza 11 (*ashamed*)

tenerle lástima 223 (*sorry*)

¡Tenga cuidado! 36 (*careful*)

terminar por 71 (*to end*)

Tirar piedras contra el propio tejado. 162 (*nose*)

tirarse al suelo de risa 128 (*to laugh*)

tocar a su fin 43 (*close*)

tomar a broma 135 (*light*)

tomar a mal 240 (*to take*)

tomar a pecho 109 (*heart*)

tomar de un golpe 238 (*swallow*)

tomar el fresco 6 (*air*)

tomar el rábano por las hojas 37 (*cart*)

tomar el sol 237 (*to sun*)

tomar en serio 207 (*seriously*)

tomar gusto a 243 (*taste*)

tomar la delantera 129 (*lead*)

tomar la palabra 86 (*floor*)

tomar nota de 163 (*note*)

tomar parte en 174 (*part*)

tomar partido 215 (*side*)

tomar por 240 (*to take*)

tomar sobre sí 241 (*to take*)

tomarle el pelo 131 (*leg*)

tomarle la delantera 146 (*march*)

tomarlo a pecho 105 (*hard*)

tomarse el trabajo de 263 (*trouble*)

tomarse la molestia de 263 (*trouble*)

tomarse un descanso 28 (*break*)

trabar amistad 90 (*friendship*)

tragar el anzuelo 113 (*hook*)

tragarse las palabras 287 (*word*)

tratar de 1 (*about*)

tratar de 3 (*to address*)

Indice

A

a 1
a laughing matter 146
A rolling stone gathers no moss.
   232
about 1
about the middle 150
above all 6
accord 1
according 1
according to 1
according to Hoyle 116
account 1
to account 2
to account for 2
accustomed 2
to acknowledge 2
to acknowledge. . . to be right
   (to agree with) 2
to acknowledge receipt 191
across 2
across from 2
across the board 25
across the street 234
act 3
to act 3
to act as 3
to act high and mighty 111
to act one's age 4
to act saintly 202
to act up 3
action 3
to add fuel to the flames 90
to add insult to injury 160
addition 3
to address 3
to address as 3
ado 4
advance 4

advantage 4
affair 4
after a fashion 80
after a (little) while 282
after all 6
after one's own heart 109
afterwards 4
against one's will 283
age 4
to agree 5
to agree to 5
agreement 5
ahead 5
ahead of time 251
to aim 5
to aim to 5
air 5
alive 6
alive and kicking 6
all 6
all alone 8
all along 8
all at once (all of a sudden) 6
All cats are alike in the dark.
   38
all day long 6
all dressed up 125
all in all 7
all in one breath 29
all of a sudden 6, 236
all of them 7
all over 7
all right 7
All that glitters is not gold. 98
All the better (worse) 7
all the same 7
an all-time high 7
all told 7
all walks of life 273

G

H

351

Indice

Indice

Indice

Indice

T

Indice

Indice

Indice

Indice

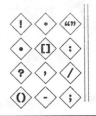